Creating Positive Support Groups for At-Risk Children

Ten Complete Curriculums for the Most Common Problems Among Elementary Students, Grades 1-8

Susan T. Dennison

Illustrations by John N. Secor, Jr.

P

Jalmar Press
Torrance, California

Creating Positive Support Groups for At-Risk Children
• *Ten Complete Curriculums for the Most Common Problems Among Elementary Students, Grades 1-8*

Copyright © 1997 by Susan Dennison, ACSW, LCSW

Jalmar Press
Permissions Dept.
Skypark Business Center
2675 Skypark Drive, Suite 204
Torrance, California 90505-5330
(310) 784-0016   FAX: (310) 784-1379

Library of Congress Cataloging-in-Publication Data

Dennison, Susan T.
    Creating positive support groups for at-risk children / by Susan Dennison.
        p. cm.
    "This book provides school guidance personnel and other mental health professionals with over 125 interventions that are therapeutically sequenced for ten different support group programs."
    Includes bibliographical references and index.
    ISBN 1-880396-26-2
    1. Socially handicapped children—United States—Psychology.
2. Self-help groups—United States.   3. Group relations training—United States.   4. Social work with children—United States.
I. Title.
HV741.D46 1993
362.7—dc20   93-27101
                                                                    CIP

Published by Jalmar Press

Creating Positive Support Groups for At-Risk Children
• *Ten Complete Curriculums for the Most Common Problems Among Elementary Students, Grades 1-8*

Author: Susan Dennison
Editor: Susan Remkus
Project Director: Jeanne Iler
Art Direction & Design: Electronic Publishing Services, Inc.
Illustrator: John N. Secor, Jr.
Manufactured in the United States of America
First edition printing: 10 9 8 7 6 5 4 3 2 1
ISBN: 1-880396-26-2

Creating Positive Support Groups for At-Risk Children

Ten Complete Curriculums for the Most Common Problems Among Elementary Students, Grades 1-8

J

Jalmar Press

Table of Contents

List of Appendices

Introduction

Creating Positive Support Groups for At-Risk Children provides school guidance personnel and other mental health professionals with over 125 interventions that are therapeutically sequenced for ten different support group programs. Here for the first time is a single text that contains all "how-to-do-it" curriculums for conducting support groups with the most common at-risk problems among elementary age students. Specific guidelines are provided for the set-up, goal development, sequencing of themes for sessions, and actual intervention ideas. This manual will quickly become a daily resource for the busy mental health professional.

Readers will be delighted to find in this manual extensive treatment ideas and resources on support groups with children. Over 50 different assessment instruments are recommended, 110 session themes (sub-goals) are suggested, 128 techniques are specifically outlined, over 160 related resources are listed, 300 bibliotherapy references are differentiated by at-risk area, and approximately 125 films/videotapes are recommended. Readers will quickly find that this manual will not only significantly impact their treatment efforts, but will save hundreds of hours in planning and preparation.

Current societal conditions have resulted in support groups as the intervention of choice for at-risk elementary age students. The reality of life is that more and more children are having to face very serious difficulties, putting a larger number of them in the at-risk category. At the same time, school districts and mental health programs are experiencing major funding cuts, resulting in fewer services for these youngsters. Again and again, support groups address the realities of these two situations. Young children usually learn and grow tremendously from effective support groups. One of the major assets of this therapeutic approach is that the youngsters are teaching many skills to one another. In addition, this treatment setting allows guidance professionals to see a larger number of youngsters.

The support group curriculums contained in this book have been intended primarily for school social workers, counselors, and psychologists. These professionals will find this material has an immediate appeal, because it addresses problems common among their students. Ten different programs are covered, so that readers will have one reference that provides the necessary information for setting up and facilitating the most commonly needed support groups in elementary schools.

Other audiences that will find this book highly relevant and useful are mental health professionals working in outpatient settings, counselors treating youngsters in residential programs, and private practitioners who conduct groups with their younger at-risk clients.

This text is intended for professionals having credentials in the mental health field and specific training in groupwork. The curriculums could be used for training purposes; however, a qualified instructor or supervisor should always be involved in monitoring usage of the interventions by inexperienced professionals or by students.

At-risk children are the targeted population for the curriculums contained in this book. The author, with 20 years of experience in school settings, has identified the following ten problem areas as those best addressed in support groups for elementary age youngsters:

1. Social skills difficulties

2. Self-esteem problems

3. Children of family life changes

4. Children of substance abusers

5. Aggressive/acting-out youngsters

6. Traumatized children (physically or sexually abused, neglected, significant loss, etc.)

7. Overly stressed youngsters

8. Children with school performance problems (learning disabilities, attention deficit disorder, and intellectually impaired children)

9. Youngsters with school motivation/attitude problems

10. Children experiencing a combination of the above problems

This list does not completely cover all the problems of childhood, but focuses on the more common ones. Professionals will find that most of their at-risk youngsters fit into one of the support group programs provided in this text.

The primary purpose of this book is to provide intervention ideas for support groups. However, it also serves several secondary purposes. In Chapter One, specific guidelines are given for setting up successful support group programs. Guidance professionals will be relieved to find in this section concrete ideas for less than ideal set-ups for these programs. Pre-group planning guidelines are provided for the environmental settings, meeting days, composition of groups, session planning/formats, the handling of problems, progress notes, and pre-/post-evaluation of the groups.

Chapter Two provides an overview of the ten curriculums and describes the consistent and easy-to-follow format of the curriculums. The Dennison Group Practice Model is introduced. This model provides the underlying rationale for the set-up and sequencing of sessions throughout the curriculums. School guidance personnel will find that this model is one of the first to combine therapeutic goals within an educational framework. This type of group counseling approach complements and integrates easily with the educational model in schools.

Furthermore, Chapter Two contains composite lists of all the group goals and their corresponding interventions from the curriculum chapters. A handy and practical planning method is introduced here; it serves to easily adapt and individualize this support group model. As a result, facilitators will be able to quickly modify and develop their own intervention ideas for similar programs.

Format of Curriculums

The heart of this book lies in Chapters Three through Thirteen. These chapters provide the actual ten curriculums for at-risk youngsters. In Chapter Three, intervention suggestions are given for the initial phase of any of the support groups addressed in this book. The next nine chapters (Chapters Four through Twelve) outline in detail the goals and interventions for the nine single problem-focused support group programs listed below.

1. Social Skills Enhancement Support Group
2. Self-Esteem Building Support Group
3. Children of Family Life Changes Support Group
4. Children of Substance Abusers Support Group
5. Anger/Conflict Resolution Support Group
6. Traumatized Children's Support Group
7. Stress Management Support Group
8. Learning Performance Support Group
9. School Motivation/Attitude Enhancement Support Group

Chapter Thirteen provides interventions for the termination phase of any of the above programs. The tenth support group curriculum (not listed above) is a general support group intended to address the needs of at-risk youngsters experiencing a combination of problems. In Chapter Two, directions are given for developing this support group through utilizing the planning method presented and extrapolating interventions with corresponding goals from Chapters Three through Thirteen.

The nine single problem-focused curriculums (Chapters Four through Twelve) follow a consistent seven component format. First, general treatment guidelines are provided for facilitating groups with each at-risk problem population. Second, a listing of typical themes for group session is provided. Third, a list of ten assessment instruments is outlined, which can be used to gather relevant content for group sessions.

The fourth component, a consistent sequenced list of support group goals, follows a therapeutic instructive step-by-step approach, one of the unique elements of this model. In the fifth component, the reader is given 12 techniques to address the middle-phase goals of a support group. Each of these techniques can be cross-referenced with eight similar techniques from the other curriculum chapters. Specifics on this cross-referencing are contained in Chapter Two.

The sixth component is a step-by-step technique instruction for each intervention. These directions (and in some cases, accompanying paper and pencil task sheets) make the techniques clear and easy to duplicate. The seventh and final component of the curriculums is a bibliography list. Here, the author has attempted to provide one of the most up-to-date how-to-do-it resource lists. Facilitators will be delighted to have so much of this reference information available in one manual.

Mental health professionals should find the curriculum chapters comprehensive and easy to follow. Experienced groupworkers will be able to immediately set up similar support group programs by following the directions in the curriculums. Much of the material necessary for interventions allows preparation time to be kept to a minimum.

Cautionary Notes

Some of the interventions look like children's game materials that are available for purchase by the general public. This similarity in format is intended to motivate youngsters to participate in group session tasks. This material should be used *only* by professionals in the field of mental health; parents and non-professionals should not use any of the technique ideas.

Teachers are cautioned to use this material only under the direct supervision of a school guidance professional experienced in groupwork. On Table VI in Chapter Two, readers will find three types of techniques (i.e., Hello Group, Instructive, and Goodbye Group) that can be most easily adapted and used in the classroom. Teachers may have to modify the presentation of some techniques in order to address the comprehension and interest levels of their students.

Educational and guidance professionals should always remember that information elicited through any of these interventions is often of a sensitive nature. An inability to process or handle emotionally charged issues could be harmful to a child or a class of students. Therefore, faculty untrained in the mental health field should always consult experienced guidance staff when selecting and modifying techniques for classroom use.

Chapter 1

Guidelines for Setting Up Support Groups

In this chapter, specific guidelines are given for 12 critical variables involved in the effective set-up of support group programs for children at-risk. Often, with this elementary age population, the quality of pre-group preparation will significantly impact a support group's ultimate success. Youngsters at this developmental level require some definite conditions for the ideal or close to ideal set-up of a group program. At times, readers may find that more energy is needed in setting up children's support groups than initially facilitating them. Facilitators should not be discouraged by this but should instead see that good preparation results in support groups that function smoothly from initiation.

Because many settings today do not have the ideal conditions for the initiation of support groups, alternative suggestions are provided for each of the 12 set-up variables. Some settings may have too many of these critical variables that are less than ideal; Appendix A therefore contains a form entitled "Dennison Ideal Group Index," which can be used to assist clinicians in deciding whether an environment is supportive enough to ensure the success of a support group program. The intent here is not to discourage clinicians from establishing groups, but rather to help them objectively evaluate whether a setting is conducive enough for support groups to be run effectively. Readers need to remember that no matter what their level of experience and skill, they still need certain minimum supports to conduct effective support group programs.

Physical Setting for Group

The ideal physical setting for most elementary age children includes an adequate size room, little stimuli on the walls or within reach, good lighting, comfortable room temperature, sound proofing from outside noises, which safeguards youngsters' confidentiality, and a generally warm atmosphere. Obviously, many clinicians will not have access to such a room for their groups. Individual evaluations will have to be made to determine whether a particular setting will be conducive to a successful support group.

Remember that youngsters, particularly ones with problems, will easily go off-task when competing visual or auditory stimuli are in the group room. Facilitators, therefore, will have to work harder to keep many members on-task. Remember that such stimuli can cause some children to engage in acting-out behavior (i.e., getting out of their seats) during the sessions. Counselors should seek as close to an ideal room as possible for their groups.

For the group room that is less than ideal, helpful suggestions include the following:

1. Cover up all materials in the room not related to the group task. This will at least keep such materials out of members' view during sessions.

2. When outside sounds can be heard, schedule groups during times that the adjoining environment is less noisy.

3. Rooms that have lots of physical stimuli can be handled by utilizing more visual aids during the group session.

4. Seat group members away from bookshelves and other places where off-task materials would otherwise be within reach.

5. When rooms are particularly less than ideal settings, schedule groups in early mornings.

6. Use assigned seating around the group circle as a way of preventing a chain reaction of members being off-task.

7. Facilitators should lower expectations of members' attention span during sessions, and tasks will need to be changed more frequently.

8. Use the environment to challenge the children to a fun game where they have to avoid off-task stimuli in order to win.

Readers should feel free to add their own ideas to the list above. There are obviously any number of creative ways to make a setting more conducive to a group. One other point to keep in mind is that it is best to use rooms the members do not typically go to for other classes. It is ideal to have a setting where the unique cues for group can be established.

When considering furniture for group use, keep in mind that youngsters respond best to sitting at a round table on heavy, hard to move chairs. Even though facilitators will find that kicking and other off-task behaviors may occur under the table, this type of furniture arrangement still offers a needed structure. Children typically require some external controls for their behavior in group. For this reason, the table and chairs offer physical limits on the youngsters' behavior.

Meeting Days/Times/Frequency/Length of Sessions

Because of their developmental level, children benefit from groups scheduled in the morning, but often school schedules prohibit such timing of sessions. Facilitators need to remember that youngsters' attention spans decrease as the day goes on. Therefore, groups scheduled in the afternoon or evening must be planned differently. Usually, such groups require more frequent changes of task, frequent use of visual aids during sessions, and different types of interventions that maintain their attention (i.e., more activity-based). Clinicians also need to change their expectations of members' on-task and off-task behavior for afternoon and evening group sessions.

There are no ideal meeting days related to good treatment practice. Counselors will need to consider a number of individual variables when scheduling meeting days. Among such variables are other scheduled classes or events, types of other activities during particular days for members (e.g., a school day that requires lots of sitting tasks before a potential group session), the facilitator's other commitments, and the consistent availability of members on particular days (for example, Fridays may not be good because the members often go on field trips).

Ideally, the more often a group meets, the better. Obviously, most settings allow for children's groups to meet only once a week. Facilitators need to remember that it will be necessary to review previous sessions at the beginning of each group meeting. Young children do not have well developed long-term memory, and therefore will often forget details from one week to the next.

Usually, the ideal length of session for a children's group is 30 to 45 minutes. Youngsters in kindergarten through third grade often need the shorter time period. The older elementary grades respond well to the 45-minute sessions, due to their increased attention span. Here again, counselors may want to consult with the teachers who can provide some specific suggestions on the overall average attention span of a particular group.

Choice of Support Group

There are two issues related to support group choice. First is the issue of closed-ended versus open-ended groups. The second issue concerns the determination of problem focus for a particular group.

In regard to the first issue, all short-term groups should ideally be closed-ended. This means that the facilitator starts and ends with the same membership. No new members are accepted into a group after it begins, and when possible, no original members are dropped. The open-ended group model allows for an ongoing flow both into and out of an existing group. When facilitating short-term groups (i.e., 12 sessions or less), it is not only ideal, but essential, that a closed-ended model be used. Clinicians need to remember that the development of group trust declines every time the membership changes. If a group has too many changes initially, eventually there will be no possibility for group cohesiveness.

The second issue related to group choice is the determination of an at-risk problem focus for a particular support program. There are any number of ways this decision can be made in a particular setting. The following is a list of suggestions for a facilitator to make this determination.

1. Sometimes, one or two whole class screening sessions can be conducted. At the end of such a meeting, the students can be asked through a confidential method (e.g., questionnaires handed back to the counselor) to indicate their interest in a particular type of group or to select from a list of possible ones.

2. Teachers and/or parents can be given a written survey to obtain their views of the most relevant at-risk problem support groups needed by the youngsters in a particular school.

3. Counselors can decide from their caseload which type of support group would be most beneficial.

4. Through a counselor's mailbox at school, children can submit their suggestions for a needed support group.

This list is not inclusive; clinicians can use other ways to determine relevant and appropriate short-term groups for a particular population. Readers are encouraged to be as creative as possible, so that support group programs best meet the individual needs of a school or agency setting. The ten curriculums have been provided for clinicians to have a full range of relevant at-risk support group programs for the elementary age population.

Composition/Screening of Group Members

To date, the studies on group composition have not been able to identify specific variables that predict a high probability of group compatibility and ultimate cohesiveness. We do know that there are three behavioral patterns in children that typically eliminate them from potential group programs. These three types include the child with psychotic behaviors that are not controlled with medication, the severely paranoid youngster who is also not controlled with medication, and the severely narcissistic student who cannot typically share with a group of peers. This data is listed on the form entitled "Group Screening Form," found in Appendix B. The facilitator should be sure to check on the existence of any of these behavioral patterns as one way of screening potential participants for a group.

Other variables to consider when composing a children's support group include the following.

1. Members should be within two years' age range so that they have similar intellectual and social/emotional levels of functioning. Obviously, there will always be exceptions to this guide, since some older children may function considerably below or above their chronological age.

2. Youngsters should have similar skills in their ability to stay in their seat for tasks.

3. Participants should have attention spans within a similar range.

4. Members should be able to share equally taking turns and listening to one another.

5. Participants should be consistently in contact with reality and thus equally affected by both the facilitator's and other members' responses.

This information is listed on the "Group Screening Form," found in Appendix B. The six behavioral areas of in-seat, attention span, social/emotional level, comprehension level, ability to share/take turns, and contact with reality should be assessed for a student's level of performance and group compatibility. The potential member's level of performance can often be gathered from relevant teachers or by the facilitator observing a classroom setting. The difficult level to assess before a group begins, however, is compatibility with one another. Often times, not until children are put together in a small group can one see, beyond the obvious variables already mentioned, whether they will be compatible and ultimately able to form a cohesive group.

Clinicians need to be aware that the most important issue to consider when placing children in the same group is compatibility, not level of functioning. It is more important that youngsters be at a similar level of functioning than at a high performance level on the six behaviors. So, for example, a potential child may be high functioning on all the six behaviors rated, yet be incompatible with a particular group because all the other youngsters are functioning considerably below his level. This is not to say such a youngster is not appropriate for a support group, but rather that he needs to be placed with members who are more compatible.

It is recommended that facilitators complete a "Group Screening Form" (Appendix B) on every child considered for a group. This form provides a consistent guide for screening and assessing youngsters for membership. In addition, the last section on page two of this form is for facilitator recommendations. Here, the group leader can indicate if a child should be placed into the group, not be placed, or be considered for another counseling service. It is important to have a brief written report such as this one to clarify the rationale behind group screening decisions and ultimate recommendations. Clinicians will be delighted to find that such a procedure helps other team members (i.e., teachers, psychologists, etc.) and parents be more understanding and supportive of treatment recommendations.

The ultimate decision for a youngster's support group placement must be determined utilizing one's clinical expertise. In other words, there are no hard and fast rules for how many of the six behaviors being assessed for group compatibility have to be incompatible before a youngster is considered inappropriate. For example, a particular child could be compatible on five behaviors but incompatible due to her contact with reality. This latter behavior could easily make this youngster inappropriate for a group. On the other hand, another child may be incompatible regarding the two behaviors of attention span and in-seat ability. In this case, the facilitator may choose to place this youngster in a group, because those two behaviors may easily improve over time with peer feedback and modeling. Counselors should use the "Group Screening Form" as a guide when making group composition decisions. This procedure must be combined with one's clinical expertise and good judgment.

Another important aspect of group composition is the size of a particular group. Generally, my experience, backed by the literature, is that children's groups should have from six to eight members. If a particular population of youngsters is having more severe difficulties, then the smaller (i.e., six member) size should be used. Also, keep in mind that if a short-term group is intended to be more educational in its focus, a larger group size can be considered.

Feedback/Support from Significant Others

It is very important to elicit relevant feedback from the other adults in members' lives. Teachers, in particular, can be very helpful in providing group functioning behaviors by following the "Group Screening" method outlined for this program. These professionals can also be invaluable in identifying common and relevant problems among a group of youngsters. Counselors have to keep in mind that teachers probably spend the most amount of group time with children. Teachers can therefore be invaluable to the facilitator in providing essential screening data and helping to formulate support group program content.

Parents can also be a tremendous resource. The counselor will find that the parents have a more historical view of how their child has functioned in group settings. Such feedback can provide previous strengths that were once in a youngster's repertoire. In addition, parents can give their impression of how they see their youngster's problems. Facilitators need to see that both parents and teachers can provide valuable feedback regarding youngsters' functioning and potential problem areas.

It is also important for the counselor to elicit parents' and teachers' support when running a group program. In order to establish consistency in gaining such support, the following guidelines are recommended.

1. Be sure to obtain both a parent's verbal and written permission to have their child in a particular support group. Even if a school or agency has earlier paperwork covering such permission, I recommend that specific clearance be obtained for each group program instituted. The reason is two-fold: first, it makes parents aware of the child's participation in a therapeutic service, keeping everything open between the youngster and parent; second, it necessitates that parents be informed of the purpose, content, and predictable outcomes of a particular group program. This helps ensure that parents are more realistic and supportive of their child's participation.

2. Facilitators should inform both parents and teachers of the specific goals of a support group program, along with some general ideas about the content of sessions. Obviously, individual disclosures made by members will need to be kept confidential. However, it is important that counselors learn to clarify their therapeutic objectives and be able to articulate how they will meet them. It is for this reason that the ten curriculums in this text were developed. Readers should feel free to share the actual relevant support group curriculum with the involved teachers and parents. Clinicians will find that such sharing generally elicits expectations of the program that are more realistic, maintain the ongoing support of members' changes, and humanize the group service so that it does not appear mysterious or magical in nature.

3. When time permits, facilitators should elicit teachers' and parents' observations of changes made by group members. Appendix C contains a form entitled "Pre/Post Evaluation of Group Progress" (described under the evaluation section of this chapter), which can be used as an efficient, effective way to gain the feedback of significant others on changes that have generalized into the classroom and home settings.

There are a number of benefits for actively engaging parents and teachers for feedback and support of a group program. We as a counseling profession need to realize that only when we are more open with our services will they appear less magical and more human. Ultimately, this ongoing eliciting of significant others' support will reinforce the members as well as the facilitators.

Facilitator/Co-facilitator Roles

This aspect of a support group program is often not within the decision-making realm of the facilitator. In many schools and mental health agencies, there are just not enough clinicians to have co-facilitators in groups. However, for readers who do have the option of a co-facilitator, this usually provides an ideal set-up in children's groups. Elementary age youngsters may need to be timed out of a session and having a co-facilitator at such times is extremely helpful. Additionally, as with any group, it is difficult and sometimes impossible for one facilitator to be aware of all significant interactions. Furthermore, having two clinicians allows for more places for children having trouble staying on-task to be seated (e.g., next to one of the co-facilitators allows for up to four members sitting next to an adult). In some activities, a co-facilitator can serve as a great model to help the primary facilitator more effectively elicit the full involvement of the membership.

If two clinicians are able to co-facilitate a support group, it will be important to establish a mutually agreed upon role differentiation. Some clinicians prefer to have one person be the primary facilitator with the other as a secondary facilitator, while others have an equal team set-up. The important point is that the two counselors make this decision together and clarify who will be doing what in the planning, preparation, and facilitating of the support group. No matter which co-facilitator model is chosen, both clinicians should make time in their schedules to assess a session and plan the next one accordingly.

Attraction Attributes of Group

It is extremely important that a facilitator determine and plan aspects of their group program to successfully attract members and maintain their maximum participation. This is easier said than done when dealing with at-risk youngsters. Counselors will often find that potential members are already turned off to therapeutic services and/or peer group settings. It can be quite challenging to overcome some children's negative expectations. Yet when clinicians are successful at engaging such youngsters, it can be enormously rewarding and be a corrective experience for youngsters.

How one engages a particular group is individualized, depending on the needs/interests of members and facilitators. I have found the following general guidelines to consistently work with the majority of elementary age youngsters placed in support groups.

1. Provide members a consistent format for each session. Specifics regarding this component can be found in the next section of this chapter (under "Session Planning"). Children enjoy the security and predictability of routines. Clinicians will find that a format usually helps youngsters to be less anxious in groups and to participate more fully. In addition, formats address children's attention span needs, providing a change of tasks throughout each session.

2. Members' average attention span must be considered when planning sessions. There will need to be changes of tasks, not too much time between participants' turns in games and sometimes backup interventions

for an off day. For details on this modification, see the "Session Planning" section in this chapter.

3. Disclosure elicited initially and during most of a short-term group should be of a positive and factual nature. Facilitators need to be sensitive to the kind of sharing they ask of participants. It is extremely important that children feel comfortable in providing the disclosure elicited. Generally, such requests should be via structured questions rather than open-ended ones. An example of each is provided below.

Open-Ended Question: How are you doing today?

Structured Positive Question: Tell me one good thing that happened to you today.

4. From the initial session and throughout a group's existence, balanced participation should always be maintained. An easy way to accomplish this is to have all members respond to tasks and questions by going around a circle, one after another. This is a time efficient method, and greatly lessens the facilitator's burden of having to monitor who has shared and who has not. The only way for *all* members to feel a part of a group is by each of them equally participating or as close to that goal as humanly possible.

5. As indicated at the beginning of this chapter, it is extremely important that an appropriate and comfortable setting be available for a group.

6. Interventions planned for members should be fun, of interest, and within their developmental abilities. Children need to feel, particularly initially, that they are going to enjoy participating with other peers in the planned activities. Facilitators may find that their best source of planning ideas is to ask the participants ahead of time to complete a check-off list of the types of activities they enjoy. An example of such a form can be found in Appendix D and is entitled "Activity Interest Questionnaire." Such a survey can ensure that interventions planned are of interest to the participants.

7. Sessions should be well planned so that a consistent routine is followed and there is variety in the activities facilitated. Much of Chapter Two focuses on details around the issue of group planning. In addition, curriculums in Chapters Three through Thirteen contain very specific interventions for each of the at-risk problem areas.

8. Facilitators should consider using visual cues as a way of keeping members on-task. This will be particularly relevant with younger children in kindergarten through third grade. Suggested ways to use visual cues are contained in the technique instructions found in Chapters Three through Thirteen.

9. Elementary age children learn best through in vivo activities. Therefore, it is important that clinicians not rely too heavily on verbal discussion interventions. Therapeutic play tasks should be planned, in which youngsters spend most of the group time experiencing the lesson being taught. Time at the end of each session can be spent having the members verbally process their experience. Specific suggestions for such tasks and later processing are contained in all the curriculums.

10. Games played in the group should always be group competitive in the first several sessions. It has been my experience that most short-term groups (i.e., 12 sessions or less) need group competition in all games played. These groups require this competition set-up as a way of building the group's cohesiveness. Otherwise the facilitator is working against the most essential part of a group, which is to create a cohesive unit.

    It is not until the middle phase that a group is ready to be challenged with team competition. In the termination phase, individual competition is most appropriate and consistent with the group getting ready for its ending. Readers have to remember that most short-term groups do not fully enter a middle phase, often terminating because their time is up. Therefore, these types of groups should adhere to a group competitive model for all activities planned. Specific ways to set up such competition in the technique instructions can be found throughout the curriculum chapters.

11. Members should be maintained on-task primarily by the session plan and the facilitator's style of running the group. It is extremely helpful to avoid disciplining in the early sessions of a group. Otherwise, a negative cue for the setting can be established and then be very difficult to change. More details on the handling of members' off-task behavior can be found later in this chapter under the subtitle "Handling of Problems."

12. Provide a structured and easy way for members to take turns being in charge of sessions. Details regarding a leader component for the format of sessions are in a later section of this chapter under "Planning Group Formats." The important point is that children love being in charge because they rarely get to take on such a role. It is essential that when members are allowed to be in charge, they can handle the task successfully. Also, the completion of such a role allows an opportunity for positive peer feedback.

13. Do not talk with the participants about group rules. Clinicians are always surprised by this suggestion. It has been my experience that most children know the rules for a group setting from their classroom experience. Their difficulty is that they cannot adhere to the rules. Facilitators may find that the one topic that turns off children and is considered quite boring is "rule talk." Ways of handling this issue are spelled out later in this chapter under "Handling of Problems."

14. Facilitators need to take an in-charge role in the group. It is essential that children's groups get off to the right start. Therefore, group leaders have to make sure everyone is following minimum rules in order to keep members on-task. This helps facilitators elicit a similar response to that obtained by teachers who are caring and warm yet set definite limits in their classrooms.

15. Support group sessions should always end on a positive note. Throughout the curriculums in this book, the technique instructions always include a way to positively end the intervention. Facilitators will find that this component adds to the attraction of the group and provides a more enjoyable way for the children to process their experiences.

16. If something is not working with a group, be sure to stop it and try another avenue. Facilitators need to be particularly careful with groups in the initial sessions, since these groups need to experience primarily positive sessions. A good rule of thumb is to always go back into a problem group with some renewed hope via a new intervention, style of facilitating, formal reinforcement, etc.

17. As a way of attracting members and maintaining their involvement, consider building in some reinforcing events or special prizes. For example, a facilitator may want to plan field trips, parties, award ceremonies, special surprise goodies for particularly difficult sessions, or other special events. These activities can greatly increase the attraction of the group and keep members' interest at an optimum level.

18. Facilitators need to be enthusiastic about their groups. Children are very perceptive and quickly pick up on a group leader's attitude. Clinicians, through their personalities and facilitating style, greatly enhance the enjoyment of the group.

There are many ways to establish an attractive group program for children. The above list is intended to provide some beginning examples of how a facilitator can increase the attractiveness of a group. Readers need to remember that although youngsters can be made to participate in a group, they may not gain from the experience. It is extremely important to hook their interest, enthusiasm, and commitment so that they will ultimately benefit from this therapeutic experience.

Session Planning and Processing

The ten support group curriculums in this book have been developed with session planning in mind. By following the directions in the next chapter (Chapter Two, Overview of Curriculums) and then choosing a relevant curriculum from one of the remaining eleven chapters (i.e., Chapters Three through Thirteen), facilitators' planning will be in near ready form. It is important that mental health professionals understand that the planning of group sessions is an integral and essential part of this support group model. The following planning guidelines should be kept in mind when determining the content of a specific support group's sessions.

1. All sessions should be planned with the details needed for new groups and younger members.

2. It is advisable to go into the first few sessions of a new group with two plans. One is the intervention initially conducted, and the second is a backup plan in case the first one is not successful. Readers need to remember that one of their primary goals in the initial phase of groups is to establish a cue for a positive experience.

3. Early phase groups and problem members usually require more variety of interventions in the initial sessions.

4. Stop using a technique that is not working, particularly during the initial phase. New groups often require facilitators to use a trial-and-error approach until effective techniques are determined for each unique membership.

5. The goals for each of the three group phases should always be kept in mind when planning sessions. This support group model directly ties interventions to specific goals for each phase. More information on this connection can be found in Chapter Two.

6. Young children's support groups should have activities planned both at their developmental level and interest range. Readers will find a great deal of therapeutic games and fun techniques throughout the curriculums. It is not advisable to plan or depend on a lot of verbal discussion with early phase children's groups, particularly with kindergarten through the third grade.

7. Group facilitators should be careful not to allow members to discuss an issue in sessions just because it surfaced spontaneously. Clinicians need to use their expertise in deciding if a group is ready to deal with a particular issue. One way to determine this is by going back to the goals of the support group in its current phase of functioning.

8. Plans for children's support groups are most effective when they involve in vivo learning. Very few elementary age youngsters change significantly through abstract discussions. This is particularly true for children under the fourth grade.

9. It is usually best not to plan more than four sessions in advance, so that a group's response to a planning style can first be assessed. By limiting future session planning, relevant issues that spontaneously surface can be considered for a group's session content.

10. Facilitators must make sure there is time to plan and prepare materials for each session. Inexperienced professionals and those with limited supplies will find this to be more time consuming. Support groups require a curriculum closet just like good teachers need for their academic classes. Many of the interventions in this book contain actual materials that can be duplicated and used for group sessions.

Facilitators must also remember to include time in their schedules for processing group sessions. This review between meetings is essential for determining the most effective way to conduct and plan content for the next session and should involve the participating co-facilitator.

Planning Group Formats

In addition to planning specific techniques for each group session, it is recommended that a consistent format be followed in each meeting. The specific routine used by the facilitator is less important than the idea that some type of predictable format is planned. There are a number of reasons for having a set routine to sessions. First, the changing of task addresses the shorter attention of children. Second, the predictable quality that is added to sessions greatly reduces the members' anxiety level. Youngsters love situations where they know the sequence of events and at the same time enjoy lots of variety within that format. Third, formats allow for group development on several levels. By having a change of task, facilitators can stimulate different learning through a variety of avenues.

Facilitators should feel free to develop a group format that meets both their needs and those of the members. A sample of such a format is found below.

Session Format
Leader Time (5-10 minutes)

Description: Each group session, a member takes a turn being the leader. Kids love this in-charge role. The facilitator gives the leader member a disclosure question to ask everyone. For younger groups (grades kindergarten through third grade), it is often helpful to have these questions written on a large sheet with a corresponding picture to enhance the concept. Older groups usually only require the question written out.

Leaders are encouraged to be polite and use good manners in their role. After everyone has answered, two compliments are given to the leader from the membership. This allows members an in vivo experience at being a leader, giving compliments, and receiving compliments. In addition, the positive, factual, and non-threatening disclosure elicited helps build a cohesive group.

Session Objective/Technique
(20-30 minutes depending on the total length of the group session)

Description: The facilitator plans a technique to address the objective of the session. These objectives and techniques are taken from the appropriate curriculum found in Chapters Three through Thirteen.

Closure
(5-10 minutes)

Description: At the end of each session, the facilitator asks members to share what they enjoyed, learned, or found most beneficial from the experience created. Readers will notice that such closures are indicated at the end of the instructions for all 120 techniques contained in the curriculums.

This way of closing sessions accomplishes several purposes. First, it helps members end the session on a positive note. Second, it provides an easy way for youngsters to process their experience. Third, the children are able to provide some valuable feedback to the facilitator in terms of what essentially is most enjoyable and effective with them as a group.

I have modified and used this sample format over the past 20 years. It has been very effective in accomplishing the purposes indicated above. Young children usually benefit from about three task changes in each group session. Clinicians are reminded that older youngsters (grades four through six) may not require as many task changes. Furthermore, on any given day a group may be ready and willing to spend an entire session on just one part of the format. Facilitators will have to use their clinical expertise in making such changes to any particular session.

Materials Preparation/Purchase

Since most children's support groups require developmentally appropriate interventions, purchase and/or preparation of the corresponding materials will be necessary. Time should be allowed within the facilitator's schedule to get such materials ready for upcoming sessions. It has been my experience that new support groups often require as much time in preparing materials as in planning sessions. This is particularly true for the counselor who does not already have a group curriculum closet. Following are some guidelines regarding the purchase and preparation of support group materials.

1. Avoid buying too many commercial games, even those intended for therapeutic usage. Many of these games are very costly, require screening of the material to make sure it is relevant and appropriate for a particular

group, and do not work well when used in a group setting (e.g., too much time between members' turns).

2. Consider joining forces with another clinician or two and develop a joint closet of group materials. This is an easy way for facilitators to share planning ideas and avoid duplicating the same types of session materials.

3. Many of the intervention ideas in the curriculums contain all the necessary materials for interventions or require items easily purchased. These curriculum plans have been developed for limited budgets.

4. When making up techniques, be sure the materials required are not too expensive, hard to find, or difficult to put together. Most mental health professionals today do not have the time to spend on such preparations.

5. Any interventions modified or modeled after ones in this book need to be developed following the general guidelines provided in Chapter Two. Also, facilitators need to be careful that the instructions for such creative activities are easy for groups to quickly understand. It is important that sessions not be spent just having members comprehend how a game is played.

6. There are lots of "how-to-do-it" books on the market today that can give facilitators other intervention ideas for any one of the at-risk problem areas. Up-to-date resources for all the curriculums are listed in the bibliographies found at the end of each. Many of the references in these lists contain lots of hands-on material that can be duplicated for sessions.

7. Never forget your own childhood memories of fun activities played with groups of youngsters. Some of those same games can be modified and successfully used for support group sessions. Sometimes we forget how little playing children do today. Many of those old games we took for granted have never been played by youngsters in this day and age.

8. Facilitators should consider their interests and natural skills when planning and preparing intervention materials. Group members always find their group leader's enthusiasm around a particular technique to be quite contagious.

Handling of Problems

Any number of problems can arise in a children's group. It is particularly important that facilitators decide ahead of time how such difficulties will be handled. I have found that the Dennison Group Practice Model followed in all ten curriculums greatly decreases the incidence of group problems. However, no model can completely eliminate the possibility of difficulties arising among youngsters in a group setting.

Clinicians will find it helpful to develop a consistent plan for dealing with individual members' off-task behavior. It is recommended that rules not be talked about in groups. Rather, facilitators should merely say that the same rules apply that are followed in the classroom. Individual participants' disruptive behavior should be handled in as brief a way as possible, so that the group's attention remains on the task of the session.

Always keep in mind the golden rule about groups, which is "You never sacrifice a group for one or two members." This differentiates this modality of treatment from individual counseling. As soon as a facilitator feels that the majority of their attention is being directed at one or two members, it is time to stop and try a different tactic.

One method I have developed for consistently handling members' off-task or disruptive behavior is a fairly simple one. The facilitator always has a pen and blank paper in front of him/her during the entire session. Whenever a member has violated a minimum rule, their name is written on the sheet, with a check mark. After the first time this method is used, the disruptive participant merely needs to be told they need to figure out a way to get rid of the check. It has been my experience that most children who are off-task know what they have done wrong. What these youngsters need is a reminder in black and white (i.e., check by their name) that they are becoming too disruptive in the group. Facilitators will be amazed at children's response to a check by their names. Since most youngsters have experienced similar programs in their classrooms, they quickly understand the meaning of a check and want to immediately get rid of it.

Another benefit of this method is that it requires very little attention from the group leader so most of his/her focus can be kept on the task at hand with the other participants. Also, the disruptive youngster has been given a reminder and the freedom to individually decide how to get rid of the check. This is an important point because it avoids the possibility of expecting too much or too little of any one child. Instead, the facilitator can individually determine when a particular youngster has done enough to get rid of his/her check. For example, one child may say "Sorry" and earn a clean slate, while another child may just need to sit quietly for a few minutes. Clinicians will find that youngsters generally respond positively to this method of getting rid of checks because it addresses them at their ability level.

In some cases a youngster may not only be unable to get rid of a check, but require a second one. When this occurs, it is a reminder to the facilitator that the child needs to be put in a time out from the group. This goes back to the golden rule that you do not sacrifice a group for one or two members. In addition, this second step often requires that a clinician have either a co-facilitator, to remove the youngster, or a class where the child can be sent. Facilitators may choose to have the youngster out for the rest of the session or allow them back for a second try at group. If the member is allowed back into the session, the clinician must remember that their slate is clean (name and check erased off the sheet) but that if one more check is acquired, they are out for the rest of that group meeting. By the time a third check is given, the youngster is saying, via his/her behavior, that they cannot handle the group setting that day.

Whenever a child is timed out for the rest of a group session, the facilitator should meet with him/her individually. During this one-to-one contact it will be important to process the incident. Also, clinicians may want to probe other reasons for the off-task problems. It has been my experience that when members who are generally on-task in group start having a difficult session, something else is bothering them. Sometimes it may be a problem that happened just before the group, or the youngster may have something upsetting on his/her mind that cannot be addressed in the session. Facilitators need to remember that children cannot always bring up problem disclosure in a short-term group, due to the very nature of this modality.

In addition to this problem handling method, readers may discover other effective ways to respond to members' off-task behavior. Whatever the method used, readers need to remember that the handling of group problems needs to be clearly outlined in this pre-group phase.

Documentation of Members' Progress

This is an age of accountability; thus, the documentation of children's progress in a group program is an absolute necessity. Since we are talking here about short-term groups (12 sessions or less), the number of progress notes required will usually be much less than in long-term groups. Readers will have to follow the documentation guidelines in their particular setting.

It is important that progress notes always address the status of goals established for a support group. The clinician will find in Appendix E a form entitled "Objectives/Progress Report for Group." This can be used for youngsters in any one of the ten types of at-risk support groups presented in this book. The form has been developed so that the group- and child-specific goals can be easily indicated. The reader will see on the second page of this form sections where the youngster's status on the group and individual goals can be documented. This report form is an example of how progress notation should tie in directly with the overall group goals.

Readers will be delighted that this "Dennison Group Practice Model" has very clear goals indicated throughout the ten curriculums. Clinicians can follow the goals developed for whatever support group they are utilizing. These goals are filled in on the "Objectives/Progress Report" found in Appendix F, saving facilitators hours of progress note writing and establishing a consistent entry form for all group members.

Facilitators should feel free to develop their own forms for progress notes. They may want to use the report form in Appendix E as a guide. The important aspects of progress note documentation that should be kept in mind include following a consistent form, indicating both the individual and group goals, documenting the youngster's progress in regard to those goals, and making future treatment recommendations. If any objective scales were used to evaluate a particular member's progress, that data should be integrated into the report.

Pre/Post Evaluation of a Group

During this pre-group phase, it is valuable to think through a plan for objectively measuring the impact of a particular support group. For this reason, a list of assessment scales has been provided for each curriculum chapter. Facilitators may choose to use one of these instruments both as a way of obtaining a baseline functioning on members and of evaluating their post-group progress. An important point about using such scales for pre/post evaluation is that some of them do not measure change over a short period of time. Readers will need to check with publishers of such instruments (see Appendix F for corresponding list of publishers for scales in Chapters Four through Twelve) to see how usable they are for short-term pre/post evaluation.

Another method for conducting before and after status on group goals is provided in Appendix C. This form, titled "Pre/Post Evaluation of Group Progress," has been developed specifically for the support group curriculums in this text. Essentially, the clinician asks significant adults in the members' lives (i.e., teachers, parents, guardians, etc.) to complete the form before the group and at its termination. The advantage of this instrument is that it ties directly into the goals of the Dennison Group Practice Model. Readers may find that this form is able to more specifically measure changes as a result of a group program. Facilitators should be aware that no reliability or validity has yet been established on this instrument.

Facilitator Enthusiasm

Last but not least, the facilitator's enthusiasm for doing a children's group will greatly enhance the success of the program. By far, the personality and style of the group leader have more impact than any other group variable. Even with a less than ideal situation for a group set-up, a warm, excited, open, and caring clinician can be successful. Never underestimate the power and influence of the facilitator on the group.

It has been my experience that what youngsters walk away most remembering from a support group is the facilitator rather than any fancy techniques. Readers can follow all the curriculums in this text exactly and still not be effective. The material in the curriculum must be combined with an experienced groupworker who knows how to work effectively with children in this modality. The impact of the facilitator's modeling will be self-evident throughout the group's development.

Group leaders will also find that the following group facilitation styles will enhance their positive impact on children:

1. Avoid disciplining as much as possible, particularly in new groups.

2. Use humor to assist a child in getting on-task or avoiding a major blow-out.

3. Avoid talking for long periods of time in the sessions.

4. Try to avoid physical confrontations with participants. Instead, use physical holding only in cases where the child is hurting themself, others, or property.

5. Stay out of control issues as much as possible (i.e., avoid saying "I'll make you do it if you don't") and instead offer choices to the member (i.e., "You have a choice, either to stop tearing the paper or give it to me").

6. Try to come to the session in a good mood, with a lot of energy and enthusiasm.

7. Be careful not to get hooked into a child's or a group's negative mood.

8. Be in touch with your feelings so that you will also know how the group is feeling.

9. Be flexible in your session to adapt to the members' needs that day (i.e., "Why don't we do this game another day since everyone is sleepy").

10. Be open to admitting you are wrong or made a mistake and realize you are also doing some valuable modeling.

11. Use body language at times rather than talking (e.g., rubbing a member's arm when he is fidgety or giving a facial reminder to another member who is calling out).

12. Look for the positive changes in members and share these observations throughout group sessions.

The facilitator's behavior has a major impact on the group's effectiveness. Therefore, it is essential that the groupworker be constantly examining what personal qualities of their style are conducive to a particular group's development.

Chapter 2

Overview of Curriculums

This chapter introduces the Dennison Group Practice Model, which provides the rationale and basic underlying structure for all the curriculums in this text. The ten at-risk support group curriculums are outlined, with some brief guidelines. Facilitators are given a very easy and time efficient planning method to use when laying out their group sessions from the curriculum chapters. As a way of complementing this material, the reader is provided a composite listing of all 128 techniques contained in the next 11 curriculum chapters of this book.

Last but not least, an overview of the seven components of each curriculum is outlined and briefly described. Readers should find that this chapter provides all the necessary directions for understanding, following, and implementing the ten support group programs provided in this manual.

Dennison Group Practice Model

The ten curriculums contained in this text follow the Dennison Group Practice Model. I originally developed this model 20 years ago. Since its inception, it has been carefully refined as it was applied to children's groups. It offers a user friendly approach to the set-up, planning, and facilitation of children's support groups.

There are six basic components to the Dennison Group Practice Model. These components are as follows:

1. Differentiation of group into three phases: initial, middle, and termination

2. A standard 12-goal sequence

3. A consistent goal focus for all groups in the initial and termination phases

4. A four-step goal sequence is followed for addressing the specific at-risk problem areas

5. Guidelines are provided for the timing of each group phase

6. Interventions are directly connected to the goals in each phase

Table I, "Dennison Group Practice Model," and Table II, "Guide for Phase Timing of a Support Group" summarize the major ingredients of these six components. As readers review these tables, it becomes evident that this is a practice-oriented model. Facilitators should find that the structure of this approach makes both the planning and facilitating of support groups easy and effective.

The first component of this model is the differentiation of group into three distinct phases. Along with other groupworkers like Yalom (Yalom, *The Theory and Practice of Group Psychotherapy,* Basic Books, 1970), I have found that the unique elements of this therapeutic approach necessitate this differentiation. The phasing of support groups is an integral part of this curriculum model; the rationale is that even short-term groups need some initial sessions that focus on relationship building (initial phase). Once a level of trust has been established, the group can address specific content related to an at-risk problem area (middle phase). At the termination of a group, there must be some closure provided for this therapeutic experience (termination phase). Readers will see in Table I, "Dennison Group Practice Model," that the initial, middle, and termination phases of a support group are indicated in the far left-hand column.

Table I also shows that there are four specific goals for each of these three phases. This sequence of 12 goals comprises the second major component of this model. Readers should note that the same 12 general goals are sequenced and consistently followed in all ten support group curriculums. This makes the curriculums very easy to follow, and thus, to duplicate in a wide variety of settings.

The third component of this model is the consistent goal focus of all support groups both in the initial and termination phases. Readers can see in Table I that the goals for those two phases are indicated in the middle column. Following this model, facilitators are directed to address the same four goals in the initial phase.

1. To provide an attractive group setting.

2. To initiate members' participation on-task and with one another.

3. To initiate trust among the members.

4. To educate members about issues and difficulties related to a specific at-risk problem area.

This structured and goal focus emphasis on relationship building in a group's initial sessions has been a unique contribution of the Dennison Model. Specifics on this phase of group are provided in Chapter Three.

The same consistent goal focus idea is utilized for the termination phase of a support group. There are four goals addressed during this ending time in a support group:

TABLE I   *Dennison Group Practice Model*

Group Phase	Group Goals	Intervention Categories
Initial	1. To provide an attractive group setting. 2. To initiate members' participation on-task and with one another. 3. To initiate trust among the membership.	**Hello Group Techniques** (Chapter Three)
	4. To educate members about issues and difficulties related to a particular at-risk problem area.	**Instructive Techniques:** a. Didactic b. Bibliotherapy/Video/Films c. Paper/Pencil Tasks
Middle	5. To increase group development goals established in initial phase (i.e., goals 1-3).	No techniques per se but follow curriculum approach.
	6. To increase members' awareness of their particular difficulties related to the at-risk problem area.	**Awareness of Self Techniques:** a. Exercises Using the Arts b. Disclosure Exercises c. Creative Exercise
	7. To provide alternative coping behaviors for the at-risk problem area.	**Alternative Coping Techniques:** a. In Vivo Exercises b. Completion Tasks c. Game Exercises
	8. To assist members in the integration of new coping behaviors into their repertoire.	**Integration Techniques:** a. Empowerment Exercises b. Check-ups/Assignments c. Confirmation Tasks
Termination	9. To have members acknowledge the value of the group. 10. To assist members in validating their changes. 11. To have members brainstorm other sources of support. 12. To have members grieve the ending of group.	**Goodbye Group Techniques** (Chapter Thirteen)

TABLE II   *Guide for Phase Timing of a Support Group*

Total # of Sessions	# of Sessions in Initial Phase	# of Sessions in Middle Phase	# of Sessions in Termination Phase
6	4	2	last part of final session
8	4	4	last part of final session
12	4	7	1
16	5	10	1
20	6	13	1
24	6	16	2

1. To have members acknowledge the value of the group.
2. To assist members in validating their changes.
3. To have members brainstorm other sources of support.
4. To have members grieve the ending of group.

The rationale is that all support groups must provide some opportunities in the ending session(s) in which members can reflect on their changes, grieve the group's termination, and think about ways to maintain their changes. This guideline applies to all support groups addressed in this book.

The fourth component of the Dennison Group Practice Model is a four-step goal sequence, which is consistently followed when addressing the specific at-risk problem area of a support group. These four goals are listed in the middle column of Table I as goals four, six, seven, and eight. For the first time, this model introduces a much more structured step-by-step format for the change process of an at-risk problem. Here again, the general sequencing of the four goals, as listed below, is consistently followed for all the support group programs in Chapters Four through Twelve. The underlined part of each of the goals below indicates where they are individualized in each curriculum, so that the specific at-risk problems can be listed.

4. To educate members about issues and difficulties related to *a particular at-risk problem area.*
6. To increase members' awareness of their particular difficulties related to *the at-risk problem area.*
7. To provide alternative coping behaviors for *the at-risk problem area.*
8. To assist members in the integration of new coping behaviors into their repertoire related to *the at-risk problem area.*

This consistent goal sequence throughout the curriculums assists facilitators in following this support group model. At the same time, school personnel have a program compatible with the educational approach. I have strived to develop a model that combines effective group therapy with a type of educational curriculum in which the goals are clearly defined and connected directly to actual session plans. Mental health professionals should find that this combination of approaches makes it easier to articulate their support group services to youngsters, parents, and other professionals.

The fifth component of the group practice model is the timing of groups in each of the three phases. Table II (Guide for Phase Timing of a Support Group) is a guide for breaking down the number of sessions to be spent in each phase, depending on the total length of a support group. As noted on this table, it is essential that a minimum of four sessions be spent in the initial phase in order to establish a beginning group relationship and level of trust. In the left column, under the initial phase, note that as the total number of sessions increases, so do the recommended number of sessions in this phase. It has been my experience that the level of group attraction and cohesiveness established in the initial phase is the single most impacting variable on members' disclosure level in the middle phase.

One can also see in Table II that in all support groups, some amount of time (dependent on total length of group as seen in right column under Termination Phase) must be spent in providing a closure experience. For the middle phase, the amount of sessions is determined by the total number of sessions available after time is spent in the initial phase and later in the termination phase.

Readers are cautioned to view this guide in Table II as a suggested framework for timing support group sessions in each phase; it is not intended as a hard and fast rule, but as a guide to be modified depending on the needs of a particular population of at-risk children. For example, youngsters having more severe difficulties may require as long as 12 sessions in the initial phase. For these children, the goal of enjoying a support group setting, participating fully, and becoming a cohesive unit would be an appropriate therapeutic accomplishment in and of itself.

The last component of the Dennison Model is the direct connection of interventions to goals in each of the three phases of a support group. This coordination of goals to actual techniques is in the right-hand column of Table I. A consistent sequencing of interventions has been developed for each of the at-risk support group curriculums. This aspect of the model results in the goals of each phase being addressed throughout a program's existence. By following the intervention plan in each curriculum chapter, facilitators will accomplish the major goals of a support group from initiation to closure.

This sixth component shows the unique combination of a therapeutic and educational approach to support group treatment. Unlike the more free flowing approach to groups, this model adheres to a structured goal focus where there is a step-by-step sequencing of goals with their corresponding interventions. This highly specific delineation of support groups is what has resulted in the *curriculum* approach

utilized in this manual. Readers will be amazed at how easy it is to follow, duplicate, and facilitate the intervention plans in each of the curriculums. At long last,
the assets of the mental health and educational fields have been combined to create
an extremely effective approach to support groups.

Ten Support Group Curriculums

The following ten support group curriculums are provided in this manual.

1. Social Skills Enhancement Support Group Curriculum

2. Self-Esteem Building Support Group Curriculum

3. Children of Family Life Changes Support Group Curriculum

4. Children of Substance Abusers Support Group Curriculum

5. Anger/Conflict Resolution Support Group Curriculum

6. Traumatized Children's Support Group Curriculum

7. Stress Management Support Group Curriculum

8. Learning Performance Support Group Curriculum

9. School Motivation/Attitude Enhancement Support Group Curriculum

10. General Support Group

The first nine curriculums listed above are single-problem focused support
group programs. I have found that these types of support groups are most ideal; for
this reason, they comprise the majority of curriculums provided. These programs
address a single at-risk problem area; thus, the impact on members is enhanced
because treatment is focusing on one area of functioning. These nine curriculums
are provided in Chapters Four through Twelve.

The tenth curriculum, the general support group, is a multi-problem focused
group. There is not a curriculum chapter per se for this type of program. Instead, as
seen on Table III, General Support Group Planning, there are two ways to set up and
plan this type of program following the Dennison Group Practice Model. First, as
seen in the top half of Table III (Plan I), facilitators may choose to plan this type of
group with no specific problem focus. The goal of such a program is to create, from
the interventions in Chapters Three and Thirteen, an attractive group where members fully participate and become a cohesive unit. With many multi-problem children, this can be a very realistic and worthwhile accomplishment for a support group
program.

The second type of set-up for a general support group is indicated in the lower
half of Table III, called Plan II. Following this plan option, the facilitator individually determines a set of at-risk problems for the focus of a group. The at-risk problems selected would be determined from the presenting issues among the membership of a particular group. Then, goals and interventions are selected from any

TABLE III *General Support Group Planning*

	Initial Phase	**Middle Phase**	**Termination Phase**
P L A N I	Hello Group Plans Chapter Three	No at-risk problem areas per se are addressed	Goodbye Group Plans Chapter Thirteen
	Session Plans	**Session Plans**	**Session Plans**
P L A N II	Hello Group Plans Chapter Three	Session themes and interventions from any of the nine single-problem focused support group curriculums (Chapters Four through Twelve). These are individually selected and planned depending on the presenting problems of group members.	Goodbye Group Plans Chapter Thirteen

combination of the nine single-problem focused curriculum chapters (Chapters Four through Twelve) for the middle phase. Interventions from Chapter Three (Hello Group Plans) and Chapter Thirteen (Goodbye Group Plans) would still be utilized for this type of support group, since it follows the Dennison Group Practice Model.

Although this type of support group is less than ideal, it is often the most practical one. Clinicians will sometimes find that they do not have enough children with any one at-risk problem to warrant putting them into a single-problem focused group. In this situation, one of these general support group plans would best serve the needs of the youngsters. School personnel often find themselves faced with this dilemma, and choose this type of support group approach for students.

Planning Support Groups from the Curriculums

As indicated earlier, a consistent and goal-oriented approach to planning has been utilized for all ten curriculums. Table I, "Dennison Group Practice Model," is an overview of the connection between group objectives and actual interventions contained in the curriculum chapters. There are a total of 12 group goals covering the initial, middle, and termination phases.

Facilitators can see that a wide variety of techniques have been provided for each goal of a support group. Examples of this feature include ten different techniques for the first three initial phase goals (i.e., Hello Group Plans techniques in Chapter Three) and the last four termination phase goals (i.e., Goodbye Group Plans techniques in Chapter Thirteen). A set of three different techniques has been provided for the instructive goal in the initial phase and the three middle phase goals (other than the first one related to group development). With these selection lists, the reader has a total of 32 different techniques for each curriculum package. In addition, several techniques from other curriculums are cross-referenced for each support group program. This variety of interventions is intended to increase the utilization of the curriculums for a larger number of settings and specific population needs.

When using the support group curriculums, readers can individually plan their sessions by following this same basic goal-directed procedure (i.e., initial phase goals to middle phase goals to termination phase goals). Facilitators should select specific techniques from each of the six categories designated for each goal area. These six categories are indicated in bold print on the far-right column of Table I. There are two intervention categories for the initial phase (Hello Group Plans techniques and Instructive techniques), three for the middle phase (Awareness of Self, Alternative Coping, and Integration), and one for the termination phase (Goodbye Group techniques).

To facilitate the selection and planning of techniques for group sessions, two forms have been provided on Tables IV (Group Session Plan I) and V (Group Session Plan II). Clinicians can use these two sheets to individually plan groups from any of the curriculum chapters. Readers will note that on Table IV, the first box is intended for initial sessions from the Hello Group Plans package (Chapter Three). As indicated in this chapter, facilitators must initially spend at least four sessions developing a positive relationship among the membership while providing instructional material on the at-risk problem area. The remaining boxes on Tables IV and V are identified and intended for planning middle phase sessions. These ten session plans should include the objectives, techniques, and any processing comments. Finally, the reader will see in Table V that the ending box has been specifically provided for the terminating sessions. The techniques selected for these final sessions in a support group should be from the Goodbye Group Plans package in Chapter Thirteen.

There is one curriculum that does not exactly follow these two planning forms (i.e., Tables IV and V). The general support group curriculum is individually developed by each facilitator. Techniques for this group are selected from any of the following eleven chapters (Chapters Three through Thirteen). These same two forms can be utilized, but the reader needs to remember that the techniques will instead

TABLE IV   *Name of Group:* _____   *Session Plan I*

Hello Group Plans Used: Session 1: _____ Session 2: _____ Session 3: _____ Session 4: _____ Processing: _____	Session: _____ Objective: _____ Technique: _____ Processing: _____
Session: _____ Objective: _____ Technique: _____ Processing: _____	Session: _____ Objective: _____ Technique: _____ Processing: _____
Session: _____ Objective: _____ Technique: _____ Processing: _____	Session: _____ Objective: _____ Technique: _____ Processing: _____

come from a wider combination of curriculums. Because it is a general support group model, the facilitator will have to more carefully plan the selection of techniques so that they are directly related to relevant issues and problems of members. Clinicians are reminded, however, that the same goal sequence procedure is followed when setting up this type of support group.

Since there is usually not enough time for planning groups in many settings, facilitators should feel free to utilize the numbering system in this text for the objectives and techniques listed on the two planning sheets (Tables IV and V). This numerical reference system allows the reader to quickly write the corresponding numbers for the objectives' and techniques' lines on the planning sheet, rather than having to write them out completely. It will still be necessary to make some quick processing notes (see last line in twelve boxes on Tables IV and V) after each session in order to remember significant group responses during the session.

TABLE V   *Name of Group:* _____   *Session Plan II*

Session: _____ Objective: _____ Technique: _____ Processing: _____	Session: _____ Objective: _____ Technique: _____ Processing: _____
Session: _____ Objective: _____ Technique: _____ Processing: _____	Session: _____ Objective: _____ Technique: _____ Processing: _____
Session: _____ Objective: _____ Technique: _____ Processing: _____	**Goodbye Group Plans Used:** Session 1: _____ Session 2: _____ Processing: _____ _____

Clinicians can now see how this planning method is structured yet flexible. Facilitators have a tremendous amount of structure and direction for their planning in all the curriculums. At the same time, a variety of techniques has been provided to attain each of the 12 objectives for a children's support group. This planning method is very practical and relevant in a wide variety of settings.

Complete List of Techniques

To help readers with an overview of the techniques in this manual, two composite listing tables have been provided. On Table VI (Technique Categories and Corresponding Technique Numbers), a complete listing of the technique categories in the left column and the corresponding technique numbers from the curriculums in the right column is provided. This particular table will help the facilitator cross-reference similar techniques between the curriculums when he or she wants to modify an intervention used with a particular support group.

TABLE VI   *Technique Categories and Corresponding Technique Numbers*

Technique Categories	Corresponding Technique Numbers
Hello Group	10 techniques in Chapter Three
Instructive	
Didactic	Technique #1 in each chapter
Bibliotherapy/Video/Films	Technique #2 in each chapter
Paper/Pencil Tasks	Technique #3 in each chapter
Self-Awareness	
Exercise Using the Arts	Technique #4 in each chapter
Disclosure Exercise	Technique #5 in each chapter
Creative Exercise	Technique #6 in each chapter
Alternative Coping	
In Vivo Exercises	Technique #7 in each chapter
Completion Tasks	Technique #8 in each chapter
Game Exercises	Technique #9 in each chapter
Integration	
Empowerment Exercises	Technique #10 in each chapter
Check-Ups/Assignments	Technique #11 in each chapter
Confirmation Tasks	Technique #12 in each chapter
Goodbye Group	10 techniques in Chapter Thirteen

Second, Table VII (Techniques in Chapters Three through Thirteen) contains a comprehensive listing of all techniques by title and corresponding number from the eleven curriculum chapters. This table will assist readers in quickly finding specific techniques in any of the curriculums. Counselors will find, in many cases, that the title alone for a particular technique will provide a general understanding of its purpose. Readers are encouraged to refer to this technique list when making modifications or creating new intervention ideas.

TABLE VII   *Techniques in Chapters Three through Thirteen*

Chapter Three: Hello Group Plans	Chapter Four: Social Skills Enhancement Support Group Curriculum
1. Getting To Know You	1. Dear Friend
2. Talk And Have Fun	2. Bibliotherapy/Video/Films
3. My Week In Cartoons	3. Tell Us Your Secret
4. Be A Copy Cat	4. Pipe Up
5. My Sticker Face Family	5. Computer Friendly
6. Pet Peeve Alert	6. Making The Grade
7. If I Were A . . .	7. Dream On
8. Leader Says	8. Target Practice
9. Your Life In Pictures	9. I'm Speechless
10. Wave Your Flag	10. Your Mission
	11. More Power To You
	12. Pack Your Bags

Chapter Five: Self-Esteem Building Support Group Curriculum	Chapter Six: Children of Family Life Changes Support Group Curriculum
1. Not A Lot Of Hot Air	1. Take A Walk Down This Road
2. Bibliotherapy/Video/Films	2. Bibliotherapy/Video/Films
3. Make Your Own Magic	3. Mixed Up Feelings
4. Cartooning Around	4. Your Sculptured Clay Family
5. Pop The Bag	5. Slice Up My Life
6. A Shopping List	6. Keeping Tabs On My Family
7. A Match-Up	7. Over And Done
8. You Liking You	8. The Family News Daily
9. Reach Out And Tell Us	9. Say It With Glasses
10. A Tune Up On Me	10. A Meditation For Me
11. Adequate And Proud Of It	11. Thumbs Up/Thumbs Down
12. A Layout Plan For A New Confident Me	12. Imagine Your Future

TABLE VII   *Techniques in Chapters Three through Thirteen—continued*

Chapter Seven: Children of Substance Abusers Support Group Curriculum	Chapter Eight: Anger/Conflict Resolution Support Group Curriculum
1. The Path Of Least Pain	1. Making Sense Of Your Anger
2. Bibliotherapy/Video/Films	2. Bibliotherapy/Video/Films
3. Guess Why?	3. Popping Your Cork
4. Scenes To Cut	4. Listen To Your Anger
5. A Book Review On Me	5. Problems And More Problems
6. Leave The Driving To Me	6. Out The Window
7. Recycle Your Problems	7. Picture This!
8. Puppet Responses	8. Be Like A Traffic Light
9. A Coping Act	9. Run With It
10. Shield Of Control	10. Group Oscar Awards
11. Facing Up To Your Worst Fear	11. Give Your Verdict
12. Teach Us	12. Wad It Up And Fly Away

Chapter Nine: Traumatized Children's Support Group Curriculum	Chapter Ten: Stress Management Support Group Curriculum
1. Disappointments In My Life	1. A Living Example
2. Bibliotherapy/Video/Films	2. Bibliotherapy/Video/Films
3. Say It With Feelings	3. Words That Spell Stress
4. My Ups And Downs	4. Picture Perfect
5. A Penny For Your Thoughts	5. Out Of Balance
6. Talk Back For Me	6. Stress Combat
7. The "Big Test"	7. Stress Counter Attack
8. Pull Me Up	8. Build A Stress Relief Ladder
9. Find The Words For You	9. What's Your Secret
10. Me Power	10. Throw Me A Line
11. Just Call Your Helper	11. Stress Check
12. An S.O.S. Code Plan	12. Prove It

TABLE VII   *Techniques in Chapters Three through Thirteen—concluded*

Chapter Eleven: Learning Performance Support Group Curriculum	Chapter Twelve: School Motivation/ Attitude Enhancement Support Group Curriculum
1. Now I See	1. Hidden Pictures/Hidden Problems
2. Bibliotherapy/Video/Films	2. Bibliotherapy/Video/Films
3. Tracking Me In School	3. Next Came . . .
4. Lightbulbs Go Off	4. A Rap Song On School
5. Pull My Leg	5. Trash It
6. Read Me Like A Comic Book	6. You Win
7. Create A Scene	7. Shadowing A Peer
8. Look For The Answer	8. Work It Out
9. X Marks The Spot	9. Opposite Day
10. Go It Alone	10. Dial . . . For A Positive School Attitude
11. Me Watching You	11. On Location
12. How Good?	12. Attitude Adjustment Quiz

Chapter Thirteen: Goodbye Group Plans

1. I.D. On Me Now
2. Remember To Write
3. People Who Will Look Out For You
4. If My Heart Could Talk
5. When This Happens, I'll Just . . .
6. Same Feeling, Different Time
7. Check It Out
8. Testing Your Memory
9. Sign On The Dotted Line
10. Party Time

Directions for Use of Curriculum

The following seven components have been provided for each of the support group curriculums.

I. *Treatment Guidelines*

Ten specific guidelines are provided for the unique planning and facilitating issues of each support group curriculum. Readers will find these suggestions to be very clearly and concisely presented. These guidelines will ensure facilitators' success in setting up any of the ten support group programs provided in this manual.

II. *Assessment Instruments*

A list of ten assessment scales has been suggested in the next section of each curriculum. These instruments are intended to give the reader a sampling of the types of objective scales available on the market to measure a specific at-risk functioning area. All instruments listed have a respectable level of reliability and validity established. In Appendix F (Publishers of Assessment Scales), the reader will find an alphabetical listing, by scale title, of all publishers of instruments listed in the curriculums throughout this text. This data will provide facilitators with mailing addresses for obtaining particular scales and the accompanying administration manuals.

III. *Relevant Session Themes*

A concise listing of the most relevant themes among children having each at-risk problem is outlined in the curriculums. Facilitators will want to review this list before setting up and conducting their support groups. This data can be helpful in identifying session topics for each meeting of a group. The latter information can also assist clinicians in developing relevant content for those sessions.

IV. *Techniques for Each At-Risk Support Group*

The fifth component of each curriculum provides an easy and quick overview of the 12 techniques for each at-risk area. This data is contained in a concise table that lists all of the session objectives for each support group, along with the techniques for each curriculum. The following 12 types of techniques have been consistently provided in each curriculum chapter to attain this therapeutic flow of objectives to interventions.

1. Didactic Techniques

2. Bibliotherapy/Videotape/Films

3. Paper and Pencil Tasks

4. Exercises Using the Arts

5. Disclosure Tasks

6. Creative Exercises

7. In Vivo Exercises

8. Completion Tasks

9. Game Exercises

10. Empowerment Exercises

11. Check-Ups/Assignments

12. Confirmation Tasks

Facilitators should feel free to use their groupwork expertise in modifying, adapting, and developing new techniques for their particular groups.

V. *Session Objectives*

Next in each curriculum, the reader will find a complete listing of session objectives by group phase. Facilitators were given specifics on the sequencing of these goals via the Dennison Short-Term Support Group Model earlier in this chapter (Dennison Group Practice Model, or Table I). These objectives are extremely important because they provide the primary focus for group sessions. Facilitators should follow the sequencing of these session objectives when developing new plans for their individual groups.

Clinicians are reminded that all interventions listed in the curriculums have been specifically developed for one of the session objectives. There is a table in each curriculum (i.e., Planning Sequence of Objectives and Techniques for a *specific at-risk problem*) that very clearly shows this connection between phase goals and interventions. This makes the planning of group sessions easy for the facilitator to follow.

VI. *Technique Instructions*

Technique instructions have been provided for each at-risk support group curriculum. Readers will find specific step-by-step directions for each of these interventions. All instructional sheets provide implementation specifics, a quick summary statement of necessary materials, and a section noting cautions/comments in regard to usage of the technique. Accompanying hands-on sheets have been provided for many of these interventions. Readers should feel free to copy these related task sheets as long as they are for use by the group members. My intent is to provide as much of the necessary material as possible for each suggested technique.

VII. *Bibliography*

The last component of each curriculum is a "how-to-do-it" bibliography. Here, the reader will find a very extensive and recent update of resources that provide guidelines and ideas for setting up and facilitating each of the at-risk support groups with children. Facilitators will find this listing helpful when looking for other ideas for their particular support group program.

Chapter 3

Hello Group Plans

The Hello Group Plans are initial phase techniques for use in the beginning sessions of all the support group programs contained in the next nine curriculum chapters. The total length and purpose of a children's support group will determine the number of sessions spent in the initial phase and the amount of techniques utilized from the plans in this chapter.

Readers may recall from Chapter Two (Table I) that the following four specific objectives are addressed in the initial phase of a support group.

1. To provide an attractive group setting.

2. To initiate members' participation on-task and with one another.

3. To initiate group cohesiveness among the membership.

4. To instruct members in difficulties that can result from an at-risk problem area.

These objectives define the primary therapeutic aspects of a group, and are the essential ingredients in any combination of youngsters becoming a cohesive unit. It is important to remember that these initial objectives are of primary emphasis in this first phase. Therefore, above all else, clinicians must aim to create attractive groups where members will fully participate and develop a high level of cohesiveness.

The Hello Group Plans outlined in this chapter address only the first three objectives on the above list. All support groups in this text require the use of intervention plans from this curriculum in order to establish a beginning relationship among members. The fourth goal, however, is attained through any one of the first three interventions listed at the beginning of each of the nine curriculum chapters (Chapters Four through Twelve). These techniques are intended to be instructive plans that address this more didactic objective for support groups. The first three objectives for this initial phase should still be of primary emphasis during the first group sessions. At the same time or soon after these initial meetings, the fourth objective can be addressed, because it does not necessitate as high a trust level among the members. Therefore, this fourth didactic objective is part of the initial phase, but the interventions to attain it are listed instead at the beginning of each curriculum chapter.

In Table II in Chapter Two, timing guidelines were given for the utilization of Hello Group Plans. For example, a six-session group needs to utilize at least four plans from this package. On the other hand, a 12-session group would require the first six sessions to be based on plans from this curriculum. Clinicians need to understand that the intent is not that support groups go through the initial phase in four sessions, but rather, to point out the need for relationship building in a support group. A more therapeutic children's group requires about eight to 12 sessions in this phase. Readers who intend to conduct such programs should feel free to use the entire Hello Group Plans for the therapy-oriented group program. Such groups are intended to elicit a more intimate level of disclosure from members. The support group model relies more on an instructive approach and less on members' actual problem disclosure.

Treatment Guidelines of Hello Group Plans

The primary purpose of this package of plans is to create an attractive setting where members fully participate and become a cohesive unit. Specific treatment guidelines when conducting support groups in this initial phase include the following.

1. Facilitators should plan fun and therapeutic play experiences during this phase. Remember, the youngsters have to be attracted to a new group program to participate.

2. Interventions should take into account members' attention span. There should be a routine change of task in each session. In addition, there should not be too long a lapse of time between participants' turns in activities.

3. All disclosure requested during this phase should be positive, factual, and non-threatening. It is extremely important that members be given the message that they will be asked to disclose at a comfortable level.

4. The logistics and physical setting will have more effect on a group in this first phase than at any other time in its development. For this reason, it is very helpful to have as close to an ideal situation as possible when starting a group. The reader is referred to Chapter One for more specifics on the ideal set-up of a support group.

5. Facilitators should initiate, elicit, and monitor balanced participation in these initial phase groups. It is essential that members be told immediately that everyone will participate equally in the sessions. Establishing this

norm at this time will allow later sessions to follow suit with little direction from the facilitator. I recommend a system of members going around the circle in order, so that the clinician does not have to constantly monitor who has responded and who has not.

6. A set format should be established at this point for all sessions. This predictable routine is comfort-producing to children and addresses their short attention spans.

7. It is extremely important at this point that all sessions be carefully planned. The ten-session plans in this chapter are provided with very specific step-by-step instructions. Clinicians who decide to modify these plans or create new ones need to follow a similar procedure in their revised planning.

8. All competition in this phase should be group based. Examples include the membership versus a timer or the facilitator in a game, or the participants trying to beat a pre-determined score. Specifics on these types of therapeutic games are provided in the technique instruction for the Hello Group Plans and all other curriculums provided in this manual.

9. Facilitators should avoid rule talk during these first few sessions. Instead, members should be reminded that the same rules as in their classrooms apply. The issue here is not that the children don't know the rules, but that they are unable to abide by them.

10. Clinicians need to take an in-charge role during these first group sessions. Just as is true with good teachers, effective facilitators should set specific limits for behavior yet convey a caring and accepting attitude toward the children.

11. Often times, it helps children in new groups to have special events or rewards planned in advance for their behavior. Clinicians in this first phase may choose to tell a group about a fun field trip, party, or award ceremony at a future session. Such an announcement adds an attractive element to the group and helps maintain on-task behavior.

12. It is imperative that facilitators be enthusiastic about their support groups from the start. Youngsters are perceptive and immediately pick up on the clinician's interest and excitement or the absence of it.

Hello Group Plans

The next several pages contain a ten-session sequencing plan for the initial sessions of any support group. Both the session objectives and interventions are indicated for all ten plans on Table IX, Hello Group Session Plans. Clinicians will recall that all of these objectives are based on the goals for the initial phase of a support group.

Facilitators will need to select interventions for their first few meetings with any group from these ten-session plans. Seasoned group clinicians should feel free to use these planning ideas as a guide to develop others.

A set format has been followed for the technique instructions. Three basic components are addressed in each of the ten session instructions. First, a quick summary of necessary materials is indicated. Second, the reader is given specific step-by-step directions to follow when utilizing a particular technique. Then, a third section on Cautions and Comments is provided, where modifications of each technique are outlined along with any particular therapeutic safety points regarding the use of the intervention. Readers are encouraged to review completely these instructional sheets before using any of the suggested session plans from this Hello Group package.

TABLE IX   *Hello Group Session Plans*

Session 1	Session 4	Session 7
Objective: Introduction to group	*Objective:* Building a trusting relationship	*Objective:* Members getting to know one another
Technique: Getting to Know You	*Technique:* Be A Copy Cat	*Technique:* If I Were A . . .
Session 2	**Session 5**	**Session 8**
Objective: Having fun as a group	*Objective:* Members getting to know one another	*Objective:* Increased interaction between members
Technique: Talk and Have Fun	*Technique:* My Sticker Face Family	*Technique:* Leader Says
Session 3	**Session 6**	**Session 9 & 10**
Objective: Members getting to know one another	*Objective:* Having fun as a group	*Objective:* Increased disclosure among members
Technique: My Week In Cartoons	*Technique:* Pet Peeve Alert	*Technique:* Your Life In Pictures & Wave Your Flag

▶ Technique #1

Title: Getting To Know You

Technique category: Paper/Pencil Task

Objective: To introduce members to one another.

Materials needed:

- Facilitators will need to plan a series of disclosure questions before this session. A sample of such questions can be found on page 42.
- Pencils

Procedure:

1. Each disclosure question is posed to the group. All members answer, with the facilitator initially modeling their response.
2. Questions are presented one at a time so commonalities can surface more clearly among members.
3. Reinforce disclosures, point out similarities, and in some instances, pose more probing questions about particular responses.
4. Process members' positive reactions to this exercise.

Cautions/comments:

This technique can be used again and again in a group. The facilitator will have to merely change the type of questions posed, depending on the specific focus of the group. It is important that facilitators exercise a great deal of thought when preparing these questions. The content must be at a surface level of disclosure and be answered comfortably by the membership.

▶ Getting to Know You Questions

Instructions: Please answer the questions below.

1. Who is in your family?

   _____

2. What is your favorite class at school?

   _____

3. What do you want to be when you grow up?

   _____

4. What are your two favorite things to do after school?

   _____

   _____

5. Where else has your family lived?

   _____

6. What is your favorite holiday?

   _____

7. Name the meal that you just love.

   _____

8. Tell us your two favorite TV shows.

   _____

   _____

9. Name one thing about your family that makes you happy.

   _____

10. What was special about your last birthday?

   _____

▸ Technique #2

Title: Talk And Have Fun

Technique category: Disclosure Exercise

Objective: To increase disclosure among the members.

Materials needed:

- Materials for game selected
- Prepare list of factual and positive disclosure questions

Procedure:

1. Before the session, the facilitator selects a game to play with the group. The game should be easily played with the size of group. Ideas for games can be found in such references as *The Incredible Indoor Games Book* (by Bob Gryso, Fearson Teacher Aids, 1982).

2. The game and corresponding rules are introduced.

3. Sometimes, it is a good idea to do a trial run of the game.

4. Members are told that an additional rule to the game is that in each round, they will have to answer a different disclosure question before their turn.

5. Game is conducted following the rules and posing a new disclosure question each round.

6. Competition should be group based (group versus facilitator) so members win as a unit. It will be important at this point in group to make sure the members win.

7. Process members' positive responses to the game at the end.

Cautions/comments:

It is advisable not to plan a game that requires too much movement. During early group sessions, members are more likely to have difficulty keeping their movement under control. When movement is required in a game, the facilitator should allow only one member out of their seat at a time to complete the required turn for the game.

▸ **Technique #3**

Title:	My Week In Cartoons
Technique category:	Exercise Using the Arts
Objective:	To provide another avenue for members to get to know one another.

Materials needed:

- Copies of the sheet entitled "Me in Cartoons," found on page 45.
- Pencils, crayons, markers

Procedure:

1. Pass out the sheet titled "Me in Cartoons" to all group members.
2. Allow 5 to 10 minutes for the completion of this task.
3. Ask everyone to share their responses by going around the circle in order. The facilitator should initially share their responses to the task sheet for purposes of modeling.
4. If time allows, pose some discussion questions related to the task sheet responses.
5. Process members' positive reactions at the end of the session.

Cautions/comments:

Incomplete cartoons are wonderful ways for youngsters to disclose and reveal some otherwise difficult things about themselves. Most children find incomplete pictures less anxiety provoking since they have to work around the picture already on the page. The beauty of this technique is its versatility. The reader can develop other cartoon completions using this sample one.

▸ Me in Cartoons

Instructions: Complete each cartoon below showing the last time you felt that way. You can either draw or write to complete these cartoons.

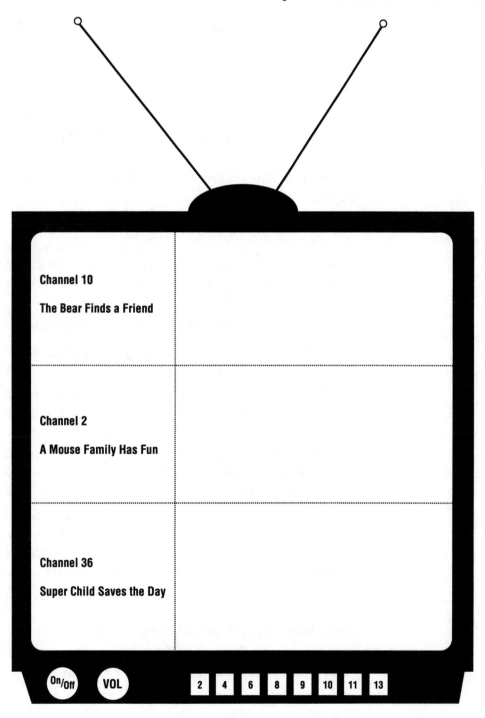

Channel 10

The Bear Finds a Friend

Channel 2

A Mouse Family Has Fun

Channel 36

Super Child Saves the Day

On/Off   VOL   2 4 6 8 9 10 11 13

▸ Technique #4

Title:	Be A Copy Cat
Technique category:	Memory Game
Objective:	To build a trusting relationship among the members.

Materials:

- Before this session, the facilitator will need to prepare disclosure questions that can be used for the game. These questions should be factual or of a positive nature.
- Copies of the form entitled "Copy Cat Game," found on page 48.
- Pencils

Procedure:

1. At the onset of this session, members are told they are going to be playing the fun game of "Copy Cat." Then, the sheet entitled "Copy Cat Game" is passed out to all members.

2. Next, the rules below are reviewed with the membership.

   - Each member will get a turn in the game by going around the circle in order, one after another.

   - When a member has his/her turn, they must share their response to a disclosure question posed by the facilitator. All participants will have to answer the same question in each round of the game.

   - After each round, the members will be given a designated period of time to write on their "Copy Cat Game" sheet all the responses they remember that were given by other members and also their own.

   - Everyone checks their own list and each time a list is complete and correct the group gets a point. Each time a list is incomplete and/or incorrect, the facilitator gets the point. The one (group or facilitator) with the most points at the end of each round wins.

   - This same format is used for all rounds played in the game.

3. The game is then conducted following the rules.

4. If time allows, discussion questions can be posed to the children in order to probe some of their earlier responses during the game.

5. At the end, everyone should be asked to complete the following sentence: "I really liked this session when _____."

Cautions/comments:

This is a wonderful intervention for eliciting disclosure from members via a fun and non-threatening game. In addition, this technique will reinforce the value of members listening to one another's responses.

▶ Copy Cat Game

Instructions: Use the spaces below to write down all the answers you remember that members gave when they answered the questions in each round of the game. This is one time you can be a copy cat.

Round One

1. _____
2. _____
3. _____
4. _____
5. _____
6. _____
7. _____
8. _____

Round Three

1. _____
2. _____
3. _____
4. _____
5. _____
6. _____
7. _____
8. _____

Round Two

1. _____
2. _____
3. _____
4. _____
5. _____
6. _____
7. _____
8. _____

Round Four

1. _____
2. _____
3. _____
4. _____
5. _____
6. _____
7. _____
8. _____

▸ Technique #5

Title:	My Sticker Face Family
Technique category:	Exercise Using the Arts
Objective:	To increase disclosure among the membership.

Materials:

- Plain white paper
- Sticker packets that include 16 faces (four each of happy, sad, angry, and afraid)
- Crayons

Procedure:

1. Members are told they are going to have an opportunity to participate in a creative exercise where they can draw a picture of their families doing something. Then, everyone is given a sticker face packet, a plain white sheet of paper, and crayons. Everyone is further instructed to use stick bodies for their families along with selecting a face from the sticker packet that best depicts each person's usual expression.

2. Members are allowed 10 to 15 minutes to complete this task.

3. After everyone is done, each child takes a turn sharing their sticker face family drawing. Facilitators should be the first to share. This will create a more comfortable setting for this disclosure.

4. Throughout the above sharing, members' commonalities and significant disclosure should be reinforced.

5. At the end, everyone is asked to share in their own creative way the most enjoyable part of this experience.

Cautions/comments:

This is a wonderful disclosure technique for eliciting members' views of their family. It is a very effective way to increase the disclosure level in a particular group. Typically, the set-up of this intervention greatly decreases the anxiety around drawing. In fact, I have found that youngsters often enjoy this alternative drawing technique. Usually, this intervention should be used after an initial relationship and level of trust have been established in a group. There is value in the very task of members doing this drawing and showing it. Even if there is not much disclosure, the non-verbal ventilation of members' feelings regarding their families can prove very beneficial.

▶ Technique #6

Title:	Pet Peeve Alert
Technique category:	Disclosure Exercise
Objective:	To assist the members in getting to know one another better through a fun game.

Materials:

- "Find Your Pet Peeve" sheet found on page 52.
- Pencils
- Large blackboard or newsprint pad

Procedure:

1. At the onset of this session, members are told they are going to be playing the fun game of Pet Peeve Alert. The form entitled "Find Your Pet Peeve" is distributed to everyone. Younger groups may require a review of this sheet to clarify "pet peeve."

2. The rules below are reviewed with the membership.

   - Each person gets a turn to pick a place (school, home, playground, park, vacation, etc.) where someone could have a pet peeve.

   - When the place is named, the group has a set period of time for all members to share their pet peeve for that particular place.

   - The game continues with everyone taking their turn to name the place for pet peeves, with the same game played after each participant's turn.

   - Each round, if the members beat the time, the group gets a point. When the participants do not beat the allotted time (i.e., all members have not been able to share their pet peeve for that place), the facilitator gets the point. Whoever (group or facilitator) has the most points at the end wins.

3. The game is then conducted following the rules.

4. If time allows, discussion questions can be posed to the children in order to probe some of their earlier responses during the game.

5. At the end, everyone should be asked to complete the following sentence: "I really liked this session when _____."

Cautions/comments:

This is a very effective way to elicit members' initial disclosure on content of a less positive or factual nature. Youngsters particularly enjoy the competitive component of this sharing, which tends to overshadow some of their anxiety regarding this more difficult disclosure. It may be helpful for facilitators to participate in this disclosure part of the game initially for modeling purposes.

▶ Find Your Pet Peeve

A "pet peeve" is something that bugs you.

Below are the places where kids might have pet peeves

Home

School

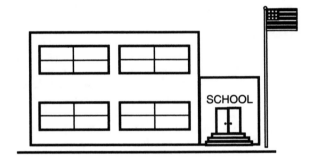

Neighborhood

Sports/Clubs

Everywhere?

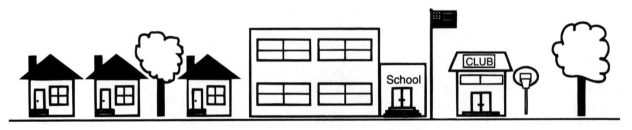

▶ Technique #7

Title:	If I Were A . . .
Technique category:	Paper/Pencil Task
Objective:	To provide an enjoyable task where members can more intimately disclose.

Materials needed:

- Copies of the sheet entitled "If I Were A . . . ," found on page 54.
- Pencils

Procedure:

1. Pass out the sheet entitled "If I Were A . . . " to all group members.
2. Allow 5 to 10 minutes for the completion of this task.
3. Ask everyone to share their responses by going around the circle in order. The facilitator should initially share their responses to the task sheet for purposes of modeling.
4. If time allows, pose some discussion questions related to the task sheet responses.
5. Process members' positive reactions at the end of the session.

Cautions/comments:

The beauty of this technique is that it usually elicits a more gut-level response from members. Typically, children will think through their past week and pick symbols regarding the highlights of that time period. Facilitators may even find that the material that surfaces could hold relevant themes for future sessions. Depending on the group, facilitators may choose to probe issues that arise during this technique.

▶ If I Were A . . .

Instructions: Complete one of the sentences below that best describes your last week. If none of the choices apply to you, feel free to write or draw one of your choices on the back of this sheet.

1.   If I were an animal last week, I would have been a _____

   because _____

   _____ .

turtle	bear	kangaroo
lion	monkey	mouse
lamb	horse	bird
giraffe	cat	rabbit
dog	elephant	cow

2.   If I were a color last week, I would have been _____

   because _____

   _____ .

red	blue	yellow
green	black	orange
purple	white	gray
pink	brown	tan

3.   If I were a vehicle last week, I would have been a _____

   because _____

   _____ .

a specific car	police car
fast sports car	van
bus	motorhome
truck	ambulance
fire engine	an antique car
an old junker	a broken down car

▸ Technique #8

Title:	Leader Says
Technique category:	In Vivo
Objective:	To increase interaction between members.

Materials:

- "Leader Says Questions" form found on page 57.
- Pencils

Procedure:

1. At the onset of this session, members are told they are going to each have a chance to be in charge of the group.

2. The rules below are reviewed with the membership.

   - Each youngster will be the leader for about five minutes and will get their turn by going around the circle in order.

   - When it is a participant's turn as leader, he/she will need to come up with a question they would like to ask everyone. The question must be an appropriate one that either requests some factual information about members or something positive in their lives. At this point, the youngsters should be shown the questions (i.e., leader says questions) to give them a better idea of what types of information should be requested. Facilitators can also allow members to select a question from this list.

   - After each member has asked everyone the same question (going around the circle in order) and thanked them, then the group is asked to give two compliments. These compliments should be given from one member to the "in charge" member so that the participants are interacting directly with one another.

3. The game is then conducted following the above rules.

4. If time allows, discussion questions can be posed to the children in order to probe some of their earlier responses during the game.

5. At the end, everyone should be asked to complete the following sentence: "I really liked this session when _____."

Cautions/comments:

Children typically love this technique. They enjoy the idea of being in charge and often come up with some better questions than adults. The beauty of this intervention is that it establishes structure for positive interaction between members. In addition, there will be a tremendous amount of disclosure in just one session, which serves to build on the group's level of cohesiveness.

▸ Leader Says Questions

Instructions: Feel free to choose your leader question from any of the suggested ones below.

1. What is the best movie you have seen lately?
2. What are your two favorite TV shows?
3. What cartoon do you always watch?
4. Name your two favorite games to play.
5. What does your family do for fun?
6. What other cities have you lived in?
7. What pets do you have or do you wish you had?
8. Which birthday was your favorite one and why?
9. What are you going to be when you grow up?
10. Name the best trip you ever went on.
11. What is your favorite class at school?
12. Tell us what would be your very favorite meal.

▶ Technique #9

Title: Your Life in Pictures

Technique category: Disclosure Exercise

Objective: To continue to build a relationship among members.

Materials:

- Facilitator's photo album. Members will have to be requested to bring in their own album.

Procedure:

1. Before this session, the facilitator will need to ask all members to bring in either a family photo album or just some family pictures. It will be important to emphasize that the facilitator is also bringing in a personal album.

2. At the beginning of the session, all members are instructed to look through their photo albums and choose three pictures they would like to share and talk about in group.

3. Next, the group is requested to be quiet as each member shares their three pictures and the story behind each one. If time permits, facilitators may want to allow questions after each presentation of pictures.

4. Members' positive responses to this technique should be processed at the end of the session.

Cautions/comments:

This is a wonderful technique for group members to get to know one another on a much more intimate level. Facilitators will be delighted to find youngsters disclosing more through this technique than any earlier one. At the same time, sensitivity should be exercised regarding members whose family may not have any photo albums or pictures. It will be important to check this out before this technique is planned. Also, in some situations, the facilitator may need to send home a note with each member indicating the request for an album or pictures. This will also assist young children in remembering their pictures for group.

▸ Technique #10

Title:	Wave Your Flag
Technique category:	Creative Task
Objective:	To increase disclosure among members.

Materials needed:

- Copies of the sheet entitled "Wave Your Flag," found on page 60.
- Pencils
- Crayons

Procedure:

1. Pass out the sheet entitled "Wave Your Flag" to all group members.
2. Allow 5 to 10 minutes for the completion of this task.
3. Ask everyone to share their responses by going around the circle in order. The facilitator should initially share their responses to the task sheet for purposes of modeling.
4. If time allows, pose some discussion questions related to the task sheet responses.
5. Process members' positive reactions at the end of the session.

Cautions/comments:

This symbolic exercise generally elicits more intimate disclosure from the participants. After a session like this one, the members will usually feel a lot closer to one another.

▸ Wave Your Flag

Instructions: Create a flag on the picture below that is symbolic of you and your life.

Chapter 4

Social Skills Enhancement Support Group Curriculum

A complete curriculum for social skills enhancement support groups is provided in this chapter. Step-by-step instructions are outlined for the unique set-up, planning, and facilitation of this type of elementary age support group. An extensive listing of assessment scales, session themes, bibliotherapy books, videotapes/films, and "how-to-do-it" references are included as part of this practical support group guide. This chapter, along with Chapters One, Two, Three, and Thirteen, will provide complete instructions for the set-up through the termination of social skill enhancement support groups.

Treatment Guidelines

Social skill difficulties are usually the most common reason for youngsters' referral to short-term support group programs. Children with such difficulties are the most ideal candidates for this treatment modality. A unique aspect of this at-risk problem area is that the participants of a group are able not only to learn about social skills, but experience them firsthand.

Today many children suffer from varying degrees of social skill deficits. One of the difficulties with treating this population is that potential members of the same group can have a wide variety of difficulties with regard to peer skills. Sometimes, one of the most valuable services a groupworker can provide for these youngsters is an assessment of their peer strengths and weaknesses. This information can be obtained through any of the suggested assessment instruments in the curriculum and through observation of the group members. In many cases, support groups begin resolving peer skill problems while clarifying each member's social skill deficit(s).

Counselors need to be aware of how important friendships are to children. Youngsters may have any number of problems out of their control. Friends can be a tremendous support and help to elementary age children who are at-risk.

Before utilizing this curriculum, the reader should review the following general treatment guidelines for working with children in a social skill support group.

1. It is essential that specifics on members' peer relationship problems be identified. Prior to the group, the counselor should obtain this information from parents and teachers on any one of the checklists or rating forms designed for such use.

2. The most ideal treatment modality for these kids is group counseling. However, some children may require individual counseling before they are ready for a group.

3. Peer pairing counseling (see references in bibliography of this curriculum) is another ideal in-between step for the child with severe peer problems. When another child or two join the youngster in a session, therapeutic activities can be planned in which peer skills are taught through firsthand experiences. Sometimes, a secondary benefit of this intervention is that the child continues such relationships outside the sessions.

4. Counselors should evaluate these youngsters' environment for "availability of peer relationships." In other words, it is important to check on the number of peers in members' neighborhoods or the kinds of relationships available at school. In some cases, a youngster may be having trouble making friends because there are few appropriate ones available. If this situation surfaces during an assessment, parents may need instruction in ways to make positive peer opportunities available for their children.

5. Another factor that may be affecting a youngster's peer relationships is the parents' response to friends. Unfortunately, it is not unusual today for parents with problems to prefer that their children not bring friends home. Instead, they choose to have their kids at home after school by themselves. There are a number of reasons behind this message, such as over protectiveness or the safeguarding of family secrets. Whatever the rationale, these parents may sabotage some of a group's impact on this problem area. When this interfering issue becomes evident, it is usually advisable to either invite the parents into counseling sessions or refer them for family counseling.

6. Assignments can be a helpful way to assist these youngsters in developing their peer relationship skills. Facilitators will want to be sure that the beginning assignments have a high probability of being carried out successfully by the youngsters. Also, it may be necessary to involve

teachers and/or parents with some assignments as a way of gaining their support and the reinforcement of members' progress in this area.

7. It is most important to ask the group members their perception of this problem area and their desired goal. Just as adults differ in their needs for friends, the same holds true with youngsters.

8. Facilitators need to be prepared for problems that may surface among members in this group. It is predictable that children with peer difficulties will usually have trouble getting along in a group setting. For this reason, you may want to have some ideas ready to implement if such difficulties arise. Examples of ways to prevent or stop these problems include: assigned seats, consistent response to rule breaking, use of time out, or having the more dysfunctional students sit next to the facilitator.

9. Children having problems with peers can learn a lot from watching good models. For this reason, interventions such as films, books (see list in bibliotherapy technique), or actual structured observations of peers in the group can be most effective.

10. Even though we are talking about peer skills here, the therapeutic relationship with the facilitator can have an enormous impact on these youngsters. Sometimes a warm, caring, and supportive therapist relationship is the first these kids have ever had with an adult. Often times, children will begin making changes initially just to please their facilitator. The bottom line is that it's okay; this can be a great use of the therapeutic relationship.

Keeping these guidelines in mind, readers are now encouraged to review the following curriculum. This support group package, along with Chapters One, Two, Three, and Thirteen, provide all the necessary information and materials to set up, plan, and facilitate a social skill support group program for elementary age students.

Assessment Instruments

1. Achenbach Child Behavior Checklist
2. Iowa Social Competency Scale: School Age
3. Matson Evaluation of Social Skills with Youngsters
4. Pupil Evaluation Inventory
5. Rochester Peer Rating Scale
6. Self-Perception Inventory
7. Social Adjustment Inventory for Children and Adolescents
8. Social Behavior Assessment
9. Social Skill Rating System
10. Young Children's Social Desirability Scale

Relevant Session Themes

Validation of feelings

Increased sense of not being alone

Skills to meet appropriate friends

Knowledge and skills to reach out to others

Skill in being able to share with friends

Positive attitude about having friends

Ability to develop common interests with peers

Family supportive of peer involvement

Age appropriate maturity

Positive sense of self (confident)

Involvement in appropriate peer situations

Realistic self-image

Sensitivity to others

Appropriate affect and communication of feelings

Effective communication skills

Assertiveness skills with peers

Motivation to interact with peers

Ability to have similar age friends

Good personal hygiene and grooming

Skill in dealing with conflictive peer situations

Increased self-awareness about friendship needs

Planning Sequence of Objectives & Techniques for Social Skills Enhancement Support Group

Group Phase	Group Goals	Intervention Categories
Initial	1. To provide an attractive group setting. 2. To initiate members' participation on-task and with one another. 3. To initiate trust among the membership.	**Hello Group Techniques** (Chapter Three)
	4. To educate members about issues and difficulties related to social skill problems.	**Instructive Techniques:** #1 Dear Friend #2 Bibliotherapy/Video/Films #3 Tell Us Your Secret
Middle	5. To increase group development goals established in initial phase (i.e., goals 1-3).	No techniques per se but follow curriculum approach.
	6. To increase members' awareness of their particular difficulties related to improving their social skills.	**Awareness of Self Techniques:** #4 Pipe Up #5 Computer Friendly #6 Making The Grade
	7. To provide alternative coping behaviors for enhanced social skills.	**Alternative Coping Techniques:** #7 Dream On #8 Target Practice #9 I'm Speechless
	8. To assist members in the integration of new coping behaviors into their repertoire.	**Integration Techniques:** #10 Your Mission #11 More Power To You #12 Pack Your Bags
Termination	9. To have members acknowledge the value of the group. 10. To assist members in validating their changes. 11. To have members brainstorm other sources of support. 12. To have members grieve the ending of group.	**Goodbye Group Techniques** (Chapter Thirteen)

▸ Technique #1

Title:	Dear Friend
Technique category:	Didactic Technique
Objective:	To instruct group members about difficulties resulting from social skill problems.

Materials needed:

- Copies of the sheet entitled "Dear Friend," found on page 67.
- Pencils

Procedure:

1. Pass out the sheet entitled "Dear Friend" to all group members.
2. Allow 5 to 10 minutes for the completion of this task.
3. Ask everyone to share their responses by going around the circle in order. The facilitator should initially share their responses to the task sheet for purposes of modeling.
4. If time allows, pose some discussion questions related to the task sheet responses.
5. Process members' positive reactions at the end of the session.

Cautions/comments:

This is an excellent technique for providing a non-threatening avenue for brainstorming solutions to common peer problems. Facilitators will typically find that this intervention surfaces some great ideas for addressing such difficulties. In addition, it is a time efficient exercise that elicits lots of disclosure around peer problems and solutions.

Readers should feel free to change the content of the letters provided on the task sheet. In fact, members can be asked to anonymously write their own letters with their actual peer problems. These letters can then be listed on a similar type of task sheet. This modification will make the group discussion even more relevant for members.

▶ Dear Friend

Instructions: Read the letters below and think about how you would help each person solve their peer problems.

Dear Friend,

No one at my school likes me. I have no children who live in my neighborhood. I want to have a friend so much. How can I get one?

David

Dear Friend,

I seem to have a lot of friends at school and in my neighborhood. But no one is really a close friend. For example, when a big event comes up, everyone else is busy with their best friend. How can I find even just one close friend?

Alice

Dear Friend,

At my school, you have to be real smart, wear cool clothes, and have money to do lots of things. Otherwise, no one wants to be your friend. You are on the outside of all the social events. What can I do about this since I want to belong but am not real smart and my family is not rich?

Steve

Dear Friend,

I get into fights with my friends on a regular basis. When I first make a friend, we do great together. But after only a few weeks we have a fight and then we are not friends anymore. I am running out of friends. What can I do to stop this pattern?

Jerry

Dear Friend,

I cannot find one friend who is always nice to me. It seems that all friends at some point have a fight with me over something. Why can't friends always agree and help each other?

Mary

Pick one of the letters from the previous page and now write a letter in response to their problem.

Dear _____,

For your problem, I think you should _____

_____

_____

_____

_____

_____

_____

_____

_____.

Sign your name:

_____

▶ Technique #2

Title:	Bibliotherapy/Video/Films
Technique category:	Bibliotherapy/Video/Films
Objective:	To instruct the group regarding peer social skills and problem areas.

Materials:

- Book, film, or videotape selected from the list on page 70.
- Equipment for film or videotape, if used.
- Prepared discussion questions related to the theme of the visual aid chosen.

Procedure:

1. Before the session, the facilitator selects a book, film, or videotape from the list on page 70.
2. Session begins with the book being read or film/videotape being shown.
3. At completion of above task, members can be asked discussion questions that surface their identification with the story. Also, some disclosure that explores the children's similar problems and struggles can be elicited.
4. Members' favorite parts of the book, film, or videotape should be processed at the end.

Cautions/comments:

Typically, members will enjoy the use of bibliotherapy materials or films/videotapes. Through these types of visual interventions, children can easily learn more about their social skills. In addition, youngsters in elementary grades typically identify with characters in books and films. As a result, they are often able to more comfortably talk about their similar issues via the story presented.

Readers are advised to select books that have colorful pictures on almost every page. Children as a whole find it easier to understand the message of a book page when a graphic design depicts the concept. Also, facilitators should be careful that books and films/videotapes selected are not too long. Again, it is important to have time in the session to pose discussion questions and process reactions among the members.

▶ Bibliotherapy

1. Berger, Terry. *Friends.* Julian Messner, Inc., 1981, ages 7-11.

2. Berger, Terry. *Special Friends.* Julian Messner, Inc., 1979, ages 8-11.

3. Bonsall, Crosby Newell. *The Goodbye Summer.* William Morrow & Company, Inc., 1979, ages 9-11.

4. Bulla, Clyde Robert. *Last Look.* Thomas Y. Crowell Company, Inc., 1979, ages 8-10.

5. Carrick, Carol. *Some Friend!* Houghton Mifflin Company, 1979, ages 9-12.

6. Conford, Ellen. *Anything for a Friend.* Little, Brown and Company, 1979, ages 9-11.

7. Delaney, Ned. *Bert and Barney.* Houghton Mifflin Company, 1979, ages 3-7.

8. DeReginers, Beatrice. *A Week in the Life of Best Friends.* Macmillan, 1986, grades 3-7.

9. Enderle, Judith. *Let's Be Friends Again.* Dandelion Press, 1987, grades K-3.

10. Fassler, Joan. *The Boy With a Problem: Johnny Learns to Share His Troubles.* Human Science Press, 1971, grades P-3.

11. Fisher, Lois. *Arianna and Me.* Dodd, 1986, grades 4-6.

12. Gaeddert, LouAnn. *Just Like Sisters.* Dutton, 1981, grades 4-6.

13. Gaeddert, LouAnn. *Your Former Friend, Matthew.* Bantam, 1985, grades 3-6.

14. Gillham, Bill. *The Rich Kid.* Andre Deutsch, 1985, grades 3-6.

15. Gonzalez, Merce. *Roncho Find a Home.* Silver, 1985, grades P-3.

16. Gormley, Beatrice. *Best Friend Insurance.* Avon, 1985, grades 3-6.

17. Greenleaf, Ann. *No Room for Sarah.* Dodd, 1983, grades P-3.

18. Henkes, Kevin. *A Weekend with Wendell.* Greenwillow, 1986, grades P-3.

19. Hermes, Patricia. *Friends Are Like That.* Scholastic, Inc., 1985, grades 5-6.

20. Kohler, Christine. *My Friend is Moving.* Concordia, 1985, grades P-4.

21. Lundell, Margo. *The Get Along Gang and the Big Bully.* Scholastic, Inc., 1984, grades P-2.

22. Matthews, Ellen. *Putting Up with Sherwood.* The Westminster Press, 1980, ages 9-11.

23. Naylor, Phyllis. *The Agony of Alice.* Macmillan, 1985, grades 4-6.

24. Ross, Pat. *Meet M and M.* Pantheon Books, 1980, ages 6-8.

25. Roth, David. *The Hermit of Fog Hollow Station.* Beaufort Books, Inc., 1980, ages 9-12.

26. Roy, Ronald. *Frankie is Staying Back.* Clarion Books, 1981, ages 8-10.

27. Sadler, Marilyn. *The Spoiled Bunny.* Random House, 1986, grades P-3.

28. Sharmat, Marjorie Weinman. *Say Hello, Vanessa.* Holiday House, Inc., 1979, ages 4-7.

29. Silverman, Maida. *The Get Along Gang and the Bad Loser.* Scholastic, Inc., 1984, grades P-2.

Videotapes

1. Beep Beep
   Churchill Films, 1975, 1 film reel (12 minutes), grades 1-6.

2. Being a Good Sport
   Coronet, 1969, 1 film reel (11 minutes), grades 1-3.

3. Buy and Buy
   National Instructional T.V., 1973, 1 film reel (15 minutes), grades 4-6.

4. Can I Help?
   National Instructional T.V., 1973, 1 film reel (15 minutes), grades 4-6.

5. Career and Costume Circus
   AIMS Media, 1970, 1 film reel (10 minutes), grades 1-6.

6. Carnival Circus
   CRM/McGraw-Hill Films, 1980, 1 film reel (23 minutes), grades 1-6.

7. Choice, The
   Phoenix/BFA Films, Inc., 1981, 1 film reel (21 minutes), grades 4-6.

8. Comes In All Colors, Shapes and Sizes
   Lucerne Films and Video, 1980, 1 film reel (24 minutes), grades 1-6.

9. Different Kind of Winning
   Learning Corporation of America/MTI, 1980, 1 film reel (27 minutes), grades 4-6.

10. Doing Things Together - A Child With Prosthetic Hand
    Encyclopedia Britannica Educational Corp., 1977, 1 film reel (6 minutes), grades K-3.

11. Fairness Game
    Coronet, 1974, 1 film reel (11 minutes), grades K-3.

12. Free To Be, You And Me: Friendship and Cooperation, Parts I, II and III
    CRM/McGraw Hill Films, 1974, 1 film reel (17 minutes), grades 4-6.

13. Friend In Deed
    Media Guild, 1979, 1 film reel (28 minutes), grades 4-6.

14. Getting Along With Others
    Encyclopedia Britannica Educational Corp., 1974, 1 film reel (28 minutes), grades K-3.

15. Getting Even
    National Instructional T.V., 1973, 1 film reel (15 minutes), grades 4-6.

16. Golden Rule Game, The
    Higgin, 1979, 1 film reel (11 minutes), grades 1-3.

17. Hopscotch
    Churchill Films, 1972, 1 film reel (12 minutes), grades 1-6.

18. It's A Thought
    Coronet, 1980, 1 film reel (22 minutes), grades 4-6.

19. Jealousy: I Won't Be Your Friend
    Guidance Associates, 1973, 1 film reel (13 minutes), grades 4-6.

20. Let's Be Friends - An Emotionally Disturbed Child
    Encyclopedia Britannica Educational Corp., 1977, 1 film reel (6 minutes), grades K-3.

21. Listen, Cindy
    Churchill Films, 1981, 1 film reel (17 minutes), grades 4-6.

22. Magic Hat, The
    CRM/McGraw Hill Films, 1980, 1 film reel (23 minutes), grades 1-6.

Films

1. *A Kid's Guide to Friendship*
   Spoken Arts, 1988, 3 films and 3 cassettes, grades K-3.

2. *Being Friends*
   Listen and Learn Company, 4 filmstrips with cassettes, grades K-4.

3. *Being Friends*
   Creative Learning, Inc., 4 filmstrips, grades K-4.

4. *Finding Friends, Keeping Friends*
   Creative Learning, Inc., 1 filmstrip, grades 5-6.

5. *Finding Friends, Keeping Friends*
   Random House Media, filmstrip/cassette, grades 5-6.

6. *First Things: You And Others*
   Guidance Associates, 13 filmstrips with cassettes, grades 2-5.

7. *Friends: How They Help...How They Hurt*
   Sunburst, 2 filmstrips/cassettes, grades 5-6.

8. *Learning About Others*
   Guidance Associates, 4 filmstrips with cassettes, grades K-2.

9. *Learning To Cooperate*
   Guidance Associates, 7 filmstrips with cassettes, grades P-2.

10. *Losing Hurts...But Not Forever*
    Marshmedia, 59 frame filmstrip/video, grades 2-4.

11. *The Group and You: Handling the Pressures*
    Sunburst, 2 filmstrips/cassettes, grades 5-6.

▶ Technique #3

Title: Tell Us Your Secret

Technique category: Paper/Pencil Task

Objective: To instruct members about peer social skills and problem areas.

Materials needed:

- Copies of the sheet entitled "Coded Message," found on page 75.
- Pencils

Procedure:

1. Pass out the sheet entitled "Coded Message" to all group members.
2. Allow 5 to 10 minutes for the completion of this task.
3. Ask everyone to share their responses by going around the circle in order. The facilitator should initially share their responses to the task sheet for purposes of modeling.
4. If time allows, pose some discussion questions related to the task sheet responses.
5. Process members' positive reactions at the end of the session.

Cautions/comments:

Paper and pencil tasks are excellent ways to have members think before they share. This technique usually assists in a more time efficient sharing among the group participants. In addition, the graphics on these task sheets usually help keep children's attention and enhance their understanding of the session theme.

Youngsters usually love doing coded messages and can get caught up in the fun of this exercise. As a result, the group often shares more easily about content that might otherwise be too threatening or difficult.

▸ Coded Message

Instructions: Use the code below and write out an important message about friends.

1	2	3	4	5	6	7	8	9	10	11	12	13	14	15	16	17	18	19	20	21	22	23	24	25	26
A	B	C	D	E	F	G	H	I	J	K	L	M	N	O	P	Q	R	S	T	U	V	W	X	Y	Z

Coded message about friends:

_____

_____

_____

_____

_____

Decode this message:

_____

_____

_____

_____

_____

▸ Technique #4

Title: Pipe Up

Technique category: Exercise Using the Arts

Objective: To increase members' awareness of their peer relationship problems.

Materials:

- Pipe cleaners of assorted colors so each member can have three
- Optional: cardboard for each child to use for making their design

Procedure:

1. Members are told they are going to have an opportunity to participate in a creative exercise where they can make a design of something with three pipe cleaners. Participants are instructed to create something symbolic of a social skill they would like to have or one they would like to better use.

2. Members are allowed 10 to 15 minutes to complete this task.

3. After everyone is done, each child takes a turn sharing their pipe cleaner design. Facilitators should be the first to share. This will create a more comfortable setting for this disclosure.

4. Throughout the sharing, members' commonalities and significant disclosure should be reinforced.

5. At the end, everyone is asked to share, in their own creative way, the most enjoyable part of this experience.

Cautions/comments:

Exercises using the arts are wonderful ways to provide non-verbal means for expressing problems or desired skills in a certain area of functioning. Usually, elementary age children love any type of artistic experience and will often disclose more via this avenue. In addition, techniques such as this will allow group participants the opportunity to think through their disclosure before sharing.

▸ Technique #5

Title: Computer Friendly

Technique category: Disclosure Task

Objective: To increase members' awareness of their peer relationship problems.

Materials needed:

- Copies of the sheet entitled "Computer Friendly," found on page 78.
- Pencils

Procedure:

1. Pass out the sheet entitled "Computer Friendly" to all group members.
2. Allow 5 to 10 minutes for the completion of this task.
3. Ask everyone to share their responses by going around the circle in order. The facilitator should initially share their responses to the task sheet for purposes of modeling.
4. If time allows, pose some discussion questions related to the task sheet responses.
5. Process members' positive reactions at the end of the session.

Cautions/comments:

This is an excellent technique for helping members identify the types of attributes they want to have as friends to others. Facilitators will usually find that the use of this computer program idea helps make the disclosure elicited less threatening. Also, it is often easier for young children to disclose what they want from friends rather than identifying their particular peer problems. This intervention is a type of back door approach that can address the same theme in the group by a less threatening approach.

▶ Computer Friendly

Instructions: Program into this computer the three most important things you want to have as a friend. Examples of such qualities could include funny, smart, kind, helpful, active, into sports, good listener, attractive, rich, talkative, quiet, or hard worker.

▸ Technique #6

Title:	Making The Grade
Technique category:	Creative Exercise
Objective:	To increase members' awareness of their peer relationship problems.

Materials needed:

- Copies of the sheet entitled "Report Card On Me," found on page 80.
- Pencils

Procedure:

1. Pass out the sheet entitled "Report Card On Me" to all group members.
2. Allow 5 to 10 minutes for the completion of this task.
3. Ask everyone to share their responses by going around the circle in order. The facilitator should initially share their responses to the task sheet for purposes of modeling.
4. If time allows, pose some discussion questions related to the task sheet responses.
5. Process members' positive reactions at the end of the session.

Cautions/comments:

Facilitators will find that creative exercises are wonderful ways for members to disclose more honestly and intimately in a group. These types of interventions offer youngsters a non-threatening way to share while increasing their own awareness level. Clinicians do need to be sensitive to the nature of disclosure being requested via this technique. Some support groups may not be ready to deal so directly with this issue of peer skill strengths and deficits. Facilitators need to use their clinical expertise in determining if a group is ready for this intervention. This technique can be modified such that members anonymously complete the report cards and the facilitator reads them all out loud. This adapted format still surfaces all members' feelings about their peer skills, and is less threatening.

▸ Report Card On Me

Instructions:

Make believe you are going to receive a report card on your friendship skills. Write below what grades you think you deserve. Be sure to write positive points in the comment section about any of the skills.

REPORT CARD		
NAME:		DATE:
FRIENDSHIP SKILL	GRADE	COMMENTS
Making Friends		
Keeping Friends		
Solving Fights		
Saying I'm Sorry		
Having a Best Friend		
Sharing with Friends		
Planning Fun with Friends		

Grading System:
A = Just doing great with this friendship skill
B = Doing pretty good with this friendship skill
C = Need to work on this particular friendship skill
? = Need to learn this friendship skill

At this time, the student should be encouraged to do the following about his/her friendship skills:

_____

_____

_____

▶ Technique #7

Title:	Dream On
Technique category:	In Vivo Exercise
Objective:	To increase members' awareness of alternative ways of handling peer problems.

Materials:

- Blackboard or newsprint pad with chalk or markers

Procedure:

1. Facilitators initially utilize a progressive relaxation method (examples in *Reducing Stress in Children Through Creative Relaxation,* by Joy and Jane Humphrey, Charles C. Thomas Publisher) to help members get into a relaxed state.

2. As everyone has their eyes closed, the youngsters should be asked to formulate what they would be doing in a dream where they are a great friend and have great friends. The children will usually need assistance in fully developing this dream. Facilitators can highlight all descriptive parts of this fantasy to help in the formulation of this dream.

3. After this fantasy state has been accomplished, the members should be asked to open their eyes and share their dreams with one another.

4. Consider listing on a blackboard or newsprint pad all the ways the children were improving their peer skills in the dreams. Facilitators should be sure to acknowledge commonalities that surface among the members.

5. At the end of the session, the youngsters should be asked to share what they enjoyed about this experience.

Cautions/comments:

Sometimes, it is easier for children to identify what they want to be different in their social life by developing a dream. This technique often surfaces needs that may not have otherwise been known or discussed by the members. It will be important during this session to have the participants fully discuss how they can go about making their dreams come true. It will also be helpful to indicate to members that dreams that are totally unrealistic may mean that they need to change their expectations of friends and of themselves.

Readers are reminded that this technique is not advisable for youngsters who have a history of psychotic behaviors. This dream state may encourage such children to lose their tenuous hold on reality. Furthermore, in some school districts specific written permission from members' parents will need to be obtained. In some areas of the country, parents see an intervention like this as an out-of-body experience. It may be necessary to educate these parents so that they fully understand the intent of this technique.

▸ Technique #8

Title:	Target Practice
Technique category:	Completion Task
Objective:	To increase members' awareness of alternative ways of handling peer problems.

Materials:

- Form entitled "Friendship Skill Practice," found on page 84.
- Pencils
- Pennies

Procedure:

1. At the onset of this session, members are told that they will be playing the fun game of target practice with pennies. Next, everyone is asked to take 5 to 10 minutes to complete the sheet entitled "Friendship Skill Practice."

2. Then, the game rules below are reviewed with the membership.

   - Show and tell the group what you wrote for your target rings.

   - After you are done sharing, place your target in the center of the table and throw two pennies on it.

   - If you follow the above two steps, you get a point and if you get at least one penny on your target, you get a second point.

   - Any points not earned by a member go to the facilitator.

   - The one (group or facilitator) with the most points at the end wins.

3. The game is then conducted following the rules.

4. If time allows, discussion questions can be posed to the children in order to probe some of their earlier responses during the game.

5. At the end, everyone should be asked to complete the following sentence: "I really liked this session when _____."

Cautions/comments:

This is an attention catching method to elicit a support group's discussion around the subject of alternative social skills. Usually, elementary age youngsters love target games and this intervention quickly decreases their anxiety around the disclosure being elicited. Some of the material that surfaces during this session could easily be addressed in future sessions.

▸ Friendship Skill Practice

Instructions: Fill in the bottom of each target ring with a friendship skill you feel would be important for solving friendship problems. Do not forget the bull's eye at the bottom.

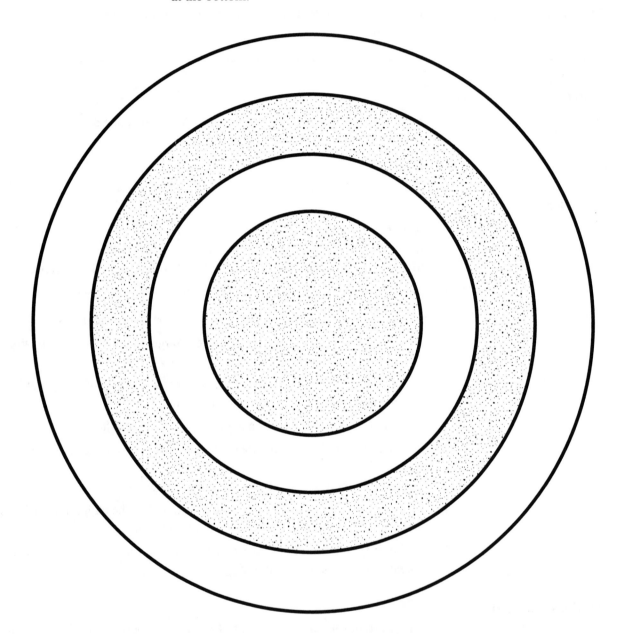

Your bull's eye: One thing I need to do to be a better friend is _____

_____ .

▸ Technique #9

Title:	I'm Speechless
Technique category:	Game Exercise
Objective:	To increase members' awareness of alternative ways to handle peer relationship problems.

Materials:

- Before this session, the facilitator will need to prepare 3"x5" cards with social skills (one per card) that are needed by group members
- Blackboard and chalk
- Timers
- Empty shoe box

Procedure:

1. At the onset of this session, members are told they are going to play a fun type of charades game combined with win, lose, or draw.

2. The rules below are reviewed with the membership.

   - Each member will get a turn in the game by going around the circle in order one after another.

   - When a member has his/her turn, they must pick a card from a box that indicates a peer relationship skill. The participant will have two minutes to act out without words the skill they selected from the box. Youngsters should also be told they can draw hints on a blackboard or large newsprint pad. The hints can only be pictures and no words. All other members can guess as often as they want by raising their hand and being called on by the facilitator.

   - A designated period of time will need to be established by the facilitator for this game. It will be important to have enough time for each member to do a charade/win, lose, or draw act. All of the details will have to be given to the group during this rule instruction time.

   - Points will be gained by the group when someone accurately guesses the skill being acted out within the two minute time limit.

   - Points will be gained by the facilitator when no one is able to guess the peer skill within the two minute period.

   - The one (group or facilitator) who has the most points at the end of the designated period wins.

3. The game is then conducted following the rules.

4. If time allows, discussion questions can be posed to the children in order to probe some of their earlier responses during the game.

5. At the end, everyone should be asked to complete the following sentence: "I really liked this session when _____."

Cautions/comments:

Participants generally love playing games in group. They get so caught up with the fun of this intervention that they forget about the potentially difficult nature of the disclosure being elicited. I feel that the experience of having fun with a group of peers is valuable in and of itself. This particular game is very effective in keeping members' attention because it relies so heavily on the children watching the youngster acting out the social skills.

▶ Technique #10

Title:	Your Mission
Technique category:	Check-Up/Assignment
Objective:	To integrate new peer skills into members' repertoires.

Materials:

- Individually prepared assignment sheet forms entitled "Your Mission," found on page 88 for each member
- Pencils

Procedure:

1. Ahead of time, the facilitator will need to develop an individualized assignment for each group member utilizing the form entitled "Your Mission."

2. These assignments are then presented in the session as a "Guess Who This Assignment is For?" game. After members have guessed each answer, everyone should be asked to identify what is going to be easy and difficult about the assignment outlined. Encourage the membership to provide support and suggestions to each child as their assignment is being addressed.

3. The facilitator passes assignments out to the appropriate members and asks them to complete the sentences at the bottom. These responses should be shared with the entire group.

4. Members are asked to take their assignment sheets home and complete the indicated task. Then, at the next group session, these assignments should be discussed in terms of how successful members have been.

5. At the end of this session, members should be asked what they feel will be helpful about their assignment for them.

Cautions/comments:

This is an excellent technique for assisting members in solidifying the changes they have made as a result of the support group. Usually, it is best to wait until this point in a group's development to give out assignments. With the cohesiveness among the members, individual youngsters should be more motivated to carry out an assignment.

It is essential that facilitators are confident that the assignments given will be successfully completed. These tasks should positively reinforce changes made by individual members as a result of the support group experience.

▶ Your Mission

Name of Child: _____

Your mission is to: _____

_____

_____

If you are successful at this mission, be sure to: _____

_____

_____

If you are not successful with this mission, then: _____

_____

_____

At the end of next week, rate how you think you did in regard to this mission.

so-so   **pretty good**   **great**

▸ Technique #11

Title:	More Power To You
Technique category:	Empowerment Exercise
Objective:	To integrate into members' repertoire new peer skills.

Materials:

- Before this session, the facilitator will need to prepare peer problem situations that are relevant to members (two for each child) on 3"x5" cards.
- Blackboard and chalk
- Timer

Procedure:

1. At the onset of this session, members are told they are going to play the fun game where they have to guess situations concerning common peer problems.

2. Then, the rules below are reviewed with the membership.

   - Each member will get a turn in the game by going around the circle in order one after another.

   - When a member has his/her turn, they will be given a card by the facilitator and need to read it out loud to the group (or it can be read to them). The participant will have two minutes to come up with a solution to the difficulty.

   - A designated period of time will need to be established by the facilitator for this game. It is important that all members get at least one turn in this exercise, and in most cases there should be enough time for at least two full rounds. All of the details will have to be given to the group during this rule coverage time.

   - Points will be gained by the group whenever a member comes up with a good solution to the peer problem within the two minute allotment. Facilitators may want to indicate this status by saying "more power to you."

   - Points will be gained by the facilitator when a member is not able to come up with a solution within the two minute allotment. Points can also be gained by the facilitator when a solution posed is not realistic or appropriate for the problem situation. The group leader can indicate this status by saying "no power to you."

- The one (group or facilitator) who has the most points at the end of the designated period wins.

3. The game is then conducted following the rules.

4. If time allows, discussion questions can be posed to the children in order to probe some of their earlier responses during the game.

5. At the end, everyone should be asked to complete the following sentence: "I really liked this session when _____."

Cautions/comments:

Participants will love playing this fun guessing game, and their answers will further solidify the knowledge and skill they have learned in the group. In addition, the youngsters will continue to learn from the responses each of them gives for their peer relationship problem. Facilitators are reminded that the problem situations developed should be as relevant as possible to members' earlier social skill difficulties. It is essential that this technique reinforce progress made as a result of the support group experience.

▶ Technique #12

Title:	Pack Your Bags
Technique category:	Confirmation Task
Objective:	To integrate into members' repertoire new peer skills.

Materials needed:

- Copies of the sheet entitled "Pack Your Bags," found on page 92.
- Pencils

Procedure:

1. Pass out the sheet entitled "Pack Your Bags" along with pencils, to all group members.
2. Allow 5 to 10 minutes for the completion of this task.
3. Ask everyone to share their responses by going around the circle in order. The facilitator should initially share their responses to the task sheet for purposes of modeling.
4. If time allows, pose some discussion questions related to the task sheet responses.
5. Process members' positive reactions at the end of the session.

Cautions/comments:

This is an excellent technique for assisting members in confirming what they have learned in the social skill support group. The symbolism utilized here offers another avenue for youngsters to become more aware of specific knowledge and skills they have learned in the group.

▸ Pack Your Bags

Instructions: Make believe you are packing a peer social skill bag below. Complete each sentence with something you have learned from your group experience.

I have cleaned up _____

I need to brush up on _____
_____

Now I can see that friends _____
_____

My ticket for social skills will be _____
_____

The one thing that holds the most promise for my friendship skills is _____
_____

▶ Bibliography

Additional references

Asher, Steven R. and Hymel, Shelley. Coaching in social skills for children who lack friends at school. *Social Work in Education* 8(4):205-218, 1986.

Biemer, David J. Shyness control: a systematic approach to social anxiety management in children. *The School Counselor* 31(1):53-60, 1983.

Bowman, R. P. and Myrick, R. D. Students as peer helpers: an untapped resource. *Social Work in Education* 7(2):124-133, 1985.

Boy, Angelo V. and Pine, Gerald J. *Fostering Psychosocial Development in the Classroom.* Springfield, Charles C. Thomas, 1984.

Camp, Bonnie W. and Bash, Ana S. *The Think Aloud Series* (Grades 1-6). Champaign, Research Press, 1985.

Canning, Judy. Peer facilitator projects for elementary and middle schools. *Elementary School Guidance & Counseling* 18(2):124-129, 1983.

Cartledge, Gwendolyn and Milburn, JoAnne Fellows. *Teaching Social Skills to Children.* New York, Pergamon Press, 1980.

Conger, Judy C. and Keane, Susan P. Social skills intervention in the treatment of isolated or withdrawn children. *Psychological Bulletin* 90:485, 1981.

Davis, Duane. *My Friends and Me.* Circle Pines, American Guidance Service, 1977.

Deitch Feshback, Norma et al. *Learning to Care: Classroom Activities for Social and Affective Development.* Culver City, Social Studies School Survey, 1983.

Dennison, Susan. *Twelve Counseling Programs for Children at Risk.* Springfield, Charles C. Thomas, 1989.

Devenenzi, Jayne and Pendergast, Susan. *Belonging.* 2960 Hawk Hill Lane, San Luis Obispo, VA, 93405, 1991.

Dinkmeyer, Don and Dinkmeyer, Don J. *Developing Understanding of Self and Others - Revised DUSO-R.* Circle Pines, American Guidance Service, 1982.

Dowrick, Peter W. *Social Survival for Children: A Trainer's Resource Book.* New York, Brunner/Mazel, 1986.

Drew, Naomi. *Learning the Skills of Peacemaking, Revised.* Torrance, CA, Jalmar Press, 1996.

Edwards, Carolyn P. *Promoting Social and Moral Development in Young Children: Creative Approaches for the Classroom.* New York, Teachers College Press, 1986.

Gazda, George M. et al. *Real Talk: Exercises in Friendship and Helping Skills.* Culver City, Social Studies School Service, 1985.

Golden, Larry B. Prosocial learning groups with young children. *Elementary School Guidance & Counseling* 22(1):31-36, 1987.

Gresham, F. M. and Nagle, R. J. Social skills training with children: responsiveness to modeling and coaching as a function of peer orientation. *Journal of Consulting and Clinical Psychology* 18:718-729, 1980.

Guerney, L. F. and Moore, Y. Phone friend: a prevention-oriented service for latchkey children. *Children Today* 12:5-10, 1983.

Hummel, J. W. A social skills training approach to the interpersonal problems of learning disabled children. *Child Welfare* 61(7):467-474, 1982.

Jackson, Nancy F., Jackson, Donald A. and Monroe, Cathy. *Getting Along with Others.* Champaign, Research Press, 1983.

Kramer, Patricia and Frazer, Linda. *The Dynamics of Relationships.* Doylestown, Marco, 1989.

L'Abate, L. and Milan, M.A. (editors). *Handbook of Social Skills Training.* New York, John Wiley and Sons, 1985.

LaGreca, A. M. and Santogrossi, D. A. Social skills training with elementary school students: a behavioral group approach. *Journal of Consulting and Clinical Psychology* 48:220-227, 1980.

LeCroy, Craig Winston. Teaching children social skills: a game format. *Social Work* 32:440-442, 1987.

Lewis, K. and Weinstein, S. Friendship skills: intense short-term interventions with latency-age children. *Social Work with Groups* 1:279-286, 1978.

Matson, Johnny L. and Alendick, Thomas. *Enhancing Children's Social Skills: Assessment and Training.* New York, Pergamon, 1988.

Matten, Darryl E. and Matten, Rosana Marie. Children who are lonely and shy: action steps for the counselor. *Elementary School Guidance & Counseling* 20(2):129-135, 1985.

McGinnis, Ellen and Goldstein, Arnold P. *Skillstreaming the Elementary School Child.* Champaign, Research Press, 1984.

Mervis, Bonnie A. The use of peer-pairing in child psychotherapy. *Social Work* 30(2):124-128, 1985.

Millyard, Anne W. and Wilks, Rick. *Getting Along.* Culver City, Social Studies School Service, 1978.

Morse, J. Thomas, et al. *Kidskills: Interpersonal Skill Series.* Stuart, Family Skills, 1985.

Oden, S. and Asher, S. R. Coaching children in social skills for friendship making. *Child Development* 48:495-506, 1977.

Peale, Janet and Tade, Carla. *In a Pickle.* Circle Pines, American Guidance Service, 1988.

Pincus, Debbie. *Sharing.* Culver City, Social Studies School Service, 1983.

Rose, Steven. Time-limited treatment groups for children. *Social Work in Groups* 8(2):17-27, 1985.

Rose, S. R. Promoting social competence in children: a classroom approach to social and cognitive skill training. *Child and Youth Services* 5:43-59, 1982.

Schilit, Rebecca and Nichols, Ann Weaver. Responses to children's loneliness, peer pressure and relationship problems. *Social Work in Education* 10:165-174, 1988.

Schmidt, Fran and Friedman, Alice. *Creative Conflict Solving for Kids.* Miami Beach, The Grace Contrino Abrams Peace Education Foundation, Inc., 1985.

Schumaker-Bragg, Jean et al. *Social Skills for Daily Living.* Circle Pines, American Guidance Service, 1988.

Sheinker, Jan and Alan. *Metacognitive Approach to Social Skill Training: A Program for Grades 4 Through 12.* Rockville, Aspen Publishers, 1988.

Sonntag, Norris. Cartooning as a counseling approach to a socially isolated child. *The School Counselor* 32(4):307-312, 1985.

Trower, Terry. *The "Kid" Counselor Curriculum.* Doylestown, Marco, 1987.

Weinstein, Matt and Goodman, Joel. *Play Fair: Everybody's Guide to Noncompetitive Play.* Culver City, Social Studies School Service, 1980.

Whittington, Ronaele. *Peace Begins With Me.* Hawaii, Waikiki Community Center, 1989.

Worzbyth, John and O'Rourke, Kathleen. *Elementary School Counseling.* Muncie, Accelerated Development, Inc., 1989.

Chapter 5

Self-Esteem Building Support Group Curriculum

A complete curriculum for self-esteem building support groups is provided in this chapter. Step-by-step instructions are outlined for the unique set-up, planning, and facilitation of this type of elementary age support group. An extensive listing of assessment scales, session themes, bibliotherapy books, video-tapes/films, and "how-to-do-it" references are included as part of this practical support group guide. This chapter, along with Chapters One, Two, Three, and Thirteen, will provide complete instructions for the set-up through the termination of self-esteem building support groups.

Treatment Guidelines

Self-esteem problems are very common today among children referred for treatment services. There are a wide variety of causes behind youngsters' self-esteem difficulties. For example, it is not unusual for children with other problems to also experience a decreased sense of self-confidence. For this reason, members of this type of support group will often have varying needs related to self-esteem problems. This is not to say that such combinations of youngsters cannot be beneficial to one another. In fact, these children can provide modeling in the group, since they will each have unique self-esteem strengths to offer one another.

A troubled self-concept is one aspect of functioning that can affect all other areas of a child's life. As a result, groups that focus on self-esteem enhancement can have multidimensional impact. Such changes can have life-long effects on a youngster's developmental and later years.

Before utilizing this curriculum, the reader should review the following general treatment guidelines for working with children in self-esteem building support groups.

1. Depending on the primary causes of a child's low self-esteem, individual or group treatment, or a combination of the two, may be the ideal treatment(s) of choice.

2. If a child's self-concept is particularly low, more frequent group sessions will be helpful. At the same time, parent and/or teacher involvement may be essential for assisting such a youngster in increasing their self-esteem. In some cases, these youngsters may need a change of school placement to increase the impact of a support group. Or a family may need to be in ongoing family counseling to accomplish the same goal.

3. Good adult and/or peer models can often teach more than all the best counseling. Therefore, facilitators should consistently try to use themselves as models for these youngsters. The support group experience itself can provide these children with excellent peer modeling, both in the group and through outside assignments.

4. Counselors should remember that some symptoms of a poor self-concept are not always so obvious. For example, youngsters who have a need to always be in charge of peer situations or who are overly controlling often do not seem to have a low self-esteem. Yet in many of these cases, the underlying problem is in fact a poor self-concept. Sometimes clinicians will need to work with involved parents and teachers to elicit a more comprehensive view of a potential group member.

5. Expectations of these group members need to be established relative to their level of functioning at support group initiation. It is particularly essential to these youngsters that they perceive significant adults as seeing them make progress. For this reason, the specific goals of this type of support group should be made clear to involved parents and teachers at the initiation of a group program.

6. Keep in mind that every youngster needs to have some area(s) of success. If this is not possible in the usual ways (i.e., academics), then it will be important to provide other potential areas of success. Support groups for these youngsters should have content that addresses this need specifically.

7. Facilitators should be sensitive to the impact their acceptance and caring will have on group members with poor self-concepts. For some youngsters, this type of relationship with a healthy adult may be the first of its kind for them. Often, the facilitator can provide children with a corrective child/adult relationship experience that will serve as an initial impetus for an increased feeling of self-worth.

8. The acceptance of a low self-esteem child by a support group of peers is therapeutic in and of itself for this youngster. Even in elementary school, one's peers greatly affect feelings of self-worth. Therefore, the creation of

a warm, caring, and trusting group will have a tremendous positive impact on most of these members' self-image.

9. Values and expectations usually play an important role in the development of a child's self-esteem. The content of some group sessions should therefore focus on these issues. Often times, elementary students have expectations too high of themselves, which result in lowered self-images.

10. Be aware that during the elementary school ages, most youngsters still have a good prognosis for improving their self-concept. Therefore, this is a crucial time to focus counseling efforts on this at-risk problem area.

Assessment Instruments

1. Coopersmith Self-Esteem Inventories

2. Culture-Free Self-Esteem Inventories for Children and Adults

3. Hare Self-Esteem Scale

4. How I Perceive Myself

5. Inferred Self-Concept

6. Piers-Harris Self-Concept Scale

7. Self-Concept Adjective Checklist

8. Self-Concept as a Learner Scale

9. Self-Concept Scale for Children

10. Self-Perception Inventory

Relevant Session Themes

Develop realistic self-image

Peer relationship skills

General communication skills

Assertiveness awareness and skills

General confidence level at school/home

Ability to trust self and others

Experience acceptance by group of peers

Developmentally appropriate interests

Positive attitude/motivation to be involved with age appropriate activities

Ability to talk up in a peer group

Increased sense of security

Identification of sources/activities that increase one's feelings of success

Increased awareness of one's competencies

Develop positive self-talk

Learn how to change undesirable behaviors

Increase awareness of expectations of oneself

Appropriate interaction skills (body language, affect, eye contact, etc.)

Develop excitement about some areas of life

Affective awareness and communication

Planning Sequence of Objectives & Techniques for Self-Esteem Building Support Group

Group Phase	Group Goals	Intervention Categories
Initial	1. To provide an attractive group setting. 2. To initiate members' participation on-task and with one another. 3. To initiate trust among the membership.	**Hello Group Techniques** (Chapter Three)
	4. To educate members about issues and difficulties related to self-esteem problems.	**Instructive Techniques:** #1 Not A Lot Of Hot Air #2 Bibliotherapy/Video/Films #3 Make Your Own Magic
Middle	5. To increase group development goals established in initial phase (i.e., goals 1-3).	No techniques per se but follow curriculum approach.
	6. To increase members' awareness of their particular difficulties related to their self-esteem.	**Awareness of Self Techniques:** #4 Cartooning Around #5 Pop The Bag #6 A Shopping List
	7. To provide alternative coping behaviors for an improved self-esteem.	**Alternative Coping Techniques:** #7 A Match-Up #8 You Liking You #9 Reach Out And Tell Us
	8. To assist members in the integration of new coping behaviors into their repertoire.	**Integration Techniques:** #10 A Tune Up On Me #11 Adequate And Proud Of . . . #12 A Layout Plan For A New Me
Termination	9. To have members acknowledge the value of the group. 10. To assist members in validating their changes. 11. To have members brainstorm other sources of support. 12. To have members grieve the ending of group.	**Goodbye Group Techniques** (Chapter Thirteen)

▶ Technique #1

Title: Not A Lot Of Hot Air

Technique category: Didactic

Objective: To instruct members on the ingredients of one's self-esteem.

Materials needed:

- Copies of the sheet entitled "Not A Lot Of Hot Air," found on page 102.
- Pencils

Procedure:

1. Pass out the sheet entitled "Not A Lot Of Hot Air" to all group members.
2. Allow 5 to 10 minutes for the completion of this task.
3. Ask everyone to share their responses by going around the circle in order. The facilitator should initially share their responses to the task sheet for purposes of modeling.
4. If time allows, pose some discussion questions related to the task sheet responses.
5. Process members' positive reactions at the end of the session.

Cautions/comments:

This particular task helps youngsters start to learn what comprises or contributes to their self-esteem. This technique is able to elicit lots of information just from members' own experiences. At the same time, clinicians can use this sharing later in the same session to show how the absence of certain uplifting behaviors contributes to a lower self-esteem. This exercise is an excellent back door entry into a subject that would otherwise be more threatening and uncomfortable to discuss initially in group.

▸ **Not A Lot Of Hot Air**

Instructions: Write as many words as possible inside the hot air balloon that are ways to lift your self-esteem.

▸ Technique #2

Title: Bibliotherapy/Video/Films

Technique category: Bibliotherapy/Video/Films

Objective: To instruct members about various aspects of their self-esteem.

Materials:

- Book, film, or videotape selected from the list on page 104.
- Equipment for film or videotape, if used.
- Prepared discussion questions related to the theme of the visual aid chosen.

Procedure:

1. Before the session, the facilitator selects a book, film, or videotape from the list on page 104.
2. Session begins with the book being read or film/videotape being shown.
3. At completion of above task, members can be asked discussion questions that surface their identification with the story. Also, some disclosure can be elicited to explore the children's similar problems and struggles.
4. Members' favorite parts of the book, film, or videotape should be processed at the end.

Cautions/comments:

Typically, members will enjoy the use of bibliotherapy materials or films/videotapes. Through these types of visual interventions, children can more easily learn about their self-esteem. In addition, youngsters in elementary grades typically identify with characters in books and films. As a result, they are often able to more comfortably talk about their similar issues via the story presented.

Readers are advised to select books that have colorful pictures on almost every page. Children as a whole find it easier to understand the message of a book page when a graphic design depicts the concept. Also, facilitators should be careful that books and films/videotapes selected are not too long. Again, it is important to have time in the session to pose discussion questions and process reactions among the members.

▶ Bibliotherapy

1. Adler, David A. *Jeffrey's Ghost and the Leftover Baseball Team.* Holt, 1984, ages 4-8.

2. Anders, Rebecca. *Look at Prejudice and Understanding.* Lerner, 1976, grades 4-6.

3. Asher, Sandra Fenichel. *Just Like Jenny.* Delacorte Press, 1982, ages 10-12.

4. Barrett, John M. *Daniel Discovers Daniel.* Human Sciences Press, 1980, ages 7-9.

5. Barrett, Judith. *I'm Too Small. You're Too Big.* Atheneum Publishers, 1981, ages 4-6.

6. Bates, Betty. *That's What T. J. Says.* Holiday House, Inc., 1982, ages 9-11.

7. Bell, Neill. *Only Human.* Little, Brown & Company, 1983, grades 4-6.

8. Berry, Joy. *Every Kid's Guide to Being Special.* Children's Press, 1987, grades 3-6.

9. Bottner, Barbara. *Dumb Old Casey is a Fat Tree.* Harper and Row Publishers, Inc., 1979, ages 6-9.

10. Brightman, Alan. *Like Me.* Little, Brown & Company, 1976, ages 4-8.

11. Brooks, Jerome. *Make Me a Hero.* E. P. Dutton & Co., Inc., 1980, ages 9-12.

12. Brown, Tricia. *Someone Special Just Like You.* Holt, 1984, grades P-2.

13. Carle, Eric. *The Mixed-Up Chameleon.* Thomas Y. Crowell Company, Inc., 1975, ages 4-8.

14. Carrick, Malcolm. *I'll Get You.* Harper & Row Publishers, Inc., 1979, ages 11-13.

15. Cohen, Barbara Nash. *The Innkeeper's Daughter.* Lothrop, Lee & Shepard Company, 1979, ages 11-14.

16. Cohen, Miriam. *So What?* Greenwillow Books, 1982, ages 4-7.

17. Delton, Judy. *I Never Win!* Caroldon Books, Inc. (PO Box 17391, Pensacola, FL 32522), 1981, ages 4-7.

18. Fassler, Joan. *Don't Worry Dear.* Behavioral Publications, Inc., 1971, ages 4-6.

19. Green, Phyllis. *Gloomy Louis.* Albert Whitman & Company, 1980, ages 8-9.

20. Greene, Laura. *I Am Somebody.* Children's Press, 1979, grades K-3.

21. Hazen, Barbara S. *The Me I See.* Abingdon, 1978, grades 1-2.

22. Hurwitz, Johanna. *Superduper Teddy.* William Morrow & Company, Inc., 1980, ages 4-7.

23. Hutchins, Pat. *Titch.* Macmillan, 1971, grades K-3.

24. Karlin, Nurit. *The Blue Frog.* Coward (Div. of Putman & Co.), 1983, ages 4-8.

25. Karlin, Nurit. *A Train for the King.* Coward, 1983, ages 4-8.

26. Kraus, Robert. *Herman the Helper.* Windmill, 1974, grades P-K.

27. Palmer, Pat. *Liking Myself.* Impact Publishers, 1982, ages 5-9.

28. Robinson, Nancy Louise. *Ballet Magic.* Albert Whitman & Company, 1981, ages 9-11.

29. Simon, Norma. *Why Am I Different?* Albert Whitman, 1976, ages 4-8.

30. Smith, Doris Buchanan. *Last Was Lloyd.* The Viking Press, Inc., 1981, ages 8-11.

Videotapes

1. Alex and the Wonderful "Doo Wah" Lamp
   CRM/McGraw-Hill Films, 1980, 1 film reel (23 minutes), grades 1-6.

2. Big People, Little People
   Sterling Educational Films, 1967, 1 film reel (9 minutes), grades 1-6.

3. Can Do/Can't Do
   National Instructional T.V., 1973, 1 film reel (15 minutes), grades 4-6.

4. Developing Self-Esteem: Living With Disabilities
   Guidance Associates, 1985, 1 film reel (6 minutes), grades K-3.

5. Developing Self-Esteem: Pride in Accomplishments
   Guidance Associates, 1985, 1 film reel (7 minutes), grades K-3.

6. Developing Self-Esteem: Self-Awareness
   Guidance Associates, 1985, 1 film reel (6 minutes), grades K-3.

7. Developing Self-Esteem: Taking Pride in Who You Are
   Guidance Associates, 1985, 1 film reel (7 minutes), grades K-3.

8. Developing Self-Esteem: There's Only One Me
   Guidance Associates, 1985, 1 film reel (7 minutes), grades K-3.

9. Developing Self-Esteem: You Can Make It If You Try
   Guidance Associates, 1985, 1 film reel (6 minutes), grades K-3.

10. Do Your Own Thing
    CRM/McGraw-Hill Films, 1975, 1 film reel (13 minutes), grades 1-6.

11. Everybody Knows That
    Phoenix/BFA Films and Video, Inc., 1984, 1 film reel (15 minutes), grades 1-6.

12. Everybody's Different and That's OK
    Barr Films, 1979, 1 film reel (15 minutes), grades 1-6.

13. Free to Be...You and Me: Expectations Part II
    CRM/McGraw-Hill Films, 1974, 1 film reel (14 minutes), grades 4-6.

14. I am Me...And I Want to Be
    Barr Films, 1975, 1 film reel (12 minutes), grades 1-6.

15. I'm Somebody Special
    AIMS Media, 1977, 1 film reel (15 minutes), grades K-3.

16. Ira Sleeps Over
    Phoenix/BFA Films and Video, Inc., 1977, 1 film reel (17 minutes),
    grades K-6.

17. Is It OK To Be Me?
    Pyramid Films and Video, 1977, 1 film reel (6 minutes), grades 1-6.

18. Just One Me
    AIMS Media, 1971, 1 film reel (11 minutes), grades 1-6.

19. Me
    Coronet, 1972, 1 film reel (17 minutes), grades 1-6.

20. Ugly Duckling, The
    Phoenix/BFA Films and Video, Inc., 1980, 1 film reel (11 minutes),
    grades 1-6.

21. What Makes Me Different?
    Pyramid Films and Video, 1977, 1 film reel (9 minutes), grades 1-6.

22. You Can Make It If You Try
    Barr Films, 1979, 1 film reel (15 minutes), grades 1-6.

Films

1. *All Kids Are Special*
   Random House Media, 6 filmstrips/cassettes, grades K-6.

2. *Being Responsible*
   Listen and Learn Company, 4 filmstrips with cassettes, grades K-4.

3. *Being You*
   Listen and Learn Company, 4 filmstrips with cassettes, grades K-4.

4. *Dealing With Handicaps*
   Coronet/MTI, 27 minute video, grades 4-6.

5. *Developing Self-Confidence*
   Creative Learning, Inc., 4 filmstrips, grades 4-6.

6. *Developing Self-Confidence*
   Listen and Learn Company, 4 filmstrips with cassettes, grades 4-8.

7. *Developing Self-Esteem*
   Guidance Associates, 7 filmstrips, grades P-2.

8. *Here's Lookin' At Me*
   Listen and Learn Company, 4 filmstrips with cassettes, grades 3-6.

9. *I Blew It!*
   Sunburst, 2 filmstrips/cassettes, grades 5-6.

10. *Journey to Success*
    Marshmedia, 51 frame filmstrip, grades K-3.

11. *Learning About Yourself*
    Guidance Associates, 3 filmstrips with cassettes, grades K-2.

12. *Knowing Me, Knowing You*
    Random House Media, 4 filmstrips/cassettes, grades K-3.

13. *Learning to Say No*
    Sun burst, 2 filmstrips (cassettes), grades 5-6.

14. *Liking Me: Building Self-Esteem*
    Creative Learning, Inc., 2 filmstrips/video, grades 5-6.

15. *Liking Me: Building Self-Esteem*
    Sunburst, 2 filmstrips/cassettes, grades 5-6.

16. *Overcoming Handicaps*
    Listen and Learn Company, 4 filmstrips with cassettes, grades 4-8.

17. *Seven Wishes of a Rich Kid*
    Coronet/MTI, 30 minute video, grades 4-6.

18. *The Importance of Being You*
    Creative Learning, Inc., 4 filmstrips, grades K-3.

19. *The Importance of You*
    Random House Media, 4 filmstrips (cassettes), grades K-3.

20. *Understanding and Accepting Yourself*
    Listen and Learn Company, 4 filmstrips with cassettes, grades 3-6.

21. *What Is A Handicap?*
    Random House Media, 4 filmstrips/cassettes, grades 4-6.

22. *What's So Great About Being Smart?*
    Listen and Learn Company, 1 filmstrip with cassette, grades 4-6.

23. *Who Am I? Looking at Self-Concept*
    Creative Learning, Inc., 2 filmstrips/video, grades 5-6.

24. *You Can Be Anything*
    Creative Learning, Inc., 4 filmstrips, grades K-6.

25. *You're Different, So Am I*
    Guidance Associates, 2 filmstrips with cassettes, grades 4-6.

▸ Technique #3

Title:	Make Your Own Magic
Technique category:	Paper/Pencil
Objective:	To instruct members on what they control around an improved self-image.

Materials needed:

- Copies of the sheet entitled "Make Your Own Magic," found on page 109.
- Pencils

Procedure:

1. Pass out the sheet entitled "Make Your Own Magic" to all group members.
2. Allow 5 to 10 minutes for the completion of this task.
3. Ask everyone to share their responses by going around the circle in order. The facilitator should initially share their responses to the task sheet for purposes of modeling.
4. The facilitator asks members to complete the outside of the magic wand on this task sheet. On the side of this wand, members are instructed to write what parts of their self-confidence dream they have ultimate control over. About ten minutes should be allowed for this completion.
5. All members are asked to share their responses to this part of the task. Facilitators should stop this sharing on a regular basis to note commonalities that surface around this crucial theme of identifying how one can control the improvement of their self-esteem. If members have difficulty with this part of the exercise, it is a good idea to have all members brainstorm some suggestions.

Cautions/comments:

This particular exercise is an excellent learning experience for helping youngsters identify how they can go about changing their self-image. The idea of first having members think about their dream or fantasy elicits some gut level feelings they have around their self-image. By completing this task with a magic wand under their control, the members start to feel an increased sense of changing their self-image.

▸ **Make Your Own Magic**

Instructions: Make a picture or write in the magic space coming out of the hat a dream you have about feeling more confident.

▶ Technique #4

Title: Cartooning Around

Technique category: Exercise Using the Arts

Objective: To increase members' awareness of their issues related to self-esteem difficulties.

Materials needed:

- Copies of the sheet entitled "Cartooning Around," found on page 111.
- Pencils

Procedure:

1. Pass out the sheet entitled "Cartooning Around" to all group members.
2. Allow 5 to 10 minutes for the completion of this task.
3. Ask everyone to share their responses by going around the circle in order. The facilitator should initially share their responses to the task sheet for purposes of modeling.
4. If time allows, pose some discussion questions related to the task sheet responses.
5. Process members' positive reactions at the end of the session.

Cautions/comments:

This is an excellent technique for having members get in touch with both their expectations of themselves and their resulting self-esteem difficulties. Youngsters usually love cartoons and often identify with these characters. This is a wonderful non-threatening way to surface such material. It will be important to point out to members that our identification with certain cartoon characters often surfaces areas of self-esteem we would like to improve.

▶ Cartooning Around

Instructions: Circle the cartoon character below that you are most like in real life. Draw you as that cartoon character in the TV and then complete the sentence at the bottom of this sheet.

Bugs Bunny

G.I. Joe	Heathcliff
Muppet Babies	Garfield
Mickey Mouse	Tom and Jerry
Popeye the Sailor	Ghostbusters
Inspector Gadget	Donald Duck
Flintstones	Teenage Mutant Ninja Turtles
Winnie the Pooh	Yogi Bear
Duck Tales	Gummi Bears
Count Duckula	Chip 'n Dale Rescue Rangers

Other: _____

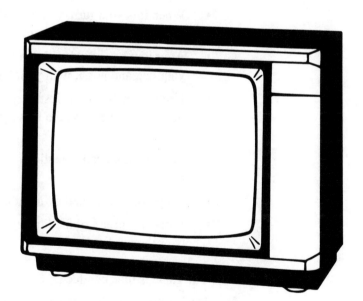

The reason I am most like _____ in real life is because:

_____

▶ Technique #5

Title:	Pop The Bag
Technique category:	Disclosure Task
Objective:	To increase members' awareness of their difficulties and strengths regarding their self-esteem.

Materials:

- Three lunch size paper bags for each member
- Chalk

Procedure:

1. At the onset of this session, members are told they are going to be playing the fun game of popping the bag. Then, three bags are passed out to each child.

2. Next, the rules below are reviewed with the membership.

   - Each member will take a turn by going around the circle.
   - When it is your turn, you must first tell us one feeling about yourself you would like to stop having or you know is not very accurate.
   - After you have disclosed that feeling, you have one chance to blow up your bag and pop it with your hands.
   - If you make your disclosure, you get a point. Then, you get a point for popping your bag on the first try and one last point for being a good sport.
   - Each member can potentially earn three points for the group when it is their turn.
   - All points not earned by members are given to the facilitator.
   - Whoever (group or facilitator) has the most points after three rounds wins the game.

3. The game is then conducted following the rules.

4. During the game, facilitators can note disclosures on a blackboard. Then, at the end of the game, members can be asked to point out commonalities among themselves and helpful ideas that surfaced.

5. At the end, everyone should be asked to complete the following sentence: "I really liked this session when _____."

Cautions/comments:

Children typically love being given permission to pop a bag. Also, they can understand better the concrete association of bag popping with getting rid of negative feelings toward self. Facilitators often find that members enjoy this activity so much that they forget about the type of disclosure being elicited.

Readers are reminded to note the tally system used in this game. The task was set up to reinforce disclosure and sportsmanship (i.e., two points given for these two behaviors out of a possible three points) versus luck (popping the bag). This game set-up is an excellent technique for reinforcing therapeutic behaviors in a support group.

▸ Technique #6

Title: A Shopping List

Technique category: Creative Exercise

Objective: To increase members' awareness of their difficulties related to their self-esteem problems.

Materials needed:

- Copies of the sheet entitled "Shopping For Me Qualities," found on page 115.
- Pencils

Procedure:

1. Pass out the sheet entitled "Shopping For Me Qualities" to all group members.
2. Allow 5 to 10 minutes for the completion of this task.
3. Ask everyone to share their responses by going around the circle in order. The facilitator should initially share their responses to the task sheet for purposes of modeling.
4. If time allows, pose some discussion questions related to the task sheet responses.
5. Process members' positive reactions at the end of the session.

Cautions/comments:

Facilitators will be delighted to find that creative exercises are wonderful ways for members to disclose more honestly and intimately in a group. Usually, these types of interventions offer youngsters a non-threatening way to share while increasing their own awareness level.

▶ Shopping For Me Qualities

Instructions: Imagine you have just gone into a store to buy qualities for yourself. Look at the list below and place a ✔ by the three you most want to buy. Be sure to tell more about that quality in the right column.

✔	QUALITY	SPELL OUT EXACTLY WHAT YOU DESIRE
	Athletic abilities	
	Physical looks	
	School work	
	Family life	
	Social skills	
	Positive feelings about self	
	Grooming/personal hygiene	
	Other talent	
	Caring, helpful, nice person	
	Other	

Have you already started to attain any of the three above qualities on your own?

___ Yes   ___ No

If yes, which ones and how did you do it?

_____

_____

_____

▸ **Technique #7**

Title:	A Match-Up
Technique category:	In Vivo Experience
Objective:	To increase members' awareness of alternative ways to enhance their self-esteem.

Materials:

- A peer helper questionnaire, found on page 118.
- Pencils

Procedure:

1. Before this group session, the facilitator will need to identify a peer helper for each group member. These peer helpers should not be members of the group and will need to be informed ahead of time their role with an assigned child. It will also be important that these peer helpers are in the same school or neighborhood so that group members have some knowledge of and easy access to them.

2. It may be time efficient to meet with all the selected peer helpers in a brief training session. During that session, the facilitator will explain that their assigned group member will be asking them questions as to how they maintain a positive view of themselves. Peer helpers should be encouraged to be honest, clear, specific, and helpful in their answers. It should be emphasized that these group members need models to show them how to improve their own self-image.

3. This session is then conducted with the facilitator explaining to the membership that they have all been assigned a peer helper to interview. The questionnaire found on the following page entitled "Your Peer Helper" is then distributed to each member.

4. Facilitators should go over this form in detail to make sure the questions are clear.

5. Participants are then given the assignment to interview their peer helper. If possible, this interviewing could be done during the group session with the assigned peer helpers present.

6. After all members have completed their interviews, the group meets as a whole to discuss the responses they elicited. It will be important to ask members the most helpful suggestions they received from these peer helpers.

Cautions/comments:

Obviously, arranging peer helpers for this technique will be considerable work for the facilitator. However, if time allows for the provision of peer helpers, the input of energy is well worth the output. Children learn so much more from a good peer model. This intervention actually provides an opportunity for members to ask peers questions that otherwise are rarely discussed between the involved youngsters. Facilitators may even find that this technique surfaces enough material to address over two sessions.

▸ **Peer Helper Questionnaire**

NAME: _____ DATE: _____

AGE: _____ GRADE: _____ INTERESTS: _____

1. Do you always feel good about yourself? _____ Yes _____ No

2. Can you tell me two ways, after a bad day, that you usually help yourself start feeling better about yourself?

   _____

   _____

3. Was there ever a grade in school when you did not feel very good about yourself? _____ Yes _____ No

4. Tell me two things you are proud of about yourself?

   _____

   _____

5. Do you have a model you look up to? _____ Yes _____ No

   If yes, could you tell me who it is? _____

6. What would you say is your golden rule for continuing to feel good about yourself?

   _____

   _____

7. Could you tell me one thing you like about me or have heard others say they like about me?

   _____

   _____

▸ Technique #8

Title:	You Liking You
Technique category:	Completion Task
Objective:	To increase members' awareness of alternative ways to enhance their self-esteem.

Materials needed:

- Copies of the sheet entitled "You Liking You," found on page 120.
- Pencils

Procedure:

1. Pass out the sheet entitled "You Liking You" to all group members.
2. Allow 5 to 10 minutes for the completion of this task.
3. Ask everyone to share their responses by going around the circle in order. The facilitator should initially share their responses to the task sheet for purposes of modeling.
4. If time allows, pose some discussion questions related to the task sheet responses.
5. Process members' positive reactions at the end of the session.

Cautions/comments:

This is an excellent technique for eliciting lots of disclosure in a time efficient manner. Facilitators will generally find that sentence completions elicit gut level responses from members while being fairly easy to complete. In some groups, the material that surfaces from this task may be enough to address over two sessions. This intervention can be modified for younger groups (i.e., kindergarten through third grade) by having fewer sentence completions on the sheet, with visual graphics to help convey the concepts.

If a group has too much anxiety around the disclosure being elicited via this technique, the sentence completion sheets can be done anonymously. The facilitator collects them and reads all the responses out loud. After this format for sharing, the members can be asked to discuss their reactions to the anonymous disclosure that surfaced.

▶ **You Liking You: A Sentence Completion**

Instructions: Complete the sentences below with the first responses that come to your mind. Do not worry about your responses, there are no right or wrong answers.

1. I usually feel good about myself when _____

   _____

2. I usually feel the least good about myself when _____

   _____

3. Compared to earlier years, this year my feelings about myself are _____

   _____

4. I know I would feel lots better about myself if only I could be more like _____

   _____

5. Other peers usually like me because _____

   _____

6. My family always says my best qualities are _____

   _____

7. Just lately I have improved my _____

   _____

8. When I start to feel bad about myself I usually _____

   _____

9. One way for me to usually start feeling better about myself is _____

   _____

10. I sure like myself lots more when I _____

   _____

▸ Technique #9

Title: Reach Out And Tell Us

Technique category: Game Exercise

Objective: To increase members' awareness of alternative ways to enhance their self-esteem.

Materials:

- A "Reach Out And Tell Us" game board
- Blindfold

Procedure:

1. Before the session, the facilitator will need to prepare this game on a large poster board. The drawing on the board should look like the picture below but on a much larger scale.

My Looks	My Family
My Friends	My After School Activities
My School Work	Other

It is suggested that tape be placed on the lines between each of the six boxes so the members can feel the division between them.

2. The group is then shown this board at the beginning of the session and it is hung at eye level on a wall in the group room. The following rules are explained to the children regarding the game they are about to play:

- Each child will get a turn by going around the circle in order.
- When it is someone's turn, that person will have a blindfold put over their eyes. Then, that person will be walked to the game board on the wall so they will know where it is located.
- Each member will be given one minute to select a box on the game poster and then must make a disclosure related to a way they can improve their self-esteem related to that aspect of their life. For this reason, members should be told to initially think through which box they could easily respond to regarding that question.
- If the youngster's disclosure matches up with the requested content of the box chosen, then he/she earns a point for the group. But if their match is not correct, then the facilitator gets the point.

- After two rounds, the one (group or facilitator) who has the most points wins.

3. After this game is completed, facilitators may want to review the disclosures shared through a more in-depth group discussion. It will be particularly helpful to note commonalities that surfaced and reinforce any particularly good ideas that youngsters shared.

4. At the end of this meeting, members should be asked to share the one thing that they found most helpful about this game exercise.

Cautions/comments:

Youngsters will usually enjoy the fun nature of this exercise. Also, by having everyone participate, members gain lots of self-esteem enhancement ideas from one another. The other beauty of this technique is that even if a child's response does not match up to the box chosen, the disclosure has still taken place. Plus, the competition of the game continues to downplay any anxiety around the disclosure being elicited.

▶ Technique #10

Title:	A Tune Up On Me
Technique category:	Empowerment Exercise
Objective:	To integrate new self-esteem enhancement skills into members' repertoire.

Materials needed:

- Copies of the sheet entitled "Me-Mobile," found on page 124.
- Pencils

Procedure:

1. Pass out the sheet entitled "Me-Mobile" to all group members.
2. Allow 5 to 10 minutes for the completion of this task.
3. Ask everyone to share their responses by going around the circle in order. The facilitator should initially share their responses to the task sheet for purposes of modeling.
4. If time allows, pose some discussion questions related to the task sheet responses.
5. Process members' positive reactions at the end of the session.

Cautions/comments:

Symbolic tasks like this one are excellent ways for members to identify changes they have made around their self-esteem. Children enjoy the association of their self-concept with something as concrete as a car. This can be a very rewarding session where members truly get in touch with their progress in this self-esteem enhancement support group.

▶ **Me-Mobile**

Instructions: Make believe this car is your self-esteem. Write out the results of your group's tune-up experience on the five point checkup.

FIVE POINT CHECKUP

1.   My battery is now all charged up so I will be trying to:_____

   _____

2.   New windows are helping me see myself: _____

   _____

3.   The body work has resulted in my feeling _____

   about my looks.

4.   Better tires will help me stop my self talk of:_____

   _____

5.   Now I know I can drive my self-confidence: _____

   _____

▶ Technique #11

Title:	Adequate And Proud Of . . .
Technique category:	Check-Ups/Assignments
Objective:	To integrate into members' repertoire self-esteem enhancement skills.

Materials:

- "Adequate And Proud Of . . ." sheet found on page 127.
- Scissors
- Pencils

Procedure:

1. The "Adequate And Proud Of . . ." sheets are passed out to members along with scissors and pencils.

2. Participants are instructed to cut out all eight of their cards from these sheets. Then, the facilitator reviews for the members how in the group they have learned that we all do some things well, other things adequately, and some things poorly.

3. Members are instructed to write on each of the eight cards one thing that they realize they do adequately. In some groups, it may be helpful to make this into a fun game by giving members only so many minutes (i.e., 10-15 minutes) to complete all eight cards.

4. After everyone has done their cards, members are asked to share their ideas of areas where they are adequate. During this sharing, it will be important to note commonalities that surface along with reinforcing good self-awareness.

5. Once members have completed reading their cards, the group is asked to think about things they do more than just adequately. This disclosure is elicited out loud from each participant.

6. Facilitators will want to summarize this session by reminding members that there are many things in this life we all do adequately and that is a fine goal to have for ourselves. Participants should be encouraged to take their cards home as a reminder that striving to be the best in everything can have a negative effect on one's self-image.

7. At the end of this session, members should be asked to share what they learned from this intervention.

Cautions/comments:

This technique can be a very effective one for helping youngsters to see that their attitude toward their abilities is often more important than the abilities themselves. This message of "adequate and proud of it" goes against many of the expectations of the greater environment for children. In many schools and homes today, the norm for kids is often that you have to be the best at everything to be good enough. Youngsters with low self-esteem need to be validated for their adequate abilities and reinforced for a positive attitude toward them.

▸ Adequate And Proud Of . . .

Adequate and Proud of:

_____

_____

_____

_____

_____

Adequate and Proud of:

_____

_____

_____

_____

_____

Adequate and Proud of:

_____

_____

_____

_____

_____

Adequate and Proud of:

_____

_____

_____

_____

_____

Adequate and Proud of:

_____

_____

_____

_____

_____

Adequate and Proud of:

_____

_____

_____

_____

_____

Adequate and Proud of:

_____

_____

_____

_____

_____

Adequate and Proud of:

_____

_____

_____

_____

_____

▶ Technique #12

Title: A Layout Plan For A New Confident Me

Technique category: Confirmation Task

Objective: To integrate into members' repertoire new self-esteem enhancement skills.

Materials needed:

- Copies of the sheet entitled "A Layout Plan For A New Confident Me," found on page 129.
- Pencils

Procedure:

1. Pass out the sheet entitled "A Layout Plan For A New Confident Me" to all group members.
2. Allow 5 to 10 minutes for the completion of this task.
3. Ask everyone to share their responses by going around the circle in order. The facilitator should initially share their responses to the task sheet for purposes of modeling.
4. If time allows, pose some discussion questions related to the task sheet responses.
5. Process members' positive reactions at the end of the session.

Cautions/comments:

This is an excellent technique for helping members summarize what they have learned about ways to improve their self-esteem. By associating this awareness with the layout of a house, children are able to more easily articulate this requested disclosure. Facilitators may also want to suggest that members take their layout plans home to keep as reminders after the support group has ended.

▸ A Layout Plan For A New Confident Me

Instructions: Write or draw in each room below something you have learned from your support group about improving your self-esteem.

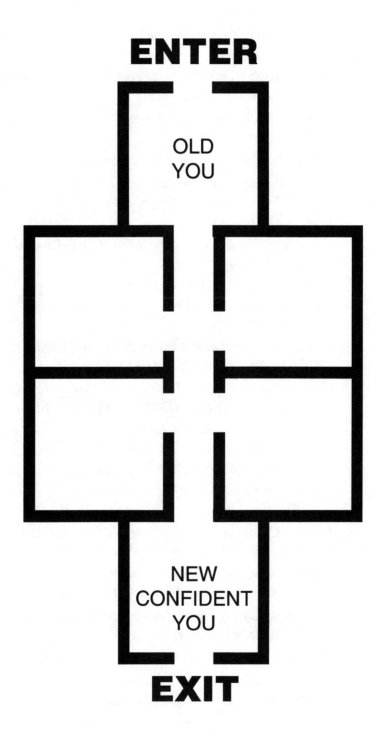

▸ Bibliography

Additional references

Allred, Carol. *Positive Action Self-Concept Curriculum.* Twin Falls, Positive Action, 1986.

Anderson, Jull. *Thinking, Changing, Rearranging.* Eugene, Timberline Press, 1985.

Berne, Patricia H. and Savary, Louis M. *Building Self-Esteem in Children.* New York, Crossroad, 1985.

Bielen, Peggy and McDaniel, Sandy. *Project Self-Esteem.* Torrance, CA, Jalmar Press, 1986.

Borba, Michele. *Esteem Builders.* Torrance, CA, Jalmar Press, 1989.

Borba, Michele and Borba, Craig. *Self-Esteem: A Classroom Affair, Volumes 1 & 2.* San Francisco, Harper & Row, 1982.

Borba, Michele and Borba, Craig. *Self-Esteem/A Classroom Affair: 101 Ways to Help Children Like Themselves.* Culver City, Social Studies School Service, 1980.

Burnett, Paul C. A self-concept enhancement program for children in the regular classroom. *Elementary School Guidance & Counseling* 18(2):101-108, 1983.

Calhoun, N. Social awareness group for girls with poor self-concept. *School Social Work Journal* 3(2):110-15, 1979.

Canfield, Jack and Wells, Harold C. *101 Ways to Enhance Self-Concept in the Classroom.* Englewood Cliffs, Prentice-Hall, Inc., 1976.

Carothers, James E. and Gasten, Ruth S. *Helping Children to Like Themselves: Activities for Building Self-Esteem.* Livermore, R. J. Associates, 1978.

Downing, C. Jerry. Affirmations: steps to counter negative, self-fulfilling prophecies. *Elementary School Guidance & Counseling* 20(3):174-179, 1986.

Farnette, Cherrie et al. *I've Got Me and I'm Glad: A Self-Awareness Activity Book.* Culver City, Social Studies School Service, 1985.

Freeman, E. M. and Smith, H. Y. Social workers can help minority students' self-esteem. *Journal of Social Welfare* 6(3):37-46, 1980.

Frey, Diane and Carlock, C. Jesse. *Enhancing Self-Esteem.* Spring Valley, Magic Circle Publishing Co., 1985.

Grim, G. and Mitchell, D. *Mostly Me.* Mount Dora, Kids Rights, 1985.

Hadley, Helen R. Improving reading scores through a self-esteem intervention program. *Elementary School Guidance & Counseling* 22(3):248-252, 1988.

Holt, Janice M. *Do I Like Myself?* Pasadena, Greenleaf Publications, 1983.

Hooker, Dennis and Gallagher, Rosemary. *I Am Gifted, Creative and Talented.* New York, Educational Design, Inc., 1984.

Kaufman, Gershen and Raphael, Lev. *Stick Up For Yourself!* Minneapolis, Johnson Institute, 1986.

Kirkland, Dianna C. *Last Year I Failed.* Oak Park, Aid-U Publishing Company, 1986.

Krughoff, G. G. et al. *Super Me-Super You: A Bilingual Activity Book for Young Children.* Washington, DC, U. S. Department of Health, Education and Welfare, 1979.

Lenett, Robin and Barthelmew, Dana. *KIDS Have Rights Too!* New York, Playmore, Inc. Publishers and Waldman Publishing Corp., 1985.

Mack, John E. and Alban, Steven L. (editors). *The Development and Sustaining of Self-Esteem in Childhood.* Madison, International University Press, 1984.

McElmurry, Mary Anne. *Caring: Learning to Value Yourself, Family, Friends and School.* Culver City, Social Studies School Service, 1981.

Morrison, Kenneth and Thompson, Marcia. *Feeling Good About Me - For Elementary School Facilitators.* Culver City, Social Studies School Service, 1985.

Morse, Carol Lynn et al. Effects of DUSO-2 and DUSO-2 Revised on children's social skills and self-esteem. *Elementary School Guidance & Counseling* 22(3):199-205, 1988.

Palmer, Pat. *Liking Myself.* Minneapolis, Johnson Institute, 1987.

Pope, Alice, et al. *Self-Esteem Enhancement with Children and Adolescents.* New York, Pergamon, 1988.

Radd, Tommie. *Grow With Guidance.* Canton, Grow With Guidance Systems, 1986.

Reasoner, Robert. *Building Self-Esteem: A Comprehensive Program.* Palo Alto, Consulting Psychologists Press, 1982.

Reider, Barbara. *A Hooray Kind of Kid: A Child's Self-Esteem and How to Build It.* El Dorado Hills, Sierra House, 1988.

Renard, Sue and Sockol, Kay. *Creative Drama-Enhancing Self-Concepts and Learning.* Minneapolis, Educational Media Corporation, 1985.

Sidley, Elayne. *Me, Myself and I.* Dominguez Hills, Educational Insights, 1980.

Sorsdahl, Sandra N. and Sanche, Robert P. The effects of classroom meetings on self-concept and behavior. *Elementary School Guidance & Counseling* 20(1):49-56, 1985.

Summerlin, Mary Lue et al. The effect of magic circle participation on a child's self-concept. *The School Counselor* 31(1):49-52, 1983.

Trower, Terry. *The Kid Counselor Curriculum.* Doylestown, Marco, 1989.

Weinhold, Barry K. and Hilferty, Judy. The self-esteem matrix: a tool for elementary counselors. *Elementary School Guidance & Counseling* 17(4):243-251, 1983.

White, Earl. *Nourishing the Seeds of Self-Esteem: A Handbook of Group Activities.* Santa Cruz, Educational and Training Services, 1980.

Worzbyt, John C. and O'Rourke, Kathleen. *Elementary School Counseling.* Muncie, Accelerated Development, 1989.

Zink, J. *Building Positive Self-Concept in Kids.* Manhattan Beach, J. Zink, 1983.

Chapter 6

Children of Family Life Changes Support Group Curriculum

A complete curriculum for children of family life changes support groups is provided in this chapter. Step-by-step instructions are outlined for the unique set-up, planning, and facilitation of this type of elementary age support group. An extensive listing of assessment scales, session themes, bibliotherapy books, videotapes/films, and "how-to-do-it" references are included as part of this practical support group guide. This chapter, along with Chapters One, Two, Three, and Thirteen, will provide complete instructions for the set-up through the termination of children of family life changes support groups.

Treatment Guidelines

Today in this country, 51% of all marriages end in divorce. As a result, over half of all American families are experiencing the difficulties involved with the breakdown of their nuclear unit. Most youngsters from these families suffer some degree of adjustment problems related to such life changes. The most difficult time in this change process will vary for these children. In some cases, it will be during the divorce, while for others it will be the remarriage. Whatever the most conflictive adjustment period, the bottom line is that most of these children need some type of assistance during this life transition experience.

Youngsters going through such family life changes often benefit from being in a support group with other peers having similar experiences. This setting helps normalize their feelings, develop coping alternatives, and establish the hope that with time things will be less painful. Peers can be wonderful models for one another as they go through the difficult changes of a family unit.

Before utilizing this curriculum, the reader should review the following general treatment guidelines for working with children in support groups where the focus is on problems related to family life changes.

1. The difficulties resulting from a family life change are varied. For this reason, it is best to ask the youngster their perception of the situation and the resulting problems. Sometimes we make inaccurate assumptions regarding these children. For example, a child from a chronically troubled marriage may in fact welcome a divorce but find visitations to be a problem. Therefore, one of the first things to elicit from such a youngster is their perception of the change, often best done in a pre-group individual session. Such disclosure can greatly assist the facilitator in developing relevant content for group sessions.

2. Young children often initially feel more comfortable talking about their family problems on a one-to-one basis. After some individual sessions, such youngsters will often be ready for a support group. In the group setting, these children are then less anxious, because of prior contact with a counselor, when discussing difficulties related to family life changes.

3. When possible, it is ideal to compose these support groups with youngsters who are at various stages of the coping process with a family life change. A mixture of such members provides helpful suggestions and can create role models.

4. Teachers should be sensitized to members' family changes so that they can be more supportive and adjust their expectations during this period. Sometimes it is advisable for teachers to keep counselors posted as to when such youngsters seem to have made a fairly good adjustment. Through this intervention, the classroom expectations can be kept in check until the major transition is made by these children.

5. As common to any grieving process, it will be important not to move members too quickly toward acceptance of a family change. Kids, just like adults, need a time to hope, fantasize, be angry, cry, and then accept. Sometimes in our society we expect everyone to make major life transitions too quickly. Divorces and remarriages are major changes in a child's life. Therefore, group sessions should initially provide support and therapeutic education to these youngsters rather than elicit lots of disclosure or confront their defense systems.

6. Assignments may serve as helpful interventions for these children. Often times, youngsters need to know alternative ways to cope with this major change. By providing structured tasks outside the group, the facilitator can teach coping alternatives through in vivo experiences. The group session time can then be used to process how the assignment worked out for the

members. Parents and teachers may need to be more directly involved in some assignments as a way of gaining their support and/or feedback.

7. Children going through family changes often experience a breakdown of their behavior in any number of different settings. It will be important for the counselor to identify the areas where regression has occurred. The group can then focus on re-establishing earlier functioning levels in those same settings. Clinicians need to remember that some children in this transition period may never regain earlier avenues of success. A continued sense of accomplishment in school, sports, clubs, or hobbies will often greatly assist a child's overall adjustment to a family life change.

8. Bibliotherapy and film/videotape interventions have been found to be very helpful for these students. These techniques provide a non-threatening format to teach youngsters about the normal steps and feelings everyone experiences during a family life change. Facilitators will find that wonderful resources of this type are now available on the market and through most libraries (see Technique #2 in this curriculum for a sample list).

9. Often, it is most effective and comfortable for these youngsters to ventilate their feelings through non-verbal indirect interventions. Several techniques of this type are contained in this curriculum. In most short-term support groups (12 sessions or less), children of family life changes are not able to fully open up about many of their conflicts and issues. It is important, however, to provide these youngsters with alternative ways of ventilating and coping with their situations.

10. The facilitator's relationship with members during this period will often be more valuable than any technique. These youngsters need to have an adult they can trust, who will give them ongoing support during this difficult adjustment period. It is important that counselors be warm, caring, and open with these students. This type of modeling often creates a similar reaction among the group members.

Assessment Instruments

1. Achenbach Child Behavior Checklist

2. Checklist of Children's Fears

3. Child's Attitude Toward Father and Mother Scales

4. Children's Version/Family Environment Scale

5. Conners' Parent and Teacher Rating Scales

6. Devereux Elementary School Behavior Rating Scale

7. Inferred Self-Concept Scale

8. Perception-of-Relationship (PORT)

9. Revised Children's Manifest Anxiety Scale

10. Reynolds Child Depression Scale

Relevant Session Themes

Normalization of feelings

Increased sense of not being alone in one's difficulties

Understand reasons behind behavioral regression at school, home, or with friends

Understand the steps in the grieving process

Learn coping skills for the various stages of family life changes

Use of effective communication skills rather than acting out behavior

Better understanding of their perception of the family change

Returning to earlier sources of success

Increased awareness of feelings

Skills in dealing with family members during this process

Learning how to ventilate feelings of depression, sadness, and guilt

Knowing how to find other supports for oneself

Role modeling on how to effectively deal with the change

Learning how to take care of one's needs in a healthy way

Maintenance of a positive self-esteem

Planning Sequence of Objectives & Techniques for Children of Family Life Changes Support Group

Group Phase	Group Goals	Intervention Categories
Initial	1. To provide an attractive group setting. 2. To initiate members' participation on-task and with one another. 3. To initiate trust among the membership.	**Hello Group Techniques** (Chapter Three)
	4. To educate members about issues and difficulties related to family life changes.	**Instructive Techniques:** #1 Take A Walk Down This Road #2 Bibliotherapy/Video/Films #3 Mixed Up Feelings
Middle	5. To increase group development goals established in initial phase (i.e., goals 1-3).	No techniques per se but follow curriculum approach.
	6. To increase members' awareness of their particular difficulties related to their family life change.	**Awareness of Self Techniques:** #4 Your Sculptured Clay Family #5 Slice Up My Life #6 Keeping Tabs On My Family
	7. To provide alternative coping behaviors for dealing with a family life change.	**Alternative Coping Techniques:** #7 Over And Done #8 The Family News Daily #9 Say It With Glasses
	8. To assist members in the integration of new coping behaviors into their repertoire.	**Integration Techniques:** #10 A Meditation For Me #11 Thumbs Up/Thumbs Down #12 Imagine Your Future
Termination	9. To have members acknowledge the value of the group. 10. To assist members in validating their changes. 11. To have members brainstorm other sources of support. 12. To have members grieve the ending of group.	**Goodbye Group Techniques** (Chapter Thirteen)

▸ Technique #1

Title:	Take A Walk Down This Road
Technique category:	Didactic
Objective:	To instruct members about the usual grieving steps one goes through when there is a family life change.

Materials:

- "Unscramble The Words" form found on page 139.
- Pencils

Procedure:

1. At the beginning of this session, members are informed that they are going to have a chance to learn more about the steps one goes through when there is a major change in a family.

2. Members are given a designated period of time to complete the paper and pencil sheet entitled "Unscramble the Words."

3. All participants are asked to share the content of these sheets by going around the circle one right after another. Some facilitators may prefer to have the content from these sheets shared one item at a time to enhance the learning experience among the participants. This is an individual decision each facilitator must make when conducting this exercise.

4. After this sharing time has been completed, the group leader should provide some summarizing of the highlights of this learning experience. It will be particularly helpful to emphasize commonalities that surfaced during the disclosure in order to normalize members' feelings and experiences.

5. At the end of the session, the participants should be asked to share the number one point they learned from this experience.

Cautions/comments:

Didactic techniques are particularly helpful interventions at the beginning of support groups because they are non-threatening. Usually, children respond to this type of intervention as if it were a classroom learning situation. This is exactly the type of feeling the facilitator wants to create.

This particular task provides youngsters a beginning awareness of why they have had some of their thoughts and behaviors regarding a family life change. At this point, members may not disclose directly about their similar experiences, but a valuable "seed planting" is accomplished through this didactic exercise.

▸ Unscramble The Words

Instructions: Unscramble the five words below that are the steps we all go through when there is a major change in our family. Hint: read the behaviors and thoughts to the right of each word to give you some extra help.

GRIEVING STEPS	BEHAVIORS AND THOUGHTS DURING THAT TIME	
Step 1: N I L A E D Answer: _____	**Behavior:** **Thought:**	Act like nothing has happened. My mom and dad will get back together.
Step 2: G E R N A Answer: _____	**Behavior:** **Thought:**	Get upset with everyone around me very easily. I hate them for what they did.
Step 3: N I B A R G A Answer: _____	**Behavior:** **Thought:**	Try to get family members back together Dear God, if you get my parents back together, I'll be good.
Step 4: O N S I S D E P R E Answer: _____	**Behavior:** **Thought:**	Do not want to participate with friends in usual activities. I am so sad because my family will never be the same again.
Step 5: A N A C C P E T C E Answer: _____	**Behavior:** **Thought:**	Back doing my usual activities again. I wish my parents had not divorced, but at least I know they still love me.

▶ Technique #2

Title:	Bibliotherapy/Video/Films
Technique category:	Bibliotherapy/Video/Films
Objective:	To instruct the group regarding the difficulties and issues related to family life changes.

Materials:

- Book, film, or videotape selected from the list on page 141.
- Equipment for film or videotape, if used.
- Prepared discussion questions related to the theme of the visual aid chosen.

Procedure:

1. Before the session, the facilitator selects a book, film, or videotape from the list on page 141.
2. Session begins with the book being read or film/videotape being shown.
3. At completion of above task, members can be asked discussion questions that surface their identification with the story. Also, some disclosure that explores the children's similar problems and struggles can be elicited.
4. Members' favorite parts of the book, film, or videotape should be processed at the end.

Cautions/comments:

Typically, members will enjoy the use of bibliotherapy materials or films/videotapes. Through these types of visual interventions, children can more easily learn about their family life change. In addition, youngsters in elementary grades typically identify with characters in books and films. As a result, they are often able to talk more comfortably about their similar issues via the story presented.

Readers are advised to select books that have colorful pictures on almost every page. Children as a whole find it easier to understand the message of a book page when a graphic design depicts the concept. Also, facilitators should be careful that books and films/videotapes selected are not too long. It is important to have time in the session to pose discussion questions and process reactions among the members.

▶ Bibliotherapy

1. Abercrombie, Barbara Mattes. *Cat-Man's Daughter.* Harper & Row Publishers, Inc., 1981, ages 11-13.

2. Anderson, Penny S. *A Pretty Good Team.* The Child's World, Inc., 1979, ages 5-8.

3. Berger, Terry. *Stepchild.* Julian Messner, Inc., 1980, ages 7-11.

4. Berger, Terry. *How Does it Feel When Your Parents Get Divorced.* Julian Messner, 1977, ages 7-10.

5. Berman, Claire. *What Am I Doing in a Step-Family?* Lyle Stuart, Inc., 1982, ages 4 and up.

6. Danziger, Paula. *The Divorce Express.* Delacorte Press, 1982, ages 11-14.

7. Davis, Diane. *Something Is Wrong At My House: A Book About Parents' Fighting.* Parenting Press, Inc., 1984, grades 1-6.

8. Drescher, Joan Elizabeth. *Your Family, My Family.* Walker and Company, 1980, ages 5-7.

9. Evans, Marla D. *This is Me and My Two Families.* Magination Press, 1986, grades 1-6.

10. Ewing, Kathryn. *Things Won't Be the Same.* Harcourt-Brace-Jovanovich, Inc., 1980, ages 8-10.

11. Gaeddert, LouAnn Bigge. *Just Like Sisters.* E. P. Dutton & Company, 1981, ages 8-12.

12. Gardner, Richard. *The Boys and Girls Book About One Parent Families.* G. P. Putnam's Sons, 1978, ages 7-14.

13. Goff, Beth. *Where is Daddy? The Story of a Divorce.* Beacon Press, 1969, ages 4-8.

14. Gregory, Diana. *There's a Caterpillar in My Lemonade.* Addison-Wesley Publishing Company, Inc., 1980, ages 10-12.

15. Helmering, Doris Wild. *I Have Two Families.* Abingdon Press, 1981, ages 6-8.

16. Irwin, Hadley, pseud. *Bring to a Boil and Separate.* Atheneum Publishers, 1980, ages 10-12.

17. Jukes, Mavis. *Like Jake and Me.* Alfred A. Knopf, 1984, ages 4 and up.

18. Krasny Brown, Laurene and Brown, Marc. *Dinosaurs Divorce.* Boston: Little Brown and Company, 1986, ages 8-12.

19. Moore, Emily. *Something to Count On.* E. P. Dutton & Company, 1980, ages 8-10.

20. Okimoto, Jean Davies. *My Mother is Not Married to My Father.* G. P. Putnam's Sons, 1979, ages 9-11.

21. Paris, Lena. *Mom is Single.* Children's Press, Inc., 1980, ages 6-8.

22. Park, Barbara. *Don't Make Me Smile.* Alfred A. Knopf, Inc., 1981, grades ages 8-11.

23. Schuchman, Joan. *Two Places to Sleep.* Carol Rhoda Books, 1979, ages 5-8.

24. Sinberg, Janet. *Divorce is a Grown-Up Problem.* Avon Books, 1978, ages 4-8.

25. Sobol, Harriet Langsan. *My Other-Mother, My Other-Father.* Macmillan, 1979, ages 8-13.

26. Stanek, Muriel. *I Won't Go Without a Father.* Albert Whitman & Company, 1972, ages 8-10.

27. Vigna, Judith. *She's Not My Real Mother.* Albert Whitman & Company, 1980, ages 4-8.

28. Wolitzer, Hilma. *Wish You Were Here.* Farrar, Straus, and Giroux, 1984, ages 10 and up.

29. Wright, Betty Ren. *My New Mom and Me.* Raintree Publishers, Inc., 1981, ages 8-10.

Videotapes

1. Breakup
   National Instructional T.V., 1973, 15 minute film, grades 4-6.

2. Divorce
   Coronet, 1981, 16 minute film, grades 4-6.

3. Divorce: Teen Perspective
   Learning Corporation of America/MTI, 1983, 15 minute film, grades 4-6.

4. Families: Growing and Changing
   Coronet, 1982, 15 minute film, grades K-6.

5. Families: Will They Survive?
   Encyclopedia Britannica Educational Corp., 1982, 23 minute film, grades 4-6.

6. Family
   Wombat Productions, Inc., 1972, 14 minute film, grades 4-6.

7. Family of Strangers
   Learning Corporation of America/MTI, 1980, 31 minute film, grades 4-6.

8. Just Like Me
   Lucerne Films and Video, 1980, 26 minute film, grades 1-6.

9. Mom and Pop Split Up
   Barr Films, 1978, 15 minute film, grades 1-6.

10. Parents - Who Needs Them?
    Coronet, 1973, 10 minute film, grades 1-6.

11. Single Parent Family
    Coronet, 1981, 15 minute film, grades 4-6.

12. The Sky is Falling: A Program for Children of Divorce
    Leane Leighton, filmstrip/videotape, grades K-5.

13. Step Family
    Coronet, 1981, 13 minute film, grades 3-6.

14. Things Are Different Now
    Media Guild, 1978, 17 minute film, grades 4-6.

15. Way It Is, The
    Churchill Films, 1986, 24 minute film, grades 4-6.

Films

1. *A Kid's Guide to Divorce*
   Spoken Arts, 1988, 4 filmstrips and cassettes, grades K-3.

2. *Coping With Your Parents' Divorce*
   Listen and Learn Company, 4 filmstrips with cassettes, grades 4-8.

3. *Dinosaurs Divorce*
   Spoken Arts, 1986, 1 filmstrip and 1 cassette, grades P-3.

4. *Don't You Love Me Anymore?*
   Listen and Learn Company, 4 filmstrips with cassettes, grades K-3.

5. *Getting Used to Divorce*
   Creative Learning, Inc., 1 filmstrip, grades 5-6.

6. *Getting Used To Divorce*
   Random House Media, filmstrip/cassette, grades 5-6.

7. *Learning About Families With the Flintstones*
   Spoken Arts, 1986, 3 filmstrips and 3 cassettes, grades K-4.

8. *Me and My Family*
   Random House Media, 6 filmstrips/cassettes, grades K-4.

9. *My Parents are Divorced* (from the kit entitled "What If a Crisis Hits Your Family?")
   Eye Gate, 1 filmstrip/cassette, grades 3-5.

10. *Surviving Your Parents' Divorce*
    Sunburst Communications, 2 filmstrips/cassettes, grades 5-8.

11. *Trouble at Home: Learning To Cope*
    Sunburst, 2 filmstrips/cassettes, grades 5-6.

12. *Understanding Changes in the Family*
    Guidance Associates, 5 filmstrips, grades K-3.

▸ Technique #3

Title:	Mixed Up Feelings
Technique category:	Paper/Pencil Task
Objective:	To instruct the group about difficulties and issues related to family life changes.

Materials needed:

- Copies of the sheet entitled "Mixed Up Feelings," found on page 146.
- Pencils

Procedure:

1. Pass out the sheet entitled "Mixed Up Feelings" to all group members.
2. Allow 5 to 10 minutes for the completion of this task.
3. Ask everyone to share their responses by going around the circle in order. The facilitator should initially share their responses to the task sheet for purposes of modeling.
4. If time allows, pose some discussion questions related to the task sheet responses.
5. Process members' positive reactions at the end of the session.

Cautions/comments:

This is an excellent technique for providing a non-threatening avenue for looking at all the feelings members are having toward family members. Facilitators will typically find that this intervention surfaces some great self-awareness among the participants. In addition, it is a time efficient exercise that elicits lots of disclosure around typical feelings kids have when they go through a family life change.

▸ **Mixed Up Feelings**

Instructions: Write all the numbers of the feelings you are having toward each family member below.

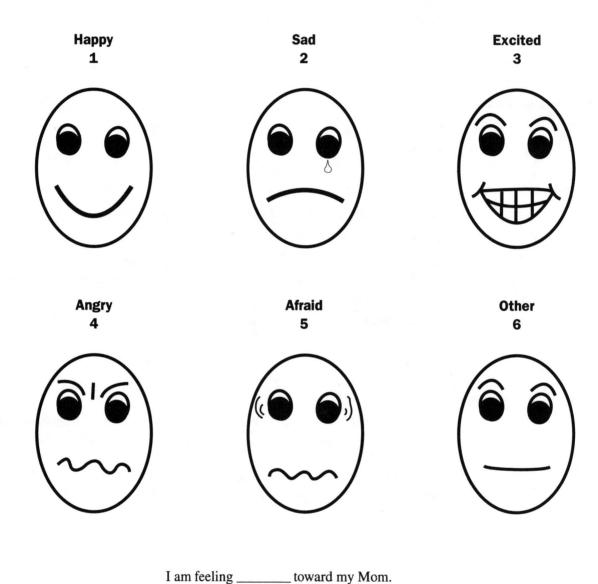

I am feeling _____ toward my Mom.

I am feeling _____ toward my Dad.

I am feeling _____ toward my Brother.

I am feeling _____ toward my Sister.

I am feeling _____ toward _____ (another person).

▶ Technique #4

Title: Your Sculptured Clay Family

Technique category: Exercise Using the Arts

Objective: To increase members' awareness of their difficulties in regard to family life change.

Materials:

- Blocks of various color clay
- Cardboard pieces

Procedure:

1. Members are told they are going to have an opportunity to participate in a creative exercise where they will sculpture their family either doing something or posing for a picture.

2. Members are allowed 10 to 15 minutes to complete this task.

3. After everyone is done, each child takes a turn sharing their clay sculptures. Members should be allowed to share as much or as little as they want in explaining their clay family model to the group. Facilitators should be the first to share. This will create a more comfortable setting for this disclosure.

4. Throughout the above sharing, members' commonalities and significant disclosure should be reinforced.

5. At the end, everyone is asked to share in their own creative way the most enjoyable part of this experience.

Cautions/comments:

Facilitators will be amazed at how much more children reveal through this clay technique than through talking about their families. They should also be sensitive to the therapeutic value of ventilating through the modeling of the clay. In some cases, there may not be a lot of verbal sharing. This does not mean that it is not a valuable experience for the youngsters: typically, children find it therapeutically helpful to have a physical and creative avenue available to express their feelings in regard to a trauma like a family life change. More and more studies in the area of childhood trauma are identifying the need for such physical outlets for traumatic feelings.

▶ Technique #5

Title:	Slice Up My Life
Technique category:	Disclosure Task
Objective:	To increase members' awareness of their difficulties in regard to their family life changes.

Materials:

- Form entitled "Slice Up My Life," found on page 149.
- Pencils

Procedure:

1. Members are given the form entitled "Slice Up My Life." In each of the two circles, the children are instructed to slice up their life, writing where and with whom they spend their time typically during the week. In older groups (fourth grade and up), facilitators may even want to have the children indicate the percentage of time they spend in each of the designated activities.

2. After everyone has completed this awareness task, each member is asked to show their drawing and to point out how their time is sliced up differently now.

3. In some groups, facilitators may want to encourage members to ask each other questions for more details related to their contrasting schedules.

4. At the end of the session, members should be asked to share what they learned from this exercise.

Cautions/comments:

This is an excellent technique for helping members look more objectively at the contrast of their time schedules before and after the family life change. As a result of this awareness task, youngsters can often better understand some of their conflicting feelings and resulting problems. Facilitators will want to emphasize that in looking at this view of their lives, the children need to identify those things they have control over. In addition, it will be important to point out all the things in their two circles that have remained the same or are similar. This awareness often helps members realize that some parts of their lives have been stable through this change.

▸ Slice Up My Life

BEFORE FAMILY CHANGE

AFTER FAMILY CHANGE

Compare how your life was sliced up before and after your family change.

▸ Technique #6

Title:	Keeping Tabs On My Family
Technique category:	Creative Exercise
Objective:	To increase members' awareness of their difficulties in regard to their family life changes.

Materials:

- Copies of the sheet entitled "Keeping Tabs On My Family," found on page 151.
- Pencils

Procedure:

1. The facilitator passes out to each participant the sheet entitled "Keeping Tabs On My Family." The group is asked to take this journal sheet home and complete it each day, using the three questions asked as a guide.

2. Then, members are given a designated period of time to brainstorm all the types of animals a family could be like on any given day.

3. After everyone is ready with some ideas, the group leader requests participants to share their responses.

4. Also, youngsters can be encouraged to give descriptive adjectives for their animals like "an angry lion" or "a mixed up bear." What members won't realize is that by coming up with these ideas for their journal sheets they will be disclosing some of their own feelings at the same time.

5. If time allows, members can be asked to discuss how they will make sure they complete their journal entry each day.

6. At the end of this session, participants should be asked to share what they think will be most helpful about this creative assignment task.

Cautions/comments:

Children of family life changes usually need an avenue for ventilating their conflicting feelings. This creative assignment can fill just that need for these students. Youngsters typically identify with animals and find this symbolic association between their family and an animal to be an easier way to convey their feelings. If a particular group seems to have trouble making this symbolic connection, then it will be helpful to hand out an accompanying sheet with examples of animals with descriptive adjectives. It will be important to spend time at the next session discussing and sharing these journal sheets.

▸ Keeping Tabs On My Family

Instructions: Each day for the next week log your feelings and thoughts on this journal page. Be sure to bring it back to our next group session so we can discuss it.

Date: _____ My day has been: _____

The animal my family has been like to me today is _____

_____

I thought about my family:

All the time	Half the time	A little

Date: _____ My day has been: _____

The animal my family has been like to me today is _____

_____

I thought about my family:

All the time	Half the time	A little

Date: _____ My day has been: _____

The animal my family has been like to me today is _____

_____

I thought about my family:

All the time	Half the time	A little

Date: _____ My day has been: _____

The animal my family has been like to me today is _____

_____

I thought about my family:

All the time	Half the time	A little

▶ Technique #7

Title:	Over And Done
Technique category:	In Vivo Exercise
Objective:	To increase members' awareness of alternative ways of handling family life changes

Materials:

- An "Over And Done" shoe box
- 3"x5" cards
- Pencils

Procedure:

1. The facilitator begins this session by showing members a shoe box that has "Over And Done" written on it. Participants are asked to imagine this as a magical box that once things are written down and placed in it, they will be put forever in the past.

2. The entire group is then asked to have an open discussion on all the things kids might want to put in the past regarding their family life change. It is suggested that these contributions be written on a blackboard to serve as a reminder for members. Also, in some groups, it may be helpful to make this discussion into a more fun brainstorming game where members have to come up with so many ideas within an allotted period of time.

3. After enough ideas have been generated from this discussion, members are given two 3"x5" cards each. They are instructed to write something that they know needs to be put in the past for them.

4. Once these cards are completed, the facilitator asks members to participate in a type of ritual for putting their issues or hopes finally in the past.

   Each participant is asked to take a turn, following the procedure below.

   - Say out loud, "I truly want to put _____ in the past."
   - "Also, I want to put _____ in the past."

     Usually, it is a good idea to offer another option so that members do not have to state the exact content of their two cards. Instead, they can say, "I truly want to put the ideas on these two cards in the past."

• Now drop both cards in the box while saying, "By putting these in this box, I am showing how much I want to rid myself of all such thoughts and actions."

• Tell the youngster to go back and sit down, and to think positive about keeping those two issues in the past.

5. At the end of the session, members should be asked to process their positive responses to this ritual experience.

Cautions/comments:

Readers will find that one of the most frequent problems among these children is their difficulty in giving up earlier family memories. Many of these kids still dream daily of their parents getting back together or a step parent not having entered their lives. For this reason, an exercise such as this can be quite effective in helping youngsters work through these unrealistic fantasies. Members may continue to use this same type of coping behavior with future unrealistic wishes that need to be put to rest.

▸ Technique #8

Title:	The Family News Daily
Technique category:	Completion Task
Objective:	To increase members' awareness of alternative ways of handling family life changes.

Materials:

- Four beginning news stories on relevant family change conflict using the form entitled "A Family News Story," found on page 156.
- Pencils

Procedure:

1. Before this session, the facilitator will need to prepare some family news stories based on relevant themes or issues of members. Such news stories should be written up as the following example:

EXTRA!! EXTRA!!

PARENTS PULL SON APART

Six months ago, Paul Andrews' parents decided to divorce. Paul is ten years old and an only child. Both of his parents want him to live with them. Mr. and Mrs. Andrews have been through several bitter courtroom battles to get Paul to reside at each of their homes.

Paul is so upset because he loves both of his parents. He has been trying to get his parents to see how difficult this situation has been on him.

Finally, a solution is reached when...

The "Family News Story" form can be used when originating these stories. Usually, it is a good idea to pair youngsters up for this exercise.

2. Teams are then assigned a story to complete, with the participants being reminded to include ending solutions that only involve things that the youngster can control.

3. After all teams have completed their news stories, the members are asked to share their stories and solutions with the entire group.

4. Members should be asked to each share at the end of the session what they learned from this exercise.

Cautions/comments:

This exercise affords an opportunity to share several coping ideas for dealing with a family life change situation. In many groups, members find themselves becoming aware of coping skills they developed from going through such an experience. Also, the nature of this task emphasizes an important point for these youngsters. They need to concentrate on these variables around their family change that they have control over.

▸ A Family News Story

Instructions: Complete the story below with a solution that will help end some of the conflict for the child. Be sure to include things that the child will have some control over in the solution.

EXTRA!! EXTRA!!
THE FAMILY NEWS DAILY

_____

_____

_____

_____

_____

_____

_____

_____

_____

_____

_____

_____

_____

_____

_____

_____

_____

_____

_____

▶ Technique #9

Title: Say It With Glasses

Technique category: Game Exercise

Objective: To increase members' awareness of alternative ways of handling family life changes.

Materials:

- Two sets of eyeglasses, one clear and the other rose-colored
- Family conflict stories developed by the facilitator (These should be relevant to members and indicate one family member's viewpoint.)

Procedure:

1. At the onset of this session, members are told they are going to be playing the fun game of "Pick the Right Set of Glasses." The facilitator then spends some time explaining the saying, "looking through rose-colored glasses." Youngsters should be instructed to make sure they understand this concept, since it will help them win the game.

2. The following rules are then reviewed with the membership.

   - Each member will have a chance at a turn by going around the circle in order.

   - The facilitator will read a family change story and then tell how one member is seeing or responding to the situation.

   - Whoever is up for a turn must pick up the glasses, clear or rose, that indicate the viewpoint the person is choosing to take. For example, if after a divorce an 8-year-old child chooses to think of his parents getting back together, then the correct glasses would be the rose-colored glasses.

   - If the member's response is correct, the group gets a point. If the response is wrong, the facilitator gets the point.

   - The one (group or facilitator) with the most points after three rounds wins.

3. The game is then conducted following the rules.

4. If time allows, discussion questions can be posed to the children in order to probe some of their earlier responses during the game.

5. At the end, everyone should be asked to complete the following sentence: "I really liked this session when _____."

Cautions/comments:

This is a very concrete way to help members learn that facing up to family life changes is usually the best response. Also, the more relevant the stories are to members' experiences, the more likely these youngsters will be able to generalize their learning from the session. Readers will find that younger children (kindergarten through third grade) enjoy using the clear and rose-colored glasses, which decreases their anxiety around the content of the stories. Facilitators will want to be sensitive to members who may become upset during a story that is very similar to their own. These youngsters may have to be seen after the group to help them process their reactions.

▸ Technique #10

Title: A Meditation For Me

Technique category: Empowerment Exercise

Objective: To integrate new coping skills for family life changes into members' repertoire.

Materials needed:

- Copies of the sheet entitled "A Meditation For Me," found on page 160.
- Pencils

Procedure:

1. Pass out the sheet entitled "A Meditation For Me" to all group members.
2. Allow 5 to 10 minutes for the completion of this task.
3. Ask everyone to share their responses by going around the circle in order. The facilitator should initially share their responses to the task sheet for purposes of modeling.
4. If time allows, pose some discussion questions related to the task sheet responses.
5. Process members' positive reactions at the end of the session.

Cautions/comments:

This is an excellent technique for helping members recount what they have learned from their support group experience. Facilitators may want to suggest that students cut out their meditation completion and put it where they will see it on a regular basis, as a reminder. By this point in a support group, facilitators will often be touched by some of the emotional growth among members as reflected in their meditations.

▶ A Meditation For Me

Instructions: Complete the following meditation for yourself as a way of helping you come to accept and handle your family life change.

May I come to accept

_____

May I begin to forgive

_____

May I start reaching out

_____

Let me now start feeling

_____

And let me now

_____

_____

Signature

_____

Date

▸ **Technique #11**

Title:	Thumbs Up/Thumbs Down
Technique category:	Check-Ups/Assignments
Objective:	To assist members in the integration of new coping skills into their repertoire.

Materials:

- Facilitators will need to prepare relevant categories of behavior changes around family life transitions. About ten to 15 of these will need to be prepared for this session.

Procedure:

1. Before this session, the facilitator may want to gather some information on specific coping skills that members have acquired or improved upon through the support group experience. After this list has been developed with at least three positive changes for each member, the facilitator will need to determine general categories in order to cover these areas of improvement. The categories can include acceptance of divorce, forgiving a parent, knowing people to turn to for support, etc.

2. The session begins with the members being told that they will have an opportunity to think about the coping skills they have learned or improved upon in the support group. Then, the following instructions for the thumbs up/thumbs down exercise are explained.

   - The facilitator will read a category of potential change such as "attitude toward divorce" and describe in more detail the progress in this area of functioning that would be involved for a child.

   - After the category and description is read, members are asked to indicate by a thumbs up sign if they feel they have made some progress and a thumbs down sign if they have made no progress. Youngsters will need to be reminded that thumbs down means no change, not even in terms of learning more about that area of functioning. (The facilitator will want to set up a situation in which most members have to use the thumbs up sign for most categories presented.)

   - This same procedure will be followed for all categories of changed behaviors, feelings, or attitudes presented.

3. At the end of this completion and awareness task, members should be asked to share how it felt having their thumbs up sign used frequently. Also, youngsters can be asked to review commonalities that surfaced during this exercise.

4. As always, it is a good idea to have the students indicate at the end of the session how this task helped them feel about all their progress around their family life change.

Cautions/comments:

This is a particularly effective intervention for summarizing the progress that members have made in a support group. Also, the use of the thumbs up/down sign is a less threatening way for elementary students to participate in this disclosure task. Usually, the concrete nature of this task is very conducive to the comprehension level of these youngsters. Many of the participants in the group will find this to be a validating experience that summarizes their progress.

▸ Technique #12

Title:	Imagine Your Future
Technique category:	Confirmation Exercise
Objective:	To assist members in the integration of new coping skills into their repertoire.

Materials:

- "My Family Five Years Later" form found on page 165.
- Pencils

Procedure:

1. This session begins with the facilitator explaining to the members that they are going to have a chance to create a future fantasy. Then, the participants are all asked to get into a relaxed position in their chairs and close their eyes. Usually, it is a good idea at this point to take a few minutes and assist members through a set of relaxation steps.

2. Once everyone seems comfortably relaxed, participants are asked to start formulating a future picture of their family life five years down the road. Typically, youngsters do better with this exercise when a series of descriptive statements is provided to help in fully formulating this look into the future. Examples of such statements are listed below.

   1. Decide who is in your family picture.
   2. Formulate an activity you all are doing.
   3. Think about how you and everyone else is feeling.
   4. Where do you see your family living?
   5. Reflect on three positive changes in your attitude toward your family at that time.

   Group members will usually require about 15 minutes to become relaxed and formulate fully this future picture of their family.

3. Next, participants are asked to draw these ideas on the form entitled "My Family Five Years Later."

4. Members are then requested to share their drawings with one another. Facilitators should allow the youngsters the freedom to share whatever they feel comfortable verbalizing to the group.

5.   Members should be asked to indicate the most beneficial part of this exercise for them.

Cautions/comments:

This is usually a very effective technique for helping members understand and accept at a gut level the changes they have made regarding their family changes. Youngsters in the midst of family life changes often find it helpful to look down the road at how much easier things will be with the passage of time. When doing this exercise, it is important that the youngsters concentrate on the things they will have control over in the future.

Facilitators will need to be prepared for some members whose future picture puts the old family unit back together. These youngsters may very well need some individual sessions following the group to continue working through these issues. Also, clinicians should only use this intervention in schools or mental health programs where families are aware of and comfortable with relaxation/fantasy techniques. Readers should be aware that in some school districts throughout the country, there is a growing concern among some parents, who see this as "out-of-body experiences." Clinicians should be aware of this situation and check to be sure their members' families understand and support the objective of this intervention.

▶ My Family Five Years Later

Instructions: In the crystal ball below, draw the picture that you just imagined of your family five years from now.

▶ Bibliography

Anderson, Ronald F. et al. The effects of divorce groups on children's classroom behavior and attitude toward divorce. *Elementary School Guidance & Counseling* 19(1):70-76, 1984.

Bebensee, B. *Loss . . . A Natural Part of Living.* Englewood Cliffs, Educational Consulting Associates, 1980.

Berry, Joy. *Every Kid's Guide to Handling Family Arguments.* Chicago, Children's Press, 1987.

Borg, Berthold. *The Changing Family Game.* Dayton, Berg, Allik and Associates, 1982.

Bowker, Marjorie A. Children and divorce: being in between. *Elementary School Guidance & Counseling* 17(3):200-207, 1983.

Brogan, John P. and Maiden, Ula. *The Kids' Guide to Divorce.* New York, Fawcett, 1986.

Brown, Laurene and Marc. *Dinosaurs Divorce: A Guide for Changing Families.* New York, Golden Books, 1985.

Cantrell, Roslyn Garden. Adjustment to divorce: three components to assist children. *Elementary School Guidance & Counseling* 20(3):163-173, 1986.

Davis, Diane. *Something is Wrong at My House.* Seattle, Parenting Press, Inc., 1984.

Dolmetsch, Paul and Shih, Alexa. *The Kids' Book About Single-Parent Families.* New York, Doubleday/Dolphin, 1985.

Engel, Rosalind. The status of the family in books for young children: a survey of literature written during the 1970's. *Child Welfare* LXI:143-151, 1982.

Evans, Marla D. *This is Me and My Single Parent.* New York, Brunner/Mazel Publishers, 1990.

Fairchild, Thomas N. (editor). *Crisis Intervention Strategies for School-Based Helpers.* Springfield, Charles C. Thomas, 1986.

Fassler, David et al. *Changing Families: A Guide for Kids and Grown-Ups.* Burlington, Waterfront Books, 1988.

Gardner, Richard. *The Storytelling Card Game.* Philadelphia, Childwork/Childplay, 1988.

Gardner, Richard. *Psychotherapy with Children of Divorce.* New York, Jason Aronson, Inc., 1976.

Gardner, Richard A. Counseling children in stepfamilies. *Elementary School Guidance & Counseling* 19(1):40-49, 1980.

Gardner, Richard A. *The Boys and Girls Book About Stepfamilies.* New York, Bantam Books, 1982.

Gardner, Richard A. *The Boys and Girls Book About Divorce.* New York, Bantam Books, 1970.

Goff, Beth. *Where is Daddy? The Story of a Divorce.* Boston, Beacon Press, 1969.

Graves, Carl M. and Morse, Linda A. *Helping Children of Divorce: A Group Leader's Guide.* Springfield, Charles C. Thomas, 1986.

Green, Barbara J. Helping children of divorce: a multimodal approach. *Elementary School Guidance & Counseling* 13(1):31-45, 1979.

Helping Children Series, Group Counseling and Classroom Guidance Programs on *Single Parent Families* and *Stepfamilies.* Doylestown, Marco, 1989.

Hodges, William F. *Interventions for Children of Divorce: Custody Access and Psychotherapy.* New York, Wiley and Sons, 1986.

Isaacs, M. D. and Levin, I. R. Who's in my family? A longitudinal study of drawings of children of divorce. *Journal of Divorce* 7(4):1-21, 1984.

Ives, Sally, Fassher, D. and Lash, M. *The Divorce Workbook.* Burlington, Waterfront Books, 1980.

Kirkland, Dianna C. *I Have a Stepfamily.* Oak Park, Aid-U Publishing Company, 1985.

Kirkland, Dianna C. *Group Counseling for Children of Stepfamilies.* Oak Park, Aid-U Publishing Company, 1985.

Kosinski, Frederick A. Improving relationships in stepfamilies. *Elementary School Guidance & Counseling* 17(3):200-207, 1983.

Lash, Michele et al. *My Kind of Family: A Book for Kids in Single Parent Homes.* Burlington, Waterfront Books, 1989.

LeShan, Eda L. *What's Going to Happen to Me? When Parents Separate or Divorce.* New York, Macmillan, 1986.

Magid, K. and Schreiberman, W. *Divorce is...A Kid's Coloring Book.* Gretna, Pelican Co., 1980.

McInnis, Kathleen M. Bibliotherapy: adjunct to traditional counseling with children of stepfamilies. *Child Welfare* LXI:153-160, 1982.

Minnick, Molly A. *Group Work with Children of Divorce.* Self-published, 1732 Coolidge Road, East Lansing, Michigan 48823, 1987.

Minnick, Molly A. *Divorce Illustrated* (workbook also). Self-published, 1732 Coolidge Road, East Lansing, Michigan 48823, 1990.

Omizo, Michael M. and Omizo, Sharon A. Group counseling with children of divorce: new findings. *Elementary School Guidance and Counseling* 22(1):46-52, 1987.

Nickman, Steven L. *When Mom and Dad Divorce.* Englewood Cliffs, Messner, 1986.

Pardeck, John T. and Pardeck, Jean A. Using bibliotherapy to help children cope with the changing family. *Social Work in Education* 10:107-116, 1987.

Ricci, Isolina. *Mom's House, Dad's House.* New York, Collier Books, 1980.

Rofes, Eric (editor). *The Kid's Book of Divorce: By, For and About Kids.* Culver City, Random House Social Studies School Service, 1982.

Seuling, B. *What Kind of Family Is This?* Racine, Western Publishing Co., 1985.

Shapiro, Lawrence. *Family Anti-Coloring Book.* Philadelphia, Center for Applied Psychology, 1982.

Shapiro, Lawrence E. *The Family "Work-Together" Workbook.* Philadelphia, Center for Applied Psychology, 1988.

Shapiro, Lawrence. *What Color Are Your Family's Dreams?* Philadelphia, Childswork/Childsplay, 1989.

Sinberg Stenson, Janet. *Now I Have a Stepparent and It's Kind of Confusing.* New York, Avon Books, 1979.

Stauss, J. B. and McGann, J. Building a network for children of divorce. *Social Work in Education* 9(2):96-105, 1987.

Tedder, Sandra L. et al. Effectiveness of a support group for children of divorce. *Elementary School Guidance & Counseling* 22(2):102-109, 1987.

> Chapter **7**

Children of Substance Abusers Support Group Curriculum

A complete curriculum for children of substance abusers support groups is provided in this chapter. Step-by-step instructions are outlined for the unique set-up, planning, and facilitation of this type of elementary age support group. An extensive listing of assessment scales, session themes, bibliotherapy books, videotapes/films, and "how-to-do-it" references are included as part of this practical support group guide. This chapter, along with Chapters One, Two, Three, and Thirteen, will provide complete instructions for the set-up through the termination of children of substance abusers support groups.

Treatment Guidelines

It is estimated that approximately five children out of every class of 25 students has a parent who is a substance abuser. Obviously, the ever increasing use of drugs and alcohol among adults in our society is directly affecting more youngsters' households today. Added to this serious situation, kids of these families are experiencing many secondary problems. These difficulties include child abuse, neglect, low self-esteem, poor peer relationships, ongoing school problems, and severe depression. Needless to say, professionals will find these youngsters showing any number of difficulties as a result of their parents' substance abuse. Unfortunately, the nature and prognosis of substance abuse will usually require long-term counseling for most of these children. Counselors will often find themselves overwhelmed with the needs of this population group. For this reason, a combination of treatment modalities are often required for the most effective intervention.

Before utilizing this curriculum, the reader should review the following general treatment guidelines for working with children in support groups whose parents are substance abusers.

1. Substance abuse is generally a family secret where verbal or non-verbal taboos have been issued not to disclose of it outside the home. Many times, it is best not to ask members to talk in direct specific terms about their own parents' substance abuse. A more indirect intervention will be less anxiety provoking for getting these kids to ventilate their difficulties. Techniques such as books and movies on substance abusing families (see lists in bibliotherapy technique of this curriculum), or family dolls acting out various situations can be examples of such indirect techniques.

2. In many school districts today, written parent permission will be necessary before a child participates in this type of support group. It is usually in the youngster's best interests to be up front with the purpose of the treatment service: readers will be amazed at the number of abusing parents who are able to acknowledge that their children need help with the ramifications of this problem area.

3. It is important that a comprehensive assessment of these youngsters be conducted. Clinicians will want to identify all areas of dysfunction that are directly or indirectly related to this issue. Group sessions then will need to focus on those areas in a step-by-step format. It is imperative that support groups address issues that are relevant to participants' difficulties.

4. Legal authorities will need to be notified when the facilitator determines that severe neglect or abuse is resulting from the parents' substance abuse. In some cases, the clinician may become aware of illegal acts occurring in the home due to this problem. Children seen in groups need to be told ahead of time that such disclosure might need to be made. This will provide some safeguard so that the members will not feel their confidentiality has been betrayed. Counselors should be sensitive to the ramifications of this disclosure on their group members. Before or during legal notification, some safeguards might have to be taken to protect an involved youngster. In such cases, the child may need to be removed from the home before or during the legal notification.

5. Teachers and other involved professionals may need to be aware of this problem for a particular child. When a facilitator sensitizes these individuals, they can provide some needed support and modify expectations of the youngsters. Clinicians should keep the confidentiality issue in mind when sharing facts about their group participants.

6. Often, parents will need to be referred for counseling or invited into sessions with the clinician. It is essential that facilitators (who are able to

tell parents that they know of the substance abuse) maintain parents' responsibility, particularly in regard to this problem area. Educating parents about the ramifications of their difficulties on their children can sometimes provide the initial impetus to begin their own change process.

7. It is very helpful in group to have these youngsters spend time identifying what they have control over in their lives. Too often these children are so overwhelmed with their parents' substance abuse that they persist on trying to get them to stop. Facilitators can assist these kids in concentrating more of their efforts on things they can change and control.

8. It is not unusual for children of substance abusers to be severely depressed or even suicidal. The clinician should be sensitive to these issues and probe for any specific plans that the youngsters may have to harm themselves. If a group member seems suicidal, the counselor will need to notify parents or guardians. Also, such youngsters may need to be referred for further evaluation (i.e., psychological or psychiatric) and possibly medication.

9. These youngsters often need the group sessions to focus on alternative ways to handle their parents' substance abuse. Counselors will want to plan sessions that provide specific suggestions as to how a child can handle such home difficulties. The books and films listed in the bibliotherapy technique of this chapter can be most helpful in this counseling goal.

10. Due to the neglect these children often experience from their parents, a nurturing relationship with the facilitator will often be the most helpful part of a support group. Counselors should keep in mind that these youngsters thrive on a caring, warm, supportive, and open relationship. Readers should not underestimate how important this relationship will be for these children. Often times, the clinician can provide a corrective adult/child experience for this youngster.

Assessment Instruments

1. Assessment of Coping Style
2. Checklist of Children's Fears
3. Child Behavior Checklist
4. Children of Alcoholics Screening Test
5. Children's Depression Inventory
6. Children's Version/Family Environment Scale
7. Coopersmith Self-Esteem Inventories
8. Family Relations Test
9. Hopeless Scale for Children
10. Revised Children's Manifest Anxiety Scale

Relevant Session Themes

Increased sense of not being alone

Validation of feelings

Normalization of feelings

Gain an awareness of things within one's control

Awareness and communication of feelings

Increased sense of self-worth

Age appropriate responsibilities

Involvement in age appropriate activities (i.e., playing)

Awareness of fears and skills in effectively dealing with them

Skill in being able to stay on desired task

Good personal and physical hygiene skills

Knowledge and solicitation of support from others in one's environment

Skills in dealing with parents' substance abuse

Realistic expectations of self

Interactive skills with peers and adults

Understanding of the effects of substance abuse in one's family

Knowledge of the disease of substance abuse

Increased awareness of one's specific difficulties

Planning Sequence of Objectives & Techniques for Children of Substance Abusers Support Group

Group Phase	Group Goals	Intervention Categories
Initial	1. To provide an attractive group setting. 2. To initiate members' participation on-task and with one another. 3. To initiate trust among the membership.	**Hello Group Techniques** (Chapter Three)
	4. To educate members about issues and difficulties related to having a substance abusing parent.	**Instructive Techniques:** #1 The Path Of Least Pain #2 Bibliotherapy/Video/Films #3 Guess Why?
Middle	5. To increase group development goals established in initial phase (i.e., goals 1-3).	No techniques per se but follow curriculum approach.
	6. To increase members' awareness of their particular difficulties related to their parents' substance abuse.	**Awareness of Self Techniques:** #4 Scenes To Cut #5 A Book Review On Me #6 Leave The Driving To Me
	7. To provide alternative coping behaviors for dealing with their parents' substance abuse.	**Alternative Coping Techniques:** #7 Recycle Your Problems #8 Puppet Responses #9 A Coping Act
	8. To assist members in the integration of new coping behaviors into their repertoire.	**Integration Techniques:** #10 Shield Of Control #11 Facing Up To Your Worst Fear #12 Teach Us
Termination	9. To have members acknowledge the value of the group. 10. To assist members in validating their changes. 11. To have members brainstorm other sources of support. 12. To have members grieve the ending of group.	**Goodbye Group Techniques** (Chapter Thirteen)

▸ Technique #1

Title: The Path Of Least Pain

Technique category: Didactic Technique

Objective: To instruct members about the typical response patterns of COAs.

Materials:

- Prepared lecture on some topic related to children of substance abusers
- Discussion questions
- Visual aid entitled "Paths of Children of Substance Abusers," found on page 176.

Procedure:

1. The facilitator will need to prepare a brief lecture ahead of time related to children of substance abusers.

2. If the group members are in grades kindergarten through third, it will be helpful to prepare visual aids to complement the lecture presentation. An example of a visual aid for this presentation is provided on the following page entitled "Paths of Children of Substance Abusers."

3. The content of this instruction will vary depending on the needs of the group. Some possible subjects to address are listed below.

Risks COAs Face

1. May become substance abusers themselves.
2. May marry a substance abuser.
3. Can have any number of emotional or physical problems in childhood.

Typical Responses of COAs

1. Need to protect family image.
2. Have trouble trusting anyone.
3. Keep all feelings to themselves.
4. Sometimes are overly responsible in various situations.
5. Try too hard to please others.
6. Take too much responsibility for others' feelings.
7. Learn to adapt to extreme situations by becoming detached.
8. Sometimes misbehave to get attention.

How COAs Can Have Happier Lives

1. Accept they have no control over parents' substance abuse.

2. Learn to be aware of and express their feelings.

3. Understand that they are not alone, and to reach out to peer group.

4. Look at the unhealthy ways they are coping and try to change them.

5. Become comfortable asking for help from adults like counselors, Al-Anon, etc.

Readers are suggested to contact the NCADI office for free material for this type of presentation. The address of NCADI is:

National Clearinghouse for Alcohol and Drug Information
PO Box 2345
Rockville, MD 20852

Note: Be sure to specifically request materials for Children of Alcoholics and Drug Abusers.

4. The didactic presentation is given and at the end, discussion questions are posed to the group.

5. At the end of the session, members should be asked to share what positive effect the lecture and discussion questions had on them.

Cautions/comments:

This technique is a non-threatening way to initiate a group's focus on the specific issues of being a child of a substance abusing parent. Many of these children will begin to feel relieved just by finding out that they are not alone. Realizing that many of their responses to this problem situation are common to other children is a normalizing experience. It is imperative to include in the lecture ways the COA can be healthier in their responses and focus on areas within their control.

▶ Paths of Children of Substance Abusing Parents

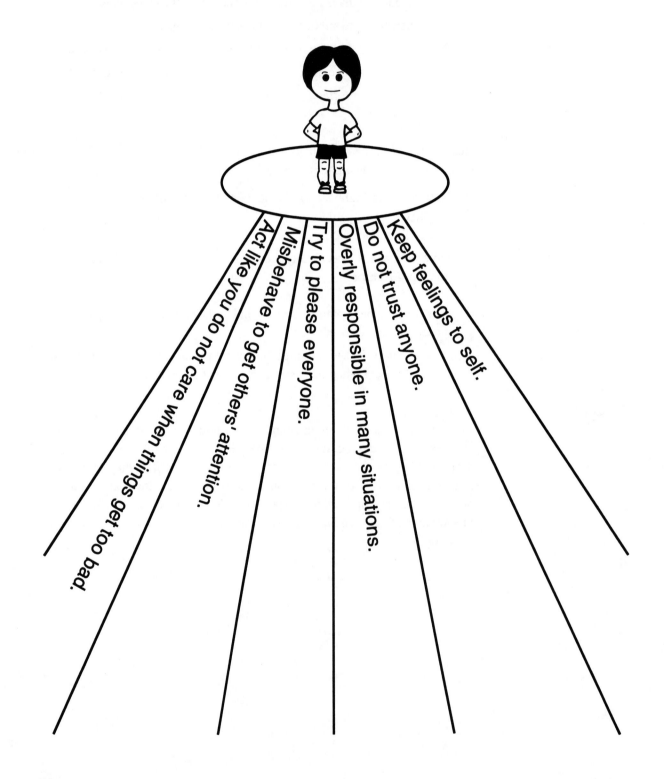

Keep feelings to self.

Do not trust anyone.

Overly responsible in many situations.

Try to please everyone.

Misbehave to get others' attention.

Act like you do not care when things get too bad.

▸ Technique #2

Title:	Bibliotherapy/Videotape/Films
Technique category:	Bibliotherapy/Videotape/Films
Objective:	To instruct members about typical problems children face when their parents are substance abusers.

Materials:

- Book, film, or videotape selected from the list on page 178.
- Equipment for film or videotape, if used.
- Prepared discussion questions related to the theme of the visual aid chosen.

Procedure:

1. Before the session, the facilitator selects a book, film, or videotape from the list on page 178.
2. Session begins with the book being read or film/videotape being shown.
3. At completion of above task, members can be asked discussion questions that surface their identification with the story. Also, some disclosure can be elicited that explores the children's similar problems and struggles.
4. Members' favorite parts of the book, film, or videotape should be processed at the end.

Cautions/comments:

Typically, members will enjoy the use of bibliotherapy materials or films/videotapes. Through these types of visual interventions, children can more easily learn about their ways to cope with substance abusing parents. In addition, youngsters in elementary grades typically identify with characters in books and films. As a result, they are often able to more comfortably talk about their similar issues via the story presented.

Readers are advised to select books that have colorful pictures on almost every page. Children as a whole find it easier to understand the message of a book page when a graphic design depicts the concept. Also, facilitators should be careful that books and films/videotapes selected are not too long. It is important to have time in the session to pose discussion questions and process reactions among the members.

▶ Bibliotherapy

1. Adler, Carole Schwerdtfeger. *The Silver Coach.* Coward, McGann & Geoghegan, Inc., 1979, ages 9-12.

2. Adler, Carole Schwerdtfeger. *In Our House Scott is My Brother.* Macmillan Publishing Company, Inc., 1980, ages 10-13.

3. Al-Anon Family Group. *What's "Drunk," Mama?* 1977, ages 6-12.

4. Black, Claudia. *My Dad Loves Me. My Dad Has a Disease.* Hazelden Educational Materials, 1979, ages 5-14.

5. Bonham, Frank. *Chief.* E. P. Dutton & Company, Inc., 1971, ages 11 and up.

6. Brooks, Jerome. *Uncle Mike's Boy.* Harper & Row Publishers, Inc., 1973, ages 11 and up.

7. Butterworth, Oliver. *A Visit to the Big House.* Families in Crisis and Junior League of Hartford, Inc., 1987, grades 4-6.

8. Corcoran, Barbara. *All the Summer Voices.* Atheneum Publishers, 1973, ages 11-14.

9. Eyerly, Jeannette Hyde. *Escape from Nowhere.* J. B. Lippincott Company, 1969, ages 12 and up.

10. Fox, Paula. *Blowfish Live in the Sea.* Bradbury Press, Inc., 1970, ages 11 and up.

11. Hall, Lynn. *Troublemaker.* Follet Publishing Company, 1974, ages 11-14.

12. Hassler, Jon Francis. *Tammy.* Atheneum Publishers, 1980, ages 11 and up.

13. Holland, Isabelle. *Heads You Win, Tails I Lose.* J. B. Lippincott Company, 1973, ages 12 and up.

14. Holland, Isabelle. *Now Is Not Too Late.* Lothrop, Lee & Shepard Company, 1980, ages 10-13.

15. Hyppo, Marion H. and Hastings, Jill M. *An Elephant in the Living Room.* Compcare Publications, 1984, grades 1-6.

16. Kenny, Kevin and Krull, Helen. *Sometimes My Mom Drinks Too Much.* Raintree Publishers, Inc., 1980, ages 5-8.

17. Miner, Jane Claypool. *A Day at a Time: Dealing With an Alcoholic.* Crestwood House, inc., 1982, ages 11 and up.

18. Norris, Gunilla Brodde. *Take My Waking Slow.* Atheneum Publishers, 1970, ages 10-13.

19. Sammuels, Gertrude. *Run, Shelly, Run!* Thomas Y. Crowell Company, 1974, ages 12 and up.

20. Schwardt, Mary Kay. *Kootch Talks About Alcoholism.* Serenity Work, 1984, grades 1-6.

21. Seixas, Judith. *Alcohol: What It Is. What It Does.* Greenwillow Books, 1977, ages 6-9.

22. Sherburne, Zoa. *Jennifer.* William Morrow & Company, Inc., 1959, ages 12 and up.

23. Summers, James L. *The Long Ride Home.* Westminster Press, 1966, ages 12 and up.

24. Thorvall, Kerstin. *And Leffe Was Instead of a Dad.* Bradbury Press, Inc., 1974, ages 10 and up.

25. Wheat, Patte. *You're Not Alone: Kids' Book on Alcoholism and Child Abuse.* National Committee for the Prevention of Child Abuse, 1985, grades 1-6.

26. Woody, Regina Llewellyn Jones. *One Day at a Time.* Westminster Press, 1968, ages 11 and up.

Videotapes

1. Alcohol: How Much Is Too Much?
   Filmfair Communications, 1981, 16 minute film, grades 4-6.

2. Drugs Are Like That
   Junior League of Miami, 1977, 16 minute film, grades 1-6.

3. Drugs: A Primary Film
   Barr Films, 1972, 9 minute film, grades 1-6.

4. Epidemic! Kids, Drugs and Alcohol
   Learning Corporation of America/MTI, 1982, 26 minute film, grades 4-6.

5. Glug, The
   Churchill Films, 1981, 15 minute film, grades 4-6.

6. How Do You Tell?
   Learning Corporation of America/MTI, 1983, 13 minute film, grades 1-6.

7. Kids and Alcohol Don't Mix
   Barr Films, 1985, 14 minute film, grades 1-6.

8. Lots of Kids Like Us
   Learning Corporation of America/MTI, 1982, 28 minute film, grades 4-6.

9. She Drinks A Little
   Learning Corporation of America/MTI, 1981, 31 minute film, grades 5-6.

10. Story About Feelings, A
    Johnson Institute, 1982, 9 minute film, grades 1-6.

11. Wasted: A True Story
    Learning Corporation of America/MTI, 1983, 24 minute film, grades 4-6.

Films

1. *A Story About Feelings*
   Johnson Institute, 10 minute film, ages 5-8.

2. *All Bottled Up*
   AIM Instructional Media, 15 minute film, ages 5-12.

3. *Hidden Alcoholics: Why Is Mommy Sick?*
   CRM/McGraw-Hill Films, 22 minute film, grades 4-6.

4. *If Someone In Your Family Drinks...*
   Sunburst, 2 filmstrips/cassettes, grades 5-6.

5. *Lots of Kids Like Me*
   Gerald T. Rogers Productions, Inc., 28 minutes film or video, all elementary ages.

6. *Should He Tell?*
   AAA Foundation for Traffic Safety, 16 minutes film or video, sixth grade.

7. *The Long Tunnel: Alcoholism, Addiction and Recovery*
   Random House Media, filmstrip/cassette, grades 5-6.

▶ Technique #3

Title: Guess Why?

Technique category: Paper/Pencil Task

Objective: To instruct members about the typical problems and feelings one has when a parent is a substance abuser.

Materials needed:

- Copies of the sheet entitled "Guess Why?" found on page 182.
- Pencils

Procedure:

1. Pass out the sheet entitled "Guess Why?" to all group members.
2. Allow 5 to 10 minutes for the completion of this task.
3. Ask everyone to share their responses by going around the circle in order. The facilitator should initially share their responses to the task sheet for purposes of modeling.
4. If time allows, pose some discussion questions related to typical feeling responses of these youngsters. Sharing that validates members' common experiences and feelings will be extremely helpful.
5. Process members' positive reactions at the end of the session.

Cautions/comments:

This is an excellent technique for teaching members about the kinds of responses kids have to parents' substance abuse problems. Usually, this indirect yet instructive technique is a less threatening way to teach this valuable lesson. Youngsters will often be able to disclose at a more intimate level because they tend to see this task as just a fun guessing game. Also, members will learn a tremendous amount from one another's sharing.

▸ Guess Why?

Instructions: Match the behaviors of children in the left column with the usual reasons behind those responses from the right column. Be sure to read through the list of behaviors before you do your matching up.

BEHAVIOR

A boy always tries to get all A's on his report card.

A girl misbehaves often at school.

A boy takes care of everything at this home even though he is only 8 years old.

A girl goes into her bedroom most of the time and plays by herself.

A boy never tells anyone how terrible he feels at times.

A girl never tells anyone about her father's alcoholism.

REASONS

Wants to stay outside the family and its troubles.

Worried that the feelings that come out will be too upsetting.

This helps the child feel in control, not having to trust anyone.

By doing this behavior, maybe the problem will go away.

Trying to make his parents be happy and stop abusing.

This way the child's parent will give some attention to him/her.

▶ Technique #4

Title: Scenes To Cut

Technique category: Exercise Using the Arts

Objective: To increase members' awareness of their problems in regard to their parents' substance abuse.

Materials:

- "Scenes To Cut" form found on page 184.
- Pencils
- Crayons

Procedure:

1. Members are told they are going to have an opportunity to participate in a creative exercise where they can make believe they are movie producers. Then, the form entitled "Scenes To Cut" is passed out to everyone.

2. Members are allowed 10 to 15 minutes to complete this task sheet.

3. After everyone is done, each child takes a turn sharing the three filmstrips they would want to cut out of their usual family life. Facilitators should be the first to share, in order to create a more comfortable setting for this disclosure.

4. Throughout the above sharing, members' commonalities and significant disclosure should be reinforced.

5. At the end, everyone is asked to share in their own creative way the most enjoyable part of this creative experience.

Cautions/comments:

This is an excellent technique for initiating members' awareness of some of their problems as a result of their parents' substance abuse. The beauty of this incomplete drawing task is that it gives youngsters an opportunity to think about what they would want to cut out of their family life. This usually makes the requested disclosure a lot less anxiety provoking. If readers want to modify this technique, they can have members anonymously complete their sheets and the facilitator can share the results. This provides an even less anxiety provoking way of eliciting members' disclosure on this topic.

▸ **Scenes To Cut**

Instructions: Pretend you are the producer of a movie about your real life family. Write or draw on the filmstrips below three scenes from your usual family life that you would want to cut out of a movie.

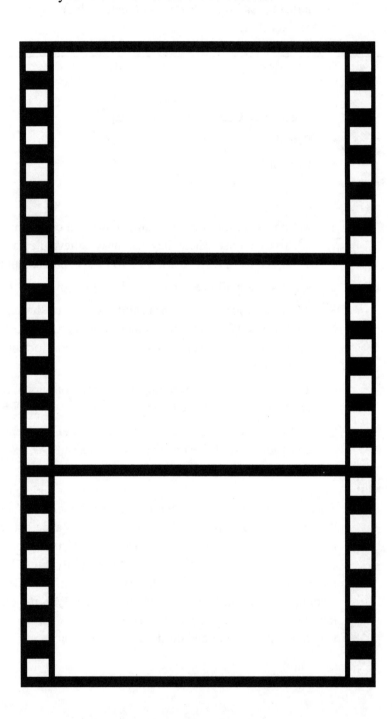

▶ Technique #5

Title:	A Book Review On Me
Technique category:	Disclosure Task
Objective:	To increase members' awareness of their problems and issues in regard to their parents' substance abuse.

Materials needed:

- Copies of the sheet entitled "A Book Review On Me," found on page 186.
- Pencils

Procedure:

1. Pass out the sheet entitled "A Book Review On Me" to all group members.
2. Allow 5 to 10 minutes for the completion of this task.
3. Ask everyone to share their responses by going around the circle in order. The facilitator should model disclosure by first sharing their responses to the task sheet.
4. If time allows, pose some discussion questions related to the task sheet responses.
5. Process members' positive reactions at the end of the session.

Cautions/comments:

This is an indirect way to elicit youngsters' disclosure of their problems related to their parents' substance abuse. This technique provides a less threatening format to conduct such a difficult discussion. In many groups, this intervention will actually help members gain an increased awareness of their difficulties.

▶ A Book Review On Me

Instructions: Complete the book titles below such that they would be based on your real life story.

A
Mystery

Title: _____

_____

An
Adventure
Story

Title: _____

_____

A
Love
Story

Title: _____

_____

A
Scary
Book

Title: _____

_____

▸ Technique #6

Title: Leave the Driving to Me

Technique category: Creative Exercise

Objective: To increase members' awareness of their difficulties in regard to their parents' substance abuse.

Materials:

- Small toy cars for all members
- Blackboard and chalk

Procedure:

1. Each participant is given a small toy car. Members are asked to hold on to their cars for a moment so some instructions for this fun task can be reviewed.

2. The group is asked to brainstorm all the problems kids can have as a result of their parents' substance abuse. These ideas are written on the blackboard with at least twenty responses being elicited.

3. Members are asked to make believe their car is a child who has a parent with a substance abuse problem. Then, the youngsters are requested to think about how they could make their car non-verbally act out one of the difficulties written on the blackboard.

4. Members are given a designated period of time to think through this task.

5. Participants are asked to act out their car driving. All other members are then given so many guesses, to see which difficulty from the blackboard is being acted out.

6. If time allows, facilitators should have some prepared discussion questions regarding the difficulties chosen for the kids' car driving act. Such questions should stimulate further disclosure among members and surface common-alities that serve to normalize everyone's feelings and reactions.

7. At the end of this session, participants should be asked to share what they consider the most beneficial part of the task.

Cautions/comments:

This technique elicits lots of disclosure from children around this issue of typical problems they face. Even though members are free to choose any problem to act out, they often do in fact select the one most relevant to their own lives. Elementary age students usually enjoy the idea of acting out symbolically via a car. Therefore, they usually disclose more than they would via a more direct discussion.

▸ Technique #7

Title:	Recycle Your Problems
Technique category:	In Vivo Experience
Objective:	To increase members' awareness of alternative ways of handling problems related to their parents' substance abuse.

Materials:

- Copies of the form entitled "Recycle Your Problems," found on page 189.
- Pencils
- Empty box

Procedure:

1. The form entitled "Recycle Your Problems" is handed out to each participant, along with a pencil.

2. Members are given a designated period of time to silently complete their sheets.

3. The facilitator instructs participants to fold up their sheets and place them in a recycling box.

4. Then, the youngsters are instructed that they will each have an opportunity to pick a sheet out of the recycling box. After a member selects a sheet, he or she must read the problem out loud.

5. The group will then be given two minutes to help that member come up with at least two ways of handling the problem posed. Participants can remain anonymous when their sheets are read. However, if individual members would like to indicate which sheet they completed, that should also be allowed. This disclosure could then give the author of the sheet an opportunity to add some reality testing to the proposed coping alternatives.

6. At the end of this session, the membership should be asked to process what they found most helpful.

Cautions/comments:

This is an excellent technique to help members feel less anxious about sharing their problems. Youngsters can be invaluable resources to one another in an exercise like this one. Facilitators will be amazed at some of the clever coping alternatives the members are able to come up with for one another's problems.

▸ Recycle Your Problems

Instructions: Write inside this make believe recycling container a problem you are having with your parents' substance abuse.

▸ Technique #8

Title: Puppet Responses

Technique category: Completion Task

Objective: To increase members' awareness of alternative ways to handle problems in regard to their parents' substance abuse.

Materials:

- Puppets with healthy responses indicated, one to each puppet
- A list of problem situations relevant to the members

Procedure:

1. Before this session, the facilitator will need to prepare some brief problem scenes relevant to the membership. Usually, two such scenes per member will be enough for this session. Puppets will need to be made or used with healthy responses indicated, one to each puppet. Examples of such responses are listed below.

    1. This is a good time to leave the house.
    2. I need to get my feelings out.
    3. I have to accept that my parent is an alcoholic or drug abuser.
    4. I am not responsible and cannot control my parents' substance abuse.
    5. I need to trust others.
    6. This is a time I need to ask for help.

2. The session begins with participants being told that they are going to have an opportunity to show how much they have learned about healthy responses to typical problems that substance abusing parents often cause.

3. Next, prepared problem situations are read, one at a time, to the group. After each one is posed, a member is asked to pick a puppet from the center of the table that would be a healthy response. Some problem scenes posed may have more than one possible response; this can be addressed by asking members if there are other ways they could handle the same problem.

4. After all problem situations have been posed, it will be important to ask the members what they have learned from this exercise.

Cautions/comments:

This is an excellent technique for teaching members other healthy ways to respond to problems caused by their parents' substance abuse. If a group has trouble attending to the situations posed, it may be necessary to make this technique into a game. One way to make such a modification is to have everyone guess, in writing, the puppet he/she will select before each child's turn. The facilitator then determines a point system for winning the game.

When working with younger groups, it may be better to have members make the puppets. It will be beneficial for them to guess all the different healthy responses. In this situation, the facilitator may not choose to pose the problem scenes. Instead, this age group can concentrate in more general terms on the most effective ways to handle problems caused by parents' substance abuse.

▸ Technique #9

Title:	A Coping Act
Technique category:	Game Exercise
Objective:	To increase members' awareness of coping alternatives for handling problems related to parents' substance abuse.

Materials:

- Large blackboard
- Chalk

Procedure:

1. At the onset of this session, members are told they are going to be playing a fun type of charades.

2. Then, the rules below are reviewed with the membership.

   - Each member will have to tell the facilitator a healthy response they have learned in regard to their parents' substance abuse. This sharing will have to be done so that none of the members hear it.

   - The member will then have two minutes to act out that response through the game of charades.

   - If the group is able to guess the healthy coping response in the two minutes, then they get the point. If no one guesses the answer correctly within the two minutes, the facilitator gets the point.

   - After everyone has done a turn at charades, the one (group or facilitator) who has the most points wins.

3. The game is then conducted following the rules.

4. If time allows, discussion questions can be posed to the children in order to probe some of their earlier responses during the game.

5. At the end, everyone should be asked to complete the following sentence: "I really liked this session when _____."

Cautions/comments:

Facilitators will find that youngsters almost always enjoy a fun game of charades. The beauty of this technique is that members enjoy reviewing what they have learned about healthy responses to problems caused by substance abusing parents. In addition, some participants may find themselves learning new coping alternatives for the first time. Usually, the nature of charades is easily conducive to keeping the attention of even younger support groups.

▶ Technique #10

Title:	Shield Of Control
Technique category:	Check-Up/Assignment
Objective:	To integrate into members' repertoire new coping skills.

Materials needed:

- Copies of the sheet entitled "Shield Of Control," found on page 195.
- Pencils

Procedure:

1. Pass out the sheet entitled "Shield Of Control" to all group members.
2. Allow 5 to 10 minutes for the completion of this task.
3. Ask everyone to share their responses by going around the circle in order. The facilitator should initially share their responses to the task sheet for purposes of modeling.
4. If time allows, pose some discussion questions related to the task sheet responses.
5. Process members' positive reactions at the end of the session.

Cautions/comments:

This is an excellent technique for reviewing and validating those things within the control of children around the issue of their parents' substance abuse. This is a crucial and relevant point for these youngsters. Most of these children need to identify and constantly remind themselves which things they have control over so that they learn to concentrate more on those areas of functioning.

▸ Shield Of Control

Instructions: Indicate on the shield below six things that you have learned you have control over in regard to your parents' substance abuse.

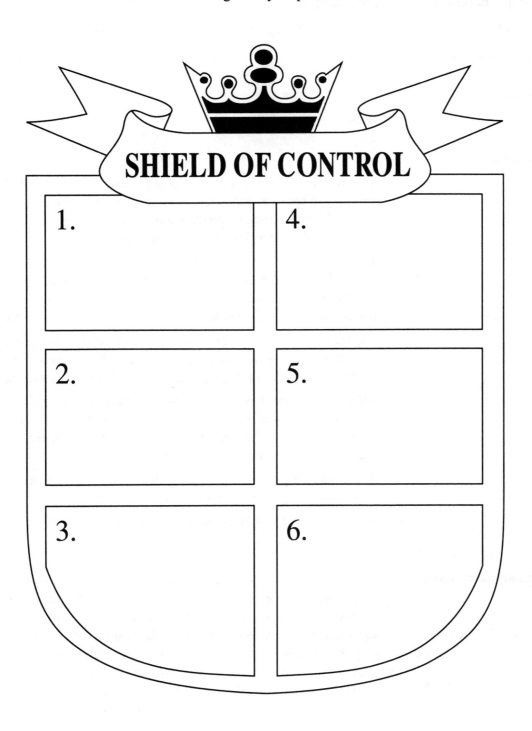

SHIELD OF CONTROL

1.

2.

3.

4.

5.

6.

▶ Technique #11

Title:	Facing Up To Your Worst Fear
Technique category:	Check-Up Exercise
Objective:	To integrate new coping skills into members' repertoire.

Materials:

- None

Procedure:

1. The facilitator begins this session by explaining to the members that they are going to have a chance to be on stage. If some members seem anxious about this announcement, the facilitator should explain that the acting they will be asked to do will be very easy for everyone.

2. Then, participants should be instructed to take a few minutes, close their eyes and think about the worst fear they have regarding their parents' substance abuse. After everyone seems to have formulated some ideas on this concept, members should be asked to share these fears with the group.

3. The facilitator requests each member to take a turn role playing their worst fear. If participants need more than just themselves in their scene, the group leader should choose other members to help in this role play.

4. After each member has completed their role play (during which specific thoughts and responses are acted out in regard to the worst fear), the facilitator asks how they feel about facing their fear. The rest of the youngsters are asked if they have had similar fears.

5. The membership is next requested to share some compliments with each participant in regard to their role play.

6. Members should be asked to process the most helpful part of these play acts.

Cautions/comments:

This is an excellent intervention for integrating new skills into children of substance abusers repertoire. Often these youngsters have a tremendous amount of unspoken fears that continue to bother and upset them. Sometimes through this role play, they find that their fears are not based on reality. Other times, however, they may see that their fears have real possibilities of becoming reality. During this exercise, it is important that youngsters be reminded about the things they do not have control over. It can be helpful for members to assist one another in brainstorming other coping skills needed in particularly tough situations.

Facilitators do need to remember that this technique can surface some very disturbing thoughts for members. It is essential that this intervention not be used in a group until the latter part of the middle phase. This intervention is intended to solidify knowledge and skills already learned in the group. Also, if a youngster becomes overly upset during the role play, it may be necessary to stop the acting and help the member identify what is so disturbing. In some cases, members may need to be seen after group in individual sessions to provide further processing and closure to this experience.

▶ Technique #12

Title: Teach Us

Technique category: Confirmation Exercise

Objective: To integrate into members' repertoire new coping responses to their parents' substance abuse.

Materials needed:

- Copies of the sheet entitled "Teach Us," found on page 199.
- Pencils

Procedure:

1. Pass out the sheet entitled "Teach Us" to all group members.
2. Allow 5 to 10 minutes for the completion of this task.
3. Ask everyone to share their responses by going around the circle in order. The facilitator should initially share their responses to the task sheet for purposes of modeling.
4. If time allows, pose some discussion questions related to the task sheet responses.
5. Process members' positive reactions at the end of the session.

Cautions/comments:

This make believe task really helps children think through all the coping skills they have either used or learned in the group. A technique like this one will usually solidify the strengths each member has acquired from their group experience. Facilitators may want to suggest that participants take home their "Teach Us" sheets as reminders of coping skills they need to keep using in their daily lives.

▸ Teach Us

Instructions: Make believe you are the teacher of this group for a session. What is something you have either learned from this group or used in the past as a skill to cope with your parents' substance abuse? Write that skill on the blackboard below.

▶ Bibliography

Ackerman, R. J. *Children of Alcoholics: A Guidebook for Educators, Therapists and Parents.* Holmes Beach, Learning Publications, 1987.

Al-Anon Family Group. *What's "Drunk," Mama?* New York, Al-Anon, 1977.

Alcohol Problems and Youth. An Annotated Reading List on Alcohol Problems and Youth. Rockville, National Clearinghouse for Alcohol and Drug Information, 1985.

A Little More About Alcohol. Lansing, Alcohol Research Information Service, 1984.

Be Smart! Don't Start! Just Say No! Rockville, National Clearinghouse for Alcohol and Drug Information, 1987.

Bissell, LeClair and Watherwax, Richard. *The Cat Who Drank Too Much.* Minneapolis, Johnson Institute, 1987.

Black, Claudia. *My Dad Loves Me, My Dad Has a Disease.* Center City, Hazelden Educational Materials, 1979.

Borba, Michele. *Esteem Builders.* Torrance, CA, Jalmar Press, 1989.

Butterworth, Oliver. *A Visit to the Big House.* Hartford, Families in Crisis, Inc. and Junior League of Hartford with the Connecticut State Department of Corrections, 1987.

Christensen, Linda and DeVol, Philip. *Elementary Student Assistance.* Minneapolis, Johnson Institute, 1990.

Davis, Ruth B. et al. Helping children of alcoholic parents: an elementary school program. *The School Counselor* 32(5):357-363, 1985.

Dennison, Susan. *Twelve Counseling Programs for Children at Risk.* Springfield, Charles C. Thomas, 1989.

Deutsch, C. *Broken Bottles, Broken Dreams.* New York: Teachers College Press, 1982.

Deutsch, C., DiCiccio, L. and Mills, D. Reach children from families with alcoholism: some innovative techniques. *Proceedings of the Twenty-Ninth Annual Meeting of Alcohol and Drug Problems Association of North America,* pp. 54-58, 1979.

DiCiccio, L., Davis, R., Hogan, Y., Maclean, A. and Orenstein, A. Group experiences for children of alcoholics. *Alcoholic Health and Research World* 8:20-24, 1984.

Edwards, Diane M. and Zander, Toni A. Children of alcoholics: background and strategies for the counselor. *Elementary School Guidance & Counseling* 20(2):121-128, 1985.

Gerne, Patricia and Gerne, Timothy. *Substance Abuse Activities for Elementary Students.* Englewood Cliffs, Prentice Hall, 1990.

Gerne, Timothy A. and Gerne, Patricia. *Substance Abuse Prevention - Activities for Elementary Children.* Englewood, Prentice-Hall, Inc., 1986.

Halprin, D. and Braheny. *Children are People Too!* Deerfield Beach, Health Communications, 1987.

Hastings, Jill M. and Hyppo, Marion H. *An Elephant in the Living Room.* Minneapolis, Compcare, 1984.

Jance, Judith. *Welcome Home. A Child's View of Alcoholism.* Mount Dora, Kids Rights, 1984.

Lane, Krist. *Feelings are Real.* Muncie, Accelerated Development, 1991.

LePantois, Joan. Group Therapy for Children of Substance Abusers. *Social Work with Groups* 9:39-51, 1986.

Manning, D. T. Books as therapy for children of alcoholics. *Child Welfare* 66(1):35-43, 1987.

McElligatt, K. Identifying and treating children of alcoholic parents. *Social Work in Education* 9(1):55-70, 1986.

Moe, Jerry and Ways, Peter. *Conducting Support Groups for Elementary Children K-6.* Minneapolis, Johnson Institute, 1991.

Moe, Jerry and Pohlman, Don. *Kids Power.* Deerfield Beach, Health Communications, 1989.

Morehouse, Ellen R. and Scola, Claire M. *Children of Alcoholics: Meeting the Needs of the Young COA in the School Setting.* South Laguna, National Association for Children of Alcoholics, 1986.

Morehouse, E. R. Working in schools with children of alcoholic parents. *Health and Social Work* 4(4):144-162, 1979.

Morris-Vann, Artie M. *My Parents are Drug Abusers.* Oak Park, Aid-U Publishing Company, 1984.

National Association for Children of Alcoholics. 31582 Coast Highway, Suite B, South Laguna, CA 92677 (714-499-3889).

National Clearinghouse for Alcohol and Drug Information, PO Box 2345, Rockville, MD 20852.

Nordi, Peter. Children of alcholics: a role-theoretical perspective. *Journal of Social Psychology* 115:237-245, 1981.

Rattray, Jamie, Howells, Bill, Siegler, Irv and Wassor, Fritz. *Kids and Alcohol: Get High on Life.* Pompano Beach, Health Communications, Inc., 1984.

Reckman, L. W. et al. Meeting the child care needs of the female alcoholic. *Child Welfare* 63(6):541-546, 1984.

Schwandt, Mary Kay. *Kootch Talks About Alcoholism.* Fargo, Serenity Work, 1984.

Seixas, Judith. *Living With a Parent Who Drinks Too Much.* New York, Morrow, 1979.

Seixas, Judith. *Alcohol: What It Is. What It Does.* New York, Greenwillow Books, 1977.

Seixas, Judith S. *What Can You Do to Help a Friend?* New York, Children of Alcoholics Foundation, 1985.

Sharp-Molchan, Deborah. *Our Secret Feelings.* Holmes Beach, Learning Publications, 1989.

Wheat, Patte. *You're Not Alone: Kids Book on Alcoholism and Child Abuse.* Chicago, National Committee for Prevention of Child Abuse, 1985.

Whitfield, Charles. Children of alcoholics: treatment issues. *Maryland State Medical Journal* 29:86-91, 1980.

Chapter 8

Anger/Conflict Resolution Support Group Curriculum

A complete curriculum for anger/conflict resolution support groups is provided in this chapter. Step-by-step instructions are outlined for the unique set-up, planning, and facilitation of this type of elementary age support group. An extensive listing of assessment scales, session themes, bibliotherapy books, videotapes/films, and "how-to-do-it" references are included as part of this practical support group guide. This chapter, along with Chapters One, Two, Three, and Thirteen, will provide complete instructions for the set-up through the termination of anger/conflict resolution support groups.

Treatment Guidelines

Elementary guidance staff are increasingly finding that children today are being referred to groups for their aggressive/acting out behaviors. Since violence in our society has steadily grown over the past twenty years, it is no surprise that youngsters' aggresive responses to anger are surfacing even as early as kindergarten.

One of the major issues related to this problem area is our society's increased acceptance of and desensitization to violence. Children are very perceptive and pick up on this change of attitude, modeling their behavior accordingly. As we all know, kids today are watching violent behaviors daily on TV, at the movies, among their peers, in the news, and in some cases, in their home and neighborhood settings. For this reason, counselors find that now more than ever they must deal with this at-risk problem area. Unfortunately, elementary schools are no longer immune from any type of violent behaviors. We are seeing an increase in murders, suicides, and severe beatings in these primary grades. Elementary counselors deal with some very serious problems among the acting out/aggressive child population.

Anger/conflict resolution support groups are often ideal settings for these youngsters. This modality provides the aggressive child with an outlet for angry feelings, an opportunity to gain support from others, and a chance to learn coping alternatives from peers having similar problems.

Before utilizing this curriculum, the reader should review the following general treatment guidelines for working with children in anger/conflict resolution support groups.

1. In order to develop a relevant sequence of session themes, it is helpful to gather referral information from members' parents and teachers. These involved adults should be asked to specify the exact problematic acting out behaviors of the students referred for this type of group. It may be easier to obtain this data on one of the rating scales provided in the curriculum.

2. This particular population needs to be sold on an attractive support group program. Many of these youngsters are already turned off to any service at school and are quite distrusting of adults. Therefore, readers are encouraged to develop non-threatening and positive names for this type of group. Titles that might be considered include clubs or buddy programs. Potential members can also be asked to share in the decision-making for an attractive name for these groups.

3. Some aggressive/acting out children are often best treated in individual counseling initially. These youngsters can be so angry when first identified that they need the one-to-one attention provided through this modality. After some time in individual counseling, these children are ready for an anger management support group. Counselors will have to use their clinical expertise in deciding the best timing for these modalities.

4. Group leaders will need to be careful in their planning of techniques for this type of support group. It will be essential that any interventions requiring movement are set up for limited and controlled movement. For example, only one member moves at one time and is seated before the next youngster engages in the same required activity.

5. Parent and teacher responsibility in the behavior change program need to be maintained. It is essential that these involved adults understand that this problem area will not usually be resolved through support groups alone. Often times, facilitators may want to incorporate behavioral programs at home and/or school as part of their session plans.

6. Facilitators need to compose their anger/conflict resolution groups carefully. It is extremely important that children with varying degrees of acting out behavior be selected for the same group. The members need to

have some skills and strengths they can share and model to one another. In addition, too many severely acting out youngsters can be very difficult to handle in the same group.

7. The aggressive child often needs to be taught alternative ways of coping with life stresses. Therefore, group sessions will need to focus on interventions around healthier responses to anger eliciting or frustrating situations. Many of these youngsters have had limited opportunities to watch the modeling of such behavioral responses.

8. School counselors should check the overall stress level of their schools when treating this population. Often, an increase in environmental stress will result in more acting out problems. It is important that teachers be made aware of this chain of events so that they can develop realistic expectations of these youngsters. At the same time, these children will need to learn other ways to handle an increase in environmental stress.

9. Facilitators should not underestimate the importance of these children having areas of success. Sometimes this population may in fact be reacting to the lack of accomplishments they are feeling in their lives. Content that focuses on this need can be most helpful to these youngsters.

10. Facilitators will find that a warm, caring and open relationship with these children will go further than all the fancy group techniques. For many acting out youngsters, there has never been an adult in their lives who provided this type of acceptance. Readers should remember that in some cases it may only take one corrective relationship experience to start a child on the path to positive change.

Assessment Instruments

1. Aggression Inventory
2. Behavior Problem Checklist
3. Burks Behavior Rating Scales
4. Child Behavior Checklist
5. Children's Action Tendency Scale
6. Children's Inventory of Anger
7. Children's Perceived Self-Control Scale
8. Conners' Teacher and Parent Rating Scales
9. Impulsivity Scale
10. Louisville Behavior Checklist

Relevant Session Themes

Normalization of feelings

Increased sense of not being alone

Increased affective awareness

Communication skills particularly around feelings

Increased awareness of problem behaviors and secondary difficulties

Skills for interacting appropriately with adults

Social skills with peers

Conflict resolution skills

Awareness of one's strengths and potential areas of success

Developing care and concern for others and their property

Ability to follow rules in various situations

Alternative coping skills for frustrations, stress, etc.

Assertive skills with peers and adults

Improved self-image

Increased awareness of the reasons behind one's anger/frustration

Planning Sequence of Objectives & Techniques for Anger/Conflict Resolution Support Groups

Group Phase	Group Goals	Intervention Categories
Initial	1. To provide an attractive group setting. 2. To initiate members' participation on-task and with one another. 3. To initiate trust among the membership.	**Hello Group Techniques** (Chapter Three)
	4. To educate members about issues and difficulties related to anger/conflict resolution problems.	**Instructive Techniques:** #1 Making Sense Of Your Anger #2 Bibliotherapy/Video/Films #3 Popping Your Cork
Middle	5. To increase group development goals established in initial phase (i.e., goals 1-3).	No techniques per se but follow curriculum approach.
	6. To increase members' awareness of their particular difficulties related to their anger/conflict resolution problems.	**Awareness of Self Techniques:** #4 Listen To Your Anger #5 Problems And More Problems #6 Out The Window
	7. To provide alternative coping behaviors for handling their anger/conflicts.	**Alternative Coping Techniques:** #7 Picture This! #8 Be Like A Traffic Light #9 Run With It
	8. To assist members in the integration of new coping behaviors into their repertoire.	**Integration Techniques:** #10 Group Oscar Awards #11 Give Your Verdict #12 Wad It Up And Fly Away
Termination	9. To have members acknowledge the value of the group. 10. To assist members in validating their changes. 11. To have members brainstorm other sources of support. 12. To have members grieve the ending of group.	**Goodbye Group Techniques** (Chapter Thirteen)

▶ Technique #1

Title: Making Sense Of Your Anger

Technique category: Didactic Technique

Objective: To instruct members about the typical response patterns to angry feelings.

Materials needed:

- Copies of the sheet entitled "You and Your Anger Questionnaire," found on page 209.
- Pencils

Procedure:

1. Pass out the sheet entitled "You and Your Anger Questionnaire" to all group members.
2. Allow 5 to 10 minutes for the completion of this task.
3. Ask everyone to share their responses by going around the circle in order. The facilitator should initially share their responses to the task sheet for purposes of modeling.
4. If time allows, pose some discussion questions related to the task sheet responses.
5. Process members' positive reactions at the end of the session.

Cautions/comments:

This particular intervention can be an effective way to begin a group's discussion on the feeling of anger and its consequences. Facilitators will generally find that members are more comfortable answering the structured questionnaire at this point in the group as opposed to a more open-ended discussion. Also, participants will be delighted to find that others share some of their same experiences with anger.

▶ You and Your Anger Questionnaire

Instructions: Read the questions below and answer them based on your experience with your anger. Be ready to discuss these answers in your group.

1. How often are you angry?

_____ Always _____ Sometimes _____ Never

2. When you do become angry, how angry do you usually get?

A little angry Pretty angry Very angry

3. Indicate below what you usually do when you are angry.

_____ Yell _____ Stop and refuse to participate in an activity

_____ Stay by yourself _____ Other:_____

_____ Start crying _____

_____ Hit someone _____

_____ Throw or break objects

4. Where do you get angry most often?

_____ Home _____ With friends

_____ School _____ With self

5. Show in this picture what anger is to you.

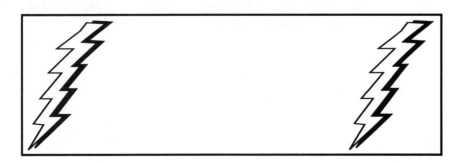

▸ Technique #2

Title: Bibliotherapy/Video/Films

Technique category: Bibliotherapy/Video/Films

Objective: To instruct members about the typical response patterns to angry feelings.

Materials:

- Book, film, or videotape selected from the list on page 211.
- Equipment for film or videotape, if used.
- Prepared discussion questions related to the theme of the visual aid chosen.

Procedure:

1. Before the session, the facilitator selects a book, film, or videotape from the list on page 211.
2. Session begins with the book being read or film/videotape being shown.
3. At completion of above task, members can be asked discussion questions that surface their identification with the story. Also, some disclosure can be elicited that explores the children's similar problems and struggles.
4. Members' favorite parts of the book, film, or videotape should be processed at the end.

Cautions/comments:

Typically, members will enjoy the use of bibliotherapy materials or films/videotapes. Through these types of visual interventions, children can more easily learn about their anger and conflict resolution skills. In addition, youngsters in elementary grades typically identify with characters in books and films. As a result, they are often able to more comfortably talk about their similar issues via the story presented.

Readers are advised to select books that have colorful pictures on almost every page. Children as a whole find it easier to understand the message of a book page when a graphic design depicts the concept. Also, facilitators should be careful that books and films/videotapes selected are not too long. It is important to have time in the session to pose discussion questions and process reactions among the members.

▶ Bibliotherapy

1. Addy, Sharon. *We Didn't Mean To.* Raintree Publishers, Inc., 1981, ages 8-10.

2. Adelman, Bab and Hall, Susan. *On and Off the Street.* The Viking Press, Inc., 1970, ages 8-10.

3. Allington, Richard L. *Feelings.* Raintree Publishers, 1985, grades K-2.

4. Barsuhn, Rochelle N. *Feeling Angry.* Childs World, 1983, grades 1-2.

5. Barsuhn, Rochelle N. *Angry.* Standard Pub., 1982, grades 1-2.

6. Bawden, Nina Mary Kark. *The Runaway Summer.* J. B. Lippincott, Company, 1969, ages 9-12.

7. Bedford, Stewart. *Tiger Juice: A Book About Stress for Kids (of All Ages).* A & S Publishers, 1981.

8. Byars, Betsy Cromer. *The 18th Emergency.* Viking Press, Inc., 1972, ages 9-11.

9. Carle, Eric. *The Grouchy Ladybug.* Thomas Y. Crowell Co., Inc., 1977, ages 3-7.

10. Carlson, Natalie Savage. *Marchers for the Dream.* Harper & Row Publishers, Inc., 1969, ages 9-11.

11. Clifford, Ethel Rosenberg. *The Wild One.* Houghton Mifflin Co., 1974, ages 11 and up.

12. Dunn, Judy. *Feelings.* Creative Educational Society, Inc., 1971, ages 3-8.

13. Fitzhugh, Louise. *The Long Secret.* Harper & Row Publishers, Inc., 1965, ages 9-12.

14. Giff, Patricia R. *Today Was a Terrible Day.* Live Oak Media, 1984, grades K-3.

15. Hitte, Kathryn. *Boy, Was I Mad!* Parents' Magazine Press, 1969, ages 5-8.

16. Hoban, Russell and Hoban, Lillian. *The Little Brute Family.* Macmillan Company, 1973, grades 1-6.

17. Hogan, Paula Z. *Sometimes I Get So Mad.* Raintree Publishers, Inc., 1980, ages 5-8.

18. Holland, Isabelle. *Amanda's Choice.* J. B. Lippincott Company, 1970, ages 10-13.

19. Kroll, Steven. *That Makes Me Mad!* Pantheon, 1976, grades K-3.

20. Maddock, Reginald. *The Dragon in the Garden.* Little, Brown and Company, 1968, ages 10-13.

21. McGovern, Ann. *Scram, Kid!* The Viking Press, Inc., 1974, ages 5-8.

22. McGovern, Ann. *Feeling Mad, Sad, Bad.* Walker & Co., 1978, grades K-3.

23. Norris, Gunilla Brodde. *The Good Morrow.* Atheneum Publishers, 1969, ages 9-11.

24. Odor, Ruth S. *Moods and Emotions.* Childs World, 1981, grades 2-6.

25. Robinson, Nancy Konheim. *Wendy and the Bullies.* Hastings House Publishers, Inc., 1980, ages 7-10.

26. Simon, Norma. *I Was So Mad.* Albert Whitman & Company, 1974, ages 4-8.

27. Skolsky, Mindy Warshaw. *Carnival and Kopeck and More About Hannah.* Harper & Row Publishers, Inc., 1979, ages 7-9.

28. Snyder, Zilpha Keatley. *The Headless Cupid.* Atheneum Publishers, 1971, ages 10-13.

29. Stolz, Mary Slattery. *Maximilian's World.* Harper & Row Publishers, Inc., 1966, ages 7-10.

30. Sugarman, Daniel A. and Hochstein, Rolaine A. *Seven Stories for Growth.* Pitman Publishing Corporation, 1965, ages 6-12.

31. Townson, Hazel. *Terrible Tuesday.* Morrow, 1986, grades P-3.

32. Udry, Janice May. *Let's Be Enemies.* Harper & Row Publishers, Inc., 1961, ages 3-7.

33. Viorst, Judith. *Alexander and the Terrible, Horrible, No Good, Very Bad Day.* Atheneum Publishers, 1972, ages 3-8.

34. Wallace, Art. *Toby.* Doubleday & Company, 1971, ages 9-11.

35. Watson, Jane Werner et al. *Sometimes I Get Angry.* Golden Press, 1971, ages 3-6.

36. Wells, Rosemary. *Benjamin and Tulip.* Dial Press, 1973, ages 3-7.

37. Wittels, Harriet and Greisman, Joan. *Things I Hate.* Behavioral Publications, Inc., 1973, ages 4-8.

38. Zolotow, Charlotte Shapiro. *The Quarreling Book.* Harper & Row Publishers, Inc., 1963, ages 4-7.

39. Zolotow, Charlotte Shapiro. *The Hating Book.* Harper & Row Publishers, Inc., 1969, ages 3-7.

Videotapes

1. Anger: Handle With Care
   Barr Films, 1983, 1 film reel (13 minutes), grades 4-6.

2. Angry Movie
   Coronet, 1978, 1 film reel (6 minutes), grades 1-3.

3. Dealing With Feelings
   Coronet, 1982, 1 film reel (15 minutes), grades K-6.

4. Don't Stay Mad
   Phoenix/BFA Films and Video, Inc., 1972, 1 film reel (15 minutes), grades 1-6.

5. Getting Angry
   Phoenix/BFA Films and Video, Inc., 1966, 1 film reel (10 minutes), grades 1-6.

6. Hating Movie, The
   Phoenix/BFA Films and Video, Inc., 1986, 1 film reel (15 minutes), grades 1-6.

7. How Do I Feel? How Do You Feel?
   Higgin, 1984, 1 film reel (13 minutes), grades 1-3.

8. I'm Feeling Sad
   Churchill Films, 1974, 1 film reel (10 minutes), grades 1-3.

9. I'm Feeling Scared
   Churchill Films, 1974, 1 film reel (9 minutes), grades 1-3.

10. I'm Mad At Me
    Churchill Films, 1974, 1 film reel (8 minutes), grades 1-3.

11. I'm Mad At You
    Churchill Films, 1974, 1 film reel (9 minutes), grades 1-3.

12. Learn From Criticism Game, The
    Higgin, 1979, 1 film reel (11 minutes), grades 1-3.

13. Learn From Disappointments, The
    Higgin, 1979, 1 film reel (11 minutes), grades 1-3.

14. Nobody Likes a Bully
    Barr Films, 1979, 1 film reel (15 minutes), grades 1-6.

15. Our Feelings Affect Each Other
    Higgin, 1984, 1 film reel (13 minutes), grades 1-6.

16. Seeds of Violence
    AIMS Media, 1983, 1 film reel (11 minutes), grades 4-6.

17. Stress: Learning How to Handle It
    AIMS Media, 1984, 1 film reel (23 minutes), grades 4-6.

18. Strong Feelings
    National Instructional T.V., 1973, 1 film reel (15 minutes), grades 4-6.

19. Tell 'Em How You Feel
    Learning Corporation of America/MTI, 1986, 1 film reel (18 minutes), grades 1-6.

20. What's Your Authority?
Encyclopedia Britannica Educational Corporation, 1972, 1 film reel (11 minutes), grades 4-6.

Films

1. *Being Courteous - Being Considerate*
Listen and Learn Company, 4 filmstrips with cassettes, grades K-4.

2. *Being Good - Being Bad*
Listen and Learn Company, 4 filmstrips with cassettes, grades K-4.

3. *Being Kind*
Listen and Learn Company, 4 filmstrips with cassettes, grades K-4.

4. *Coping With Anger, Embarrassment, Frustration and Jealousy*
Creative Learning, Inc., 4 filmstrips, grades 3-6.

5. *Developing Self-Discipline*
Listen and Learn Company, 4 filmstrips with cassettes, grades 4-8.

6. *Fighting, Bullying, Gossiping and Teasing People*
Listen and Learn Company, 4 filmstrips with cassettes, grades 4-8.

7. *Think, Talk and Do*
Listen and Learn Company, 8 filmstrips with cassettes, grades P-4.

8. Trower, Terry. *Self-Control Sound Filmstrip*
2 filmstrip/cassette, grades K-4.

9. *Truancy, Disrespect, Clowning and Goofing Off*
Creative Learning, Inc., 4 filmstrips, grades 4-6.

10. *Understanding Right and Wrong*
Listen and Learn Company, 4 filmstrips with cassettes, grades 3-6.

11. *Understanding Your Feelings*
Listen and Learn Company, 2 filmstrips with cassettes, grades 3-6.

12. *What Should I Do?*
Walt Disney Educational Media, 5 filmstrips, grades K-3.

13. *Winnie the Pooh and the Right Thing to Do*
Walt Disney Educational Media, 5 filmstrips, grades K-3.

▶ Technique #3

Title:	Popping Your Cork
Technique category:	Paper/Pencil Exercise
Objective:	To educate members about the typical response patterns to angry feelings.

Materials needed:

- Copies of the sheet entitled "Popping Your Cork," found on page 216.
- Pencils

Procedure:

1. Pass out the sheet entitled "Popping Your Cork" to all group members.
2. Allow 5 to 10 minutes for the completion of this task.
3. Ask everyone to share their responses by going around the circle in order. The facilitator should initially share their responses to the task sheet for purposes of modeling.
4. If time allows, pose some discussion questions related to the task sheet responses.
5. Process members' positive reactions at the end of the session.

Cautions/comments:

This is an excellent technique for helping members understand some of the reasons behind aggressive/acting out behavior. The graphic association of a bottle cork popping shows the youngsters that when feelings build up too long the result is often an out of control response. The completion of the task sheet for this exercise will help increase members' awareness of things that make kids angry.

▸ **Popping Your Cork**

Instructions: Fill up all lines inside this bottle with things that generally result in kids feeling angry.

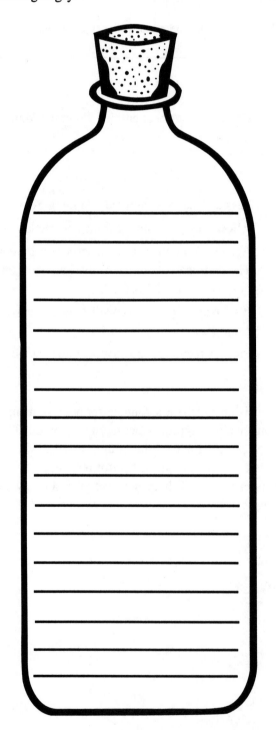

▶ Technique #4

Title:	Listen To Your Anger
Technique category:	Exercise Using the Arts
Objective:	To increase members' awareness of their anger/conflict resolution problems.

Materials:

- Music related to the session theme. Ideas for music selections to use in this session can be obtained from the following references:

    Berenzon, Rolando. *Music Therapy Manual.* Springfield: Charles C. Thomas, 1981.

    Plach, Tom. *The Creative Use of Music in Group Therapy.* Springfield: Charles C. Thomas, 1980.

- Necessary equipment to play music

Procedure:

1. Before this session, the facilitator will need to select some music that will assist members in becoming more aware of their anger and responses to it. Some readers may choose to use music pieces that contrast calming tunes with more aggressive or upsetting tunes.

2. At the onset of the session, members are asked to relax by closing their eyes and listening to a calming tune. During this part of the exercise, participants should be instructed to think of recent times in which they had the same type of feeling that the music is eliciting. Sometimes, it is best to use music with no words for this free association. (Otherwise, the youngsters may get too caught up with the words.)

3. Next, the facilitator plays a musical selection that conveys a feeling of anger or aggressiveness. Here again, members are asked to think of a recent time they experienced a similar feeling. The children should also be instructed to reflect on their behavioral responses to such a feeling. Another type of music to use for this exercise would be the song entitled "Work the Anger Out" by Jack Hartmann (published by Educational Activities, PO Box 392, Freeport, NY 11520) which has specific words to help members think through their angry feelings. When using a record such as this, it is best to have the group respond directly to the words and instructions.

4. The facilitator asks members to share with one another either their free associations or general responses to the music. It will be important that discussion questions posed during this component focus on increasing members' awareness of their anger and their usual responses to it.

5. Participants should be asked to indicate what they enjoyed most about this music exercise.

Cautions/comments:

Truly, music is the window to the soul. Many youngsters will respond at more of a gut level after listening to some relevant and moving musical piece. Also, facilitators will often find that calming music has a settling down effect on acting out youngsters. Usually, they enjoy not only listening to the tune or words but feel the relaxing impact it has on them. For this reason, the more calming music should be played first. Group members themselves can be asked to bring in their favorite music and share why they like it. A secondary benefit of this intervention is that members can learn how listening to music can be another way of working out their anger.

▶ Technique #5

Title:	Problems And More Problems
Technique category:	Disclosure Task
Objective:	To increase members' awareness of their anger/conflict resolution problems.

Materials:

- Blackboard
- Chalk

Procedure:

1. At the onset of this session, members are told they are going to be doing a competitive task as a group.

2. Then, the rules below are reviewed with the membership.

   - The group will be given so much time (10 to 15 minutes) to brainstorm a predetermined amount of problems that can result from anger not handled effectively.

   - Each member will have an equal opportunity to share their contributions to the list by going around the circle.

   - If a member does not have any new problems to add to the list when it is his/her turn, that member can pass to the next participant.

   - All problems brainstormed should be written on the blackboard by the facilitator in order to make sure there are no repeats.

   - If the group comes up with the desired number of problems, the members win the game. If they are not able to come up with the predetermined number of problems, the facilitator wins.

3. The game is then conducted following the rules.

4. At the end, members are asked to carefully look over the list of problems they developed. All youngsters are asked to identify three of the problems on the list that they have experienced or are currently experiencing. All members are then requested to share their three problems with the entire group.

5. At the end, everyone should be asked to complete the following sentence: "I really liked this session when _____."

Cautions/comments:

This fun exercise can be a non-threatening way for group members to share in more depth their acting out problems as a result of anger control difficulties. Facilitators will be amazed how much easier it will be for youngsters to respond to this difficult theme via this technique. It is advisable to keep members' lists of problems, to assist in planning future relevant group meetings.

▶ Technique #6

Title: Out The Window

Technique category: Creative Exercise

Objective: To increase members' awareness of their anger control problems.

Materials:

- Form entitled "Out The Window," found on page 222.
- Pencils

Procedure:

1. The facilitator passes out to each participant the sheet entitled "Out The Window." The group is asked to write or draw on this form an anger control problem they would like to throw out the window or stop doing. Facilitators should further clarify these instructions by noting that the behavior indicated should be an ineffective response to angry feelings. It will also be important to emphasize that no one in the group will know what everyone has written down since the facilitator will read the responses anonymously.

2. Members are given a designated period of time to complete this task.

3. The group leader requests participants to fold up their papers. Then, each youngster is asked to try their skill at tossing their folded up sheet into a box, symbolic of a window, held by the facilitator (i.e., tossing a problem out the window).

4. The facilitator reads and notes on a blackboard the problems written down. It will be important during this sharing to note commonalities that surface.

5. If time permits, facilitators should have some prepared discussion questions regarding these responses. Such questions should stimulate further disclosure that will serve to normalize everyone's feelings and reactions.

6. At the end of this session, participants should be asked to share the most beneficial part of the task.

Cautions/comments:

This technique is extremely effective in surfacing lots of disclosure from the membership. Youngsters typically love the creative idea of tossing a problem out the window without having to tell anyone about it. Even though group members will be making this disclosure anonymously, this exercise still serves as a means for ventilating some tough acting out difficulties. In addition, this intervention will help all participants feel that they are not alone with their problems.

▶ Out The Window

Instructions: Write in between the hands below an anger control problem you would like to get rid of and throw out the window.

▶ Technique #7

Title:	Picture This!
Technique category:	In Vivo Experience
Objective:	To increase members' awareness of alternative ways to cope with their anger.

Materials:

- Videotape camera, VCR, TV set, and blank tape
- 3"x5" cards
- Pencils

Procedure:

1. Members are informed that they will be having an opportunity to do some acting in front of a video camera. Also, it will be important to emphasize that the youngsters will have a chance to watch how they do in their performances.

2. All the participants are asked to write down on a 3"x5" card a situation that is typically problematic for them in regard to their anger control. These cards are passed to the facilitator once they are completed.

3. Members are then instructed to listen to each problem situation as it is read, so that they can decide which one they would like to act out for possible alternative responses. All participants may volunteer for one of the card situations posed. If not, the facilitator may have to do some assigning.

4. Members are given a few minutes to prepare their responses and think about the details around their play acts.

5. Participants are each asked to act out their responses to the problematic situations in front of the video camera. If other people are needed for the play acts, the facilitator should assign parts to other members. In some instances, the group leader may want to do the other talking part in each play act, for time efficiency purposes.

6. After all members have conducted their play acts (a limit of about 5 minutes will need to be placed on these play acts), the group is given an opportunity to view themselves on tape.

7. Either during the videotape viewing or after, the facilitator should have structured discussion questions to pose to the group. These questions

should focus on processing both the content and acting ability of the members.

8.   At the end of the session, it will be important to ask participants what coping alternatives they viewed as most helpful.

Cautions/comments:

This is an excellent technique for members to share coping skills via their modeling of alternative responses to anger eliciting situations. Facilitators may find that some participants are at first shy about acting in front of a camera. However, after watching other eager members, they will often be more comfortable with this request. Readers will have to remember that this particular exercise may take two sessions for a group of eight to complete.

▸ Technique #8

Title:	Be Like A Traffic Light
Technique category:	Completion Task
Objective:	To increase members' awareness of alternative ways to cope with their anger.

Materials:

- Eight to ten problematic situations relevant to the group in regard to anger control problems
- The visual aid entitled "Be Like A Traffic Light," found on page 227.

Procedure:

1. Before this session, the facilitator will need to have prepared some problematic situations relevant to the group members. It will be necessary to have about eight to ten of these situations.

2. The session begins with members being told they are going to be playing a fun game in the group. But before they will have a chance to enjoy the game, they must first listen to a short lecture to help them win when they do play. The facilitator then conducts a brief presentation (about 10 minutes) on one of the methods for managing one's anger, which is to stop, think, and then act.

   For younger children (third grade and under), visual aids will be helpful to complement this lecture. The sheet entitled "Be Like A Traffic Light" can be used for this purpose. Some good refer-ences with didactic material ideas include Dr. Camp and M.A. Bash's *Think Aloud Program*, Dr. Ritchey and W. Isaacs' book entitled *"I Think I Can, I Know I Can,"* and Dr. Berg's *The Self-Control Workbook.* These three books are fully referenced in the bibliography at the back of this curriculum.

3. After this short lecture has been given, the youngsters are instructed in the following rules for playing the game.

   - An anger eliciting situation will be read by the facilitator to the group.
   - Members will be given an opportunity to volunteer to go through the steps of Stop, Think, and Act in regard to the problematic situation posed.

- The participants who volunteer for each situation will be given 2 to 3 minutes to go through the three steps and show at each point how a youngster establishes a more effective response to an angry situation.

- When members act out the three steps, they will need to think out loud for the second step (Think) the two possible responses, and they must choose one to act out for the third step (Act).

- Members should only be allowed to volunteer for one play act opportunity so that everyone has a chance to participate in this experience.

- If members are able to do the three steps in the time period, a point is given to the group. But if they cannot complete all three steps, the point goes to the facilitator. The one (group or facilitator) at the end with the most points wins.

4. The task is then conducted following the rules.

5. At the end of this fun competition, members are asked to share which alternative responses used would be most helpful for them.

Cautions/comments:

This is a fun and non-threatening way for members to learn the three step alternative approach for dealing with anger. Facilitators will find that children learn this material quickly because it is associated with a fun game. Often times, youngsters with anger control problems fail to think before they act. In many instances, they are impulsive in their responses, which accounts for their unhealthy patterns of handling such situations. Clinicians may well find that a particular group will benefit from practicing this technique over a period of two or more sessions.

▸ Be Like A Traffic Light

Instructions: Think of yourself as a traffic light so you can remember the three steps for best handling your anger.

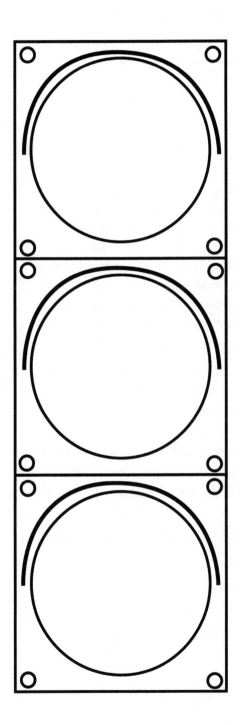

STOP

Make yourself stop before you act.

THINK

Think through all the ways you could respond to the situation. Be sure to also think about the consequences for each behavior.

ACT

Once you have stopped and thought about ways to respond to a situation where you feel angry, act. Do something that will effectively get your anger out but is not harmful to you or others.

▶ **Technique #9**

Title: Run With It

Technique category: Game Exercise

Objective: To increase members' awareness of alternative ways to cope with their anger.

Materials:

- Blackboard
- Chalk

Procedure:

1. Members are informed at the beginning of this session that they will be having an opportunity to show off their memory and running skills. But, before they play this fun game utilizing these skills, they must first brainstorm all the alternative ways one can respond to an anger eliciting situation. Participants then take turns one at a time going around the circle telling ways children can respond to anger more effectively.

2. After a long list of answers (i.e., about 20) has been developed, the group is given the following rules to play this game.

    - Each member has to run up to the blackboard and write one of the alternative responses given and say it out loud when it is their turn. The response shared must not have been given yet by any other member in the game.

    - Once the member has completed this task, they sit down and the next youngster gets up, runs, and writes on the board the same way.

    - The total group is given a designated period of time to complete one round of turns.

    - If the group completes a round in the time period, they win. If they do not, the facilitator wins.

3. The game is then played following the rules.

4. At the end, members should be asked to share what they enjoyed and which alternative responses to anger were new ones for them to try out.

Cautions/comments:

This is a fun and easy way for members to learn alternative ways to respond to situations that elicit anger. Facilitators will find that often times, regardless of the members' academic levels, participants can and do have good memory skills. The review nature of this activity helps reinforce the teaching of new coping responses to anger. In addition, this population will enjoy the idea of combining learning with a running task.

▸ Technique #10

Title:	Group Oscar Awards
Technique category:	Empowerment Exercise
Objective:	To integrate into members' repertoire alternative responses to their anger.

Materials:

- Award certificates (like the one found on page 231) prepared for each member indicating the significant progress they have made in regard to their anger management skills

Procedure:

1. Before this group session, the facilitator will need to prepare award certificates for each member utilizing the form found on the following page. These awards should be for new behavioral responses the participants have learned and demonstrated in regard to their anger management skills.

2. The session then begins with members being informed that they are each going to receive an award today for positive changes they have made regarding the handling of their anger. As a way of keeping members' attention and having them share in this reinforcement ceremony, the participants are told that they are going to have to guess who gets each award. When facilitating groups under third grade, it may be advisable to keep count of the score (each wrong guess gives a point to the facilitator and each right guess gives a point to the group) in order to enhance this fun competitive component.

3. After each award receiver is guessed, the facilitator hands the certificate to that member.

4. At the end of the session, members should be asked to share what meant the most to them about this award ceremony.

Cautions/comments:

This is a very nurturing and reinforcing way for members to solidify the changes they have made in this type of support group. Youngsters usually enjoy the guessing component of this exercise and in so doing add peer reinforcement to the facilitator's feedback. Group leaders will be amazed at the impact of this technique for many members, who have rarely — if ever — received positive feedback for their progress.

OSCAR AWARD

FOR: _____

Who has shown great progress in regard to

_____

_____

_____

Date: _____

Awarded by: _____

▶ **Technique #11**

Title:	Give Your Verdict
Technique category:	Check-Up/Assignment
Objective:	To integrate into members' repertoire alternative responses to their anger.

Materials needed:

- Copies of the sheet entitled "Give Your Verdict," found on page 233.
- Pencils

Procedure:

1. Pass out the sheet entitled "Give Your Verdict" to all group members.
2. Allow 5 to 10 minutes for the completion of this task.
3. Ask everyone to share their responses by going around the circle in order. The facilitator should initially share their responses to the task sheet for purposes of modeling.
4. If time allows, pose some discussion questions related to the task sheet responses.
5. Process members' positive reactions at the end of the session.

Cautions/comments:

This verdict technique provides a non-threatening way for acting out youngsters to discuss alternatives to handling one's anger. The youngsters enjoy the idea of being a jury so much that they forget how much they are learning about alternative ways of responding to upsetting situations. Facilitators should feel free to modify this intervention by making up cases more relevant to the membership's experiences. This change will usually enhance the impact of this instructive technique.

▸ **Give Your Verdict**

Instructions: Read the stories below and decide with a ✔ if the youngster's response was *guilty* for the crime of an anger control problem or *not guilty.*

CASE #1:

A child breaks another friend's toy because that friend accidentally broke his favorite toy.

Your verdict: _____ Not Guilty   _____ Guilty

CASE #2:

A youngster defends himself in a fight after school that was started by a class bully.

Your verdict: _____ Not Guilty   _____ Guilty

CASE #3:

A boy threatens another child for constantly teasing him.

Your verdict: _____ Not Guilty   _____ Guilty

CASE #4:

A girl is very upset with a friend who stole her money but will not admit it. She decided to ask her mom to help solve the problem.

Your verdict: _____ Not Guilty   _____ Guilty

▶ Technique #12

Title: Wad It Up And Fly Away

Technique category: Confirmation Task

Objective: To integrate into members' repertoire alternative coping responses to the management of anger.

Materials:

- Blank paper
- Pencils

Procedure:

1. In the first part of this exercise, participants are each given a blank sheet of paper and asked to write one response to their anger that they have stopped doing or intend to stop in the near future.

2. Next, the members are given a two minute period to wad up their papers into balls and throw them at one another. It will be essential that the youngsters know ahead of time that they must remain in their seats during the throwing of these paper balls.

3. After the two minute period, the youngsters are asked to stop their throwing and to pick up the paper ball that is nearest them. Then, each participant unfolds their ball and reads out loud what has been written on it. Facilitators, at this point, will want to note any commonalities that arise during this sharing and reinforce the self-awareness of members.

4. The next part of this exercise will require the participants to write down on another blank sheet of paper a more effective response to anger that they have learned in the group.

5. Once everyone has written down their statements, members are asked to fold these into paper airplanes. After these planes are ready, participants are given a two minute period to fly these planes toward one another. Again, the same rule will have to be instituted where members have to remain in their chairs while making their planes fly.

6. Once the two minute period is up, the participants are instructed to pick up the paper plane nearest them and read the contents. Here again, facilitators will want to note commonalities that surface during this sharing and

reinforce positive changes made. As each paper is read, it is advisable to ask who in the group wrote the change indicated. Through this disclosure, everyone can directly reinforce the others' changes.

7. At the end of this session, members should be asked to share what they enjoyed.

Cautions/comments:

These movement games are excellent for acting out youngsters. They allow the children an opportunity to physically express themselves and combine those responses with verbal confirmations of their changes. Typically, youngsters love this intervention. They are able to quickly identify the concrete association of dysfunctional coping behaviors with wadded up paper balls and the healthy coping behaviors with paper airplanes that glide away so easily.

▶ Bibliography

Berg, Barthen. *Anger Control Workbook and Game.* Los Angeles, Western Psychological Services, 1989.

Boswell, Judy. Helping children with their anger. *Elementary School Guidance & Counseling* 18(1):278-287, 1982.

Buffington, P. W. and Stilwell, W. E. Self-control and affective education: a case of omission. *Elementary School Guidance & Counseling* 15(2):152-159, 1980.

Cain, Barbara C. *Double-Dip Feelings.* New York, Magination Press, 1990.

Camp, Bonnie W. Verbal mediation in young aggressive boys. *Journal of Abnormal Psychology* 86:145-153, 1977.

Camp, Bonnie and Bash, Mary Ann. *Think Aloud.* Champaign, Research Press, 1985.

Cooper, JoAnn et al. *Helping Children Series* (pamphlet on Disruptive Behaviors). Doylestown, Marco, 1986.

Downing, C. Jerry. Affirmations: steps to counter negative, self-fulfilling prophecies. *Elementary School Guidance & Counseling* 21(2):174-179, 1986.

Drew, Naomi. *Learning the Skills of Peacemaking, Revised.* Torrance, CA, Jalmar Press, 1996.

Duncan, Riana. *When Emily Woke Up Angry.* Hauppauge, Barron, 1989.

Fairchild, Thomas N. *Crisis Intervention Strategies for School Based Helpers.* Springfield, Charles C. Thomas, 1986.

Fleischman, M. J. A replication of Patterson's "Intervention for boys with conduct problems." *Journal of Consulting and Clinical Psychology* 49(3):342-51, 1981.

Fry-Miller, Kathleen and Myers-Wells, Judith. *Young Peacemakers Project Book.* Elgin, Brethren Press, 1988.

Fugitt, Eva. *He Hit Me Back First!* Torrance, CA, Jalmar Press, 1982.

Gaushell, W. Harper and Lawson, David M. Using a checksheet with misbehaviors in school: parent involvement. *School Counselor* 36(3):208-213, 1989.

Goff, G. A. and Demetral, G. D. A home-based program to eliminate aggression in the classroom. *Social Work in Education* 6(1):5-14, 1983.

Golant, Mitch. *Sometimes It's OK to be Angry.* New York, Tom Doherty Associates, 1987.

Hawley, Susan and Hawley, Robert C. *Ten Steps for Disciplining Difficult Students.* Amherst, Educational Research Associates, 1985.

Isaacs, Susan and Ritchey, Wendy. *I Think I Can, I Know I Can.* New York, St. Martin, 1989.

Kaufman, Gershen and Raphael, Lev. *Stick Up For Yourself!* Minneapolis, Educational Media, 1988.

Kreidler, William. *Creative Conflict Resolution.* Mount Dora, Kids Rights, 1989.

Lalli, Judy. *Feeling Alphabet.* Torrance, CA, Jalmar Press, 1984.

Lane, Kristi. *Feelings are Real.* Muncie, Accelerated Development, 1991.

McElmurry, Mary Anne. *Feelings.* Carthage, Good Apple, 1984.

Nelsen, Jane. *Positive Discipline: Teaching Children Self-Discipline, Responsibility, Cooperation and Problem Solving Skills.* Fair Oaks, Sunrise Press, 1985.

Onizo, Michael M. et al. Teaching children to cope with anger. *Elementary School Guidance & Counseling* 22(3):241-245, 1988.

Palmares, Waldo and Logan, Ben. *A Curriculum Guide on Conflict Management.* San Diego, Human Development Training Institute, 1975.

Polisar, Barry Louis. *Don't Do That!* Silver Spring, Rainbow Morning Music, 1986.

Radd, Tommie. *Grow with Guidance Classroom Activities File.* Canton, Grow With Guidance, 1986.

Schmidt, Fran and Friedman, Alice. *Creative Conflict Solving for Kids.* Miami Beach, The Grace Contrino Abrams Peace Education Foundation, Inc., 1985.

Schmidt, Fran and Friedman, Alice. *Peacemaking Skills for Little Kids.* Miami Beach, The Grace Abrams Peace Education Foundation, Inc., 1986.

Taber, Sara Mansfield. Cognitive-behavior modification treatment of an aggressive 11-year-old boy. *Social Work Research and Abstracts* 17(2):13-23, 1981.

Taylor, John. *Anger Control Training for Children and Adolescents.* Doylestown, Marco Products, 1991.

Trower, Terry. *Furious Fables.* Doylestown, Marco, 1987.

Whittington, Ronaele et al. *Peace Begins With Me.* Honolulu, Waikiki Community Center, 1988.

Wohl, Agnes and Kaufman, Bobbie. *Silent Screams and Hidden Cries.* New York, Brunner/Mazel, 1985.

Workman, Edward A. *Teaching Behavioral Self-Control to Students.* Culver City, Social Studies School Service, 1982.

Chapter 9

Traumatized Children's Support Group Curriculum

A complete curriculum for traumatized children's support groups is provided in this chapter. Step-by-step instructions are outlined for the unique set-up, planning, and facilitation of this type of elementary age support group. An extensive listing of assessment scales, session themes, bibliotherapy books, video-tapes/films, and "how-to-do-it" references are included as part of this practical support group guide. This chapter, along with Chapters One, Two, Three, and Thirteen, will provide complete instructions for the set-up through the termination of traumatized children's support groups.

Treatment Guidelines

The amount and type of trauma young children face today is enormous compared to earlier generations. Elementary students are experiencing murders in their families, the incarceration of significant others, divorce, the blending of new family units, deaths, suicides, and any number of other serious tragedies. Counselors working with these young children often find themselves having to provide coping mechanisms for some pretty overwhelming crises. One of the major difficulties with traumatized youngsters is that the precipitating event is usually not a minor one nor an isolated tragedy. Typically, these kids are having to cope with any number of serious problems simultaneously. For this reason, treatment services for these elementary age children may require long-term counseling.

Youngsters who have had trauma in their lives will at some point benefit from a support group program. Often such a service is best provided after the youngster has made an initial adjustment to the traumatic event — usually through individual counseling. The child can then be an excellent candidate for a support group. They can form a close relationship with other children in this setting and their mutual sharing can help normalize feelings and reactions to a traumatic experience. In addition, they can be excellent models for other members in terms of coping skills. Many traumatized children are positively impacted by seeing and hearing how peers in similar situations have learned to cope effectively.

Before utilizing this curriculum, the reader should review the following general treatment guidelines for working with traumatized children in support groups.

1. A careful assessment of the causes of a child's trauma will need to be made by the counselor. As indicated earlier, a youngster can be experiencing any number of serious problems simultaneously. Sometimes the more obvious ones may not, in fact, be the major causes of the current difficulties. It will be important that the facilitator explore these other possible causes carefully with parents, teachers, and the child before a group service is initiated.

2. Youngsters in the first three grades are usually not able initially to talk very openly about their feelings regarding a trauma. Typically, non-verbal interventions need to be utilized in a support group with these children. Facilitators need to have realistic expectations about the level of disclosure that can be elicited in a short-term support group. These youngsters do not do a lot of intimate sharing regarding their trauma in this type of counseling program. They will, however, benefit from therapeutic instruction around this subject, the support from peers, and the sharing of alternative coping ideas.

3. Even with elementary age students, it is important to check on their thoughts regarding severe depression or suicide during or after a traumatic event. As we know, young children are increasingly resorting to these coping behaviors. If a youngster appears severely depressed or suicidal, it is imperative that counselors share this information with the child's parents and other involved professionals. Often times it will be necessary to provide these adults with immediate suggestions to monitor the youngster. Students at this level of functioning generally should not be seen in a group, but rather on a one-to-one basis.

4. The timing of a counseling intervention is more crucial with these children. Kids, like adults, are more vulnerable and subsequently more open at the time of the trauma. Individual counseling at this time will usually have an increased impact on the child's coping style. Usually, it is only after an initial adjustment to the trauma that these young children are ready for a support group.

5. Counselors who have had previous relationships with children involved in a trauma will find that these youngsters can more easily open up regarding their problems and feelings. At the same time, these students may not be able to be as open in a support group. Counselors need to be sensitive to settings where traumatized children can be most revealing.

6. Facilitators need to be careful about the type of disclosure they elicit in a group setting. Readers have to remember the developmental stage of elementary age students. These youngsters should not be asked to handle certain types of disclosure just because they are in a support group together. This is particularly relevant with this population because it may mean that it is best to not have members talk in very direct terms about their traumatic experiences. We should not put such responsibilities on these young shoulders. Instead, the group leader may need to address this at-risk problem from a more instructive standpoint.

7. Facilitators will find that when some children experience a traumatic event, they remember earlier tragedies in their lives. The ones most often recalled are those that were not fully resolved for the youngster. In support groups, counselors will need to be prepared for these earlier unresolved traumas in members' lives. One of the positive aspects of a trauma for a child is that it is often an opportunity to work through some earlier unresolved ones.

8. Often times, we forget the obvious with children. For example, traumatized youngsters need to be asked their perception of the situation and the resulting problems. Sometimes, even counselors assume children are having the same reaction to a crisis as the involved adults. What might be most problematic about the tragedy for an adult may not be the same for a child. It is a good rule of thumb to elicit the youngster's view of a traumatic event before making any assumptions around areas of difficulty. This disclosure should be elicited before a student is placed in a support group. The material surfaced from this probing can provide excellent relevant content for group sessions.

9. Some of the most effective interventions to use with this population in groups are exercises utilizing the arts. These techniques provide non-threatening ways to indirectly elicit disclosure from these youngsters. Many of the group members will benefit from these artistic avenues for expressing feelings that otherwise would be difficult to convey.

10. Remember the value of touch for traumatized youngsters. Children who are open to such contact can sometimes benefit greatly from an appropriate hug or a comforting squeeze. In this day and age, many helping professionals are being very cautious about any touching of children. However, in our efforts to protect ourselves from accusations, we are withholding one of the most important supports during a crisis. Just as with adults, sometimes what kids need most during a tragedy is a caring touch. While maintaining appropriate precautions, counselors need to make this part of the helping relationship available to these youngsters. Let's not get so carried away with litigation concerns that we forget our humanness and sensitivity.

Assessment Instruments

1. Assessment of Coping Style
2. Bellevue Index of Depression
3. Checklist of Children's Fears
4. Child Behavior Checklist
5. Reynolds Child Depression Scale

6. Revised Children's Manifest Anxiety Scale
7. Hopelessness Scale for Children
8. Kiddie-SADS
9. Stress Response Scale
10. What I Think and Feel

Relevant Session Themes

Awareness of feelings

Learning to communicate one's feelings

Skill in asking to have one's needs met

Learning how to take better care of oneself

Increasing one's motivation to be involved in earlier activities

Expression of one's sadness either directly or indirectly

Increased sense of hope

Skill in talking with involved family about tragedy

Understanding the normal reactions to a tragedy

Knowing how to find support from others

Normalization of one's feelings and reactions

A sense of not being alone

Learning to feel that with time things will be easier

Alternative outlets for one's anger, hurt, sadness

Engagement in relationships with peers

Identification of things within one's control around a tragedy

Maintenance of a positive self-esteem

Alternative coping skills for dealing with a past trauma

Planning Sequence of Objectives & Techniques for Traumatized Children's Support Group

Group Phase	Group Goals	Intervention Categories
Initial	1. To provide an attractive group setting. 2. To initiate members' participation on-task and with one another. 3. To initiate trust among the membership.	**Hello Group Techniques** (Chapter Three)
	4. To educate members about issues and difficulties related to past trauma.	**Instructive Techniques:** #1 Disappointments In My Life #2 Bibliotherapy/Video/Films #3 Say It With Feeling
Middle	5. To increase group development goals established in initial phase (i.e., goals 1-3).	No techniques per se but follow curriculum approach.
	6. To increase members' awareness of their particular difficulties related to past trauma.	**Awareness of Self Techniques:** #4 My Ups And Downs #5 A Penny For Your Thoughts #6 Talk Back For Me
	7. To provide alternative coping behaviors for dealing with problems related to trauma.	**Alternative Coping Techniques:** #7 The "Big Test" #8 Pull Me Up #9 Find The Words For You
	8. To assist members in the integration of new coping behaviors into their repertoire.	**Integration Techniques:** #10 Me Power #11 Just Call Your Helper #12 An S.O.S. Code Plan
Termination	9. To have members acknowledge the value of the group. 10. To assist members in validating their changes. 11. To have members brainstorm other sources of support. 12. To have members grieve the ending of group.	**Goodbye Group Techniques** (Chapter Thirteen)

▶ Technique #1

Title: Disappointments In My Life

Technique category: Didactic Technique

Objective: To instruct members about some of the difficulties youngsters can have as a result of a trauma.

Materials:

- Copies of the form entitled "Disappointments In My Life," found on page 246.
- Pencils

Procedure:

1. At the beginning of this session, members are informed that they are going to have a chance to learn more about disappointments that youngsters can experience in life, via a helpful didactic technique.

2. The form entitled "Disappointments in My Life" is passed out to all members.

3. Members are given a designated period of time to anonymously complete this paper and pencil task. Once the allotted time is up, all participants are asked to fold up their sheets and pass them to the facilitator.

4. The group leader summarizes the content of sheets by noting the results graphically on a large blackboard. This visual aid is very helpful to younger support groups (grades kindergarten through third). It will be particularly important to indicate members' coping responses to the sentence completion on this sheet.

5. After the facilitator has tabulated the results of this anonymous questionnaire, it will be helpful to pose discussion questions to the group similar to the ones below.

   - What do you think about the sharing provided on these questionnaires?
   - Name one positive feeling you have after learning what everyone disclosed.
   - Did someone give you a helpful coping suggestion? If yes, which one?

6. At the end of the session, the participants should be asked to indicate the number one point they learned from this experience.

Cautions/comments:

This is a particularly good task for eliciting some intimate disclosure initially from members without causing too much anxiety. Facilitators will be delighted to find that this intervention is instructive in and of itself — members will benefit just from learning all the disappointments they have each experienced and some of their coping responses.

▶ Disappointments In My Life

Instructions: Place a ✔ next to each disappointment you have had in life. Then, complete the sentence at the bottom.

____ Moving away from a favorite school or city that I liked.

____ My parents not having enough time for me.

____ My mom or dad being unfair to me when they get angry.

____ A close family member or friend has died.

____ Feeling like I cannot do well at school.

____ Other: _____

_____

When I think about these disappointments, I sometimes cause myself more problems by:

_____

_____

_____

As I think about these disappointments, I know the best way for me to cope with them has been:

_____

_____

_____

▸ Technique #2

Title: Bibliotherapy/Video/Films

Technique category: Bibliotherapy/Video/Films

Objective: To instruct members about some of the difficulties that can result from a trauma in life.

Materials:

- Book, film, or videotape selected from the list on page 248.
- Equipment for film or videotape, if used.
- Prepared discussion questions related to the theme of the visual aid chosen.

Procedure:

1. Before the session, the facilitator selects a book, film, or videotape from the list on page 248.
2. Session begins with the book being read or film/videotape being shown.
3. At completion of above task, members can be asked discussion questions that surface their identification with the story. Also, some disclosure can be elicited that explores the children's similar problems and struggles.
4. Members' favorite parts of the book, film, or videotape should be processed at the end.

Cautions/comments:

Typically, members will enjoy the use of bibliotherapy materials or films/videotapes. Through these types of visual interventions, children can more easily learn about alternative coping skills for common traumas in their lives. In addition, youngsters in elementary grades typically identify with characters in books and films. As a result, they are often able to more comfortably talk about their similar issues via the story presented.

Readers are advised to select books that have colorful pictures on almost every page. Children as a whole find it easier to understand the message of a book page when a graphic design depicts the concept. Also, facilitators should be careful that books and films/videotapes selected are not too long. It is important to have time in the session to pose discussion questions and process reactions among the members.

▶ Bibliotherapy

Losses in Childhood

1. Armstrong, W. *Sounder.* Harper & Row Publishers, Inc., 1973, grades 1-6.

2. Berger, Terry. *I Have Feelings.* Human Sciences, 1971, grades K-5.

3. Bernstein, J. *Loss: And How to Cope With It.* Seabury, 1977, grades 4-6.

4. Berry, Joy. *Teach Me About Crying.* Children's Press, 1986, grades P-2.

5. Berry, Joy. *Teach Me About Separation.* Children's Press, 1986, grades P-2.

6. Berry, Joy. *Every Kid's Guide to Coping With Childhood Trauma.* Children's Press, 1988, grades 3-6.

7. Berry, Joy. *Every Kid's Guide to Understanding Nightmares.* Children's Press, 1987, grades 3-6.

8. Blue, R. *Grandma Didn't Wave Back.* Franklin Watts, 1972, grades K-3.

9. Bunting, Anne Evelyn. *The Happy Funeral.* Harper & Row Publishers, Inc., 1982, ages 5-9.

10. Byars, Betsy Cromer. *Goodbye, Chicken Little.* Harper & Row Publishers, Inc., 1979, ages 9-11.

11. Carrick, Carol. *The Accident.* Seabury Press, 1976, ages 5-8.

12. Coerr, Eleanor. *Sadako and the Thousand Paper Canes.* C. P. Putnam's Sons, 1979, grades 4-6.

13. Collier, J. L. *Danny Goes to the Hospital.* Grosset and Dunlap, 1970, ages 5-8.

14. Donnelly, Effie. *So Long, Grandpa.* Crown Publishers, Inc., 1981, ages 9-11.

15. Hermes, Patricia. *You Shouldn't Have to Say Goodbye.* Harcourt-Brace-Jovanovich, Inc., 1982, ages 10-13.

16. Jones, A. *So, Nothing is Forever.* Houghton-Mifflin, 1974, grades 1-6.

17. Jones, Penelope. *Holding Together.* Bradbury Press, Inc., 1981, ages 9-11.

18. Krementz, Jill. *How It Feels When a Parent Dies.* Alfred A. Knopf, Inc., 1981, ages 8 and up.

19. LeShan, Eda. *Learning to Say Goodbye When a Parent Dies.* Macmillan Publishing Co., 1976, ages 5-8.

20. McLendon, Gloria Houston. *My Brother Joey Died.* Julian Messner, Inc., 1982, ages 9-11.

21. Miles, M. *Annie and the Old One.* Atlantic Monthly Press, 1971, ages 6-9.

22. Osborne, Mary Pope. *Run, Run, As Fast As You Can.* The Dial Press, Inc., 1982, ages 9-12.

23. Quinlan, Patricia. *My Dad Takes Care of Me.* Annick Press, 1987, grades 4-8.

24. Rabin, G. *Changes.* Harper & Row Publishers, Inc., 1973, age 12.

25. Riley, Sue and Tester, Sylvia R. *What Does It Mean?* (set of 12 books on feelings). Children's Press, 1980-87, grades P-2.

26. Sharmat, M. W. *I Want Mama.* Harper & Row Publishers, Inc., 1974, ages 4-8.

27. Smith, D. B. *A Taste of Blackberries.* Thomas Y. Crowell, 1973, ages 8-11.

28. Stevens, Margaret. *When Grandpa Died.* Children's Press, Inc., 1979, ages 4-8.

29. Tester, Sylvia Root. *Sometimes I'm Afraid.* Children's Press, 1979, grades P-2.

30. Wolfe, B. *Don't Feel Sorry for Paul.* J. B. Lippincott, 1974, ages 8-12.

31. Wright, Betty Ren. *I Like Being Alone.* Raintree, 1981, grades K-3.

32. Yep, L. *Dragon Wings.* Harper & Row Publishers, Inc., 1975, grades 1-6.

Physically Abused/Neglected Children

1. Alda, Arlene. *Sonya's Mommy Works.* Simon & Schuster, Inc., 1982, ages 4-7.

2. Alexander, Anne. *To Live a Lie.* Atheneum, 1975, grades 4-6.

3. Armstrong, Louise. *Saving the Big-Deal Baby.* E. P. Dutton & Company, Inc., 1980, ages 10 and up.

4. Ashley, Bernard. *Break in the Sun.* S. G. Phillips, Inc., 1980, ages 11 and up.

5. Barshun, Rochelle Nielsen. *Feeling Afraid.* Children's Press, 1983, grades P-2.

6. Barshun, Rochelle Nielsen. *Feeling Angry.* Children's Press, 1983, grades P-2.

7. Bauer, Caroline Feller. *My Mom Travels a Lot.* Frederick Warne & Company, Inc., 1981, ages 5-8.

8. Berry, Joy. *Alerting Kids to the Dangers of Abuse and Neglect.* Word Publishing Company, 1984, grades 1-6.

9. Berry, Joy Wilt. *Living Skills.* Children's Press, 1987, grades 3-6.

10. Blue, Rose. *Wishful Lying.* Human Sciences Press, 1980, ages 6-9.

11. Carlson, Natalie Savage. *Runaway Marie Louise.* Charles Scribner & Sons, Inc., 1977, ages 3-6.

12. Cleary, Beverly Bunn. *Ramona Quimby, Age 8.* William Morrow & Company, Inc., 1980, ages 8-10.

13. Cleary, Beverly Bunn. *Ramona and Her Mother.* William Morrow & Company, Inc., 1979, ages 7-10.

14. Culin, Charlotte. *Cages of Glass, Flowers of Time.* Bradbury Press, 1979, ages 12 and up.

15. Ensign, B. J. *Waldamare and Wally.* Parents Anonymous of Delaware, Inc., 1980, ages 4-10.

16. Family Information Systems, Inc. *Sometimes It's OK to Tattle.* Massachusetts Society for the Prevention of Child Abuse, 1982, ages 5-10.

17. Gerson, Corinne. *Son for a Day.* Atheneum Publishers, 1980, ages 10-12.

18. Gilbert, Sara. *By Yourself.* Lothrop, 1983, grades 4-6.

19. Haskins, James and Connolly, Pat. *The Child Abuse Help Book.* Addison, 1982, grades 5-6.

20. Hill, Margaret. *Turn the Page, Wendy.* Abingdon Press, 1981, ages 10-14.

21. Hoban, Russell. *The Little Brute Family.* Macmillan, 1969, grades K-3.

22. Holz, Loretta. *Foster Child.* Messner, 1984, grades 4-6.

23. Kyte, Kathy S. *In Charge: A Complete Handbook for Kids With Working Parents.* Knopf, 1983, grades 5-6.

24. Laiken, Deidre S. and Schneider, Alan J. *Listen to Me, I'm Angry.* Lothrop, 1980, grades 5-6.

25. Levinson, Nancy Smiler. *Silent Fear.* Crestwood House, Inc., 1981, ages 10-13.

26. Luttrell, Ida. *Lonesome Lester.* Harper, 1984, grades P-3.

27. Moncure, Jane Belk. *Courage.* Children's Press, 1981, grades P-3.

28. Paris, Lena. *Mom is Single.* Children's Press, 1980, grades K-3.

29. Piepgras, Ruth. *My Name is Mike Trumsky.* The Child's World, Inc., 1979, ages 5-8.

30. Reuter, Margaret. *My Mother is Blind.* Children's Press, 1979, grades K-3.

31. Sarnoff, Jane. *That's Not Fair.* Scribners LB, 1980, grades P-2.

32. Seixas, Judith S. *Living With a Parent Who Drinks Too Much.* Greenwillow, 1979, grades 4-6.

33. Sharmat, Mitchell. *Come Home Wilma.* Whitman, 1980, grades P-1.

34. Simon, Norma. *All Kinds of Families.* Whitman, 1976, grades 4-6.

35. Smith, Lucia B. *My Mom Got a Job.* Holt, Rinehart and Winston, Inc., 1979, ages 5-8.

36. Smith, Nancy Covert. *The Falling-Apart Winter.* Walker and Company, 1982, ages 10-13.

37. Stanek, Muriel. *Don't Hurt Me, Mama.* Whitman, 1983, grades 1-3.

38. Swartley, David Warren. *My Friend, My Brother.* Herald Press, 1980, ages 9-11.

39. Wakcher, Bridget. *Child Abuse - Is It Happening to You?* Teknek, 1984, ages 3-8.

40. Wheat, Patte. *Why Does It Hurt to be You?* Parents Anonymous (Los Angeles), 1981, ages 4-12.

41. White, Laurie and Spencer, Steven L. *Take Care With Yourself.* Take Care With Yourself (Flint, Michigan), 1983, ages 3-10.

Sexually Abused Children

1. Barshun, Rochelle Nielsen. *Feeling Afraid.* Children's Press, 1983, grades P-2.

2. Bassett, Kerry. *My Very Own Special Body Book.* Hawthorne Press, 1983, grades 4-6.

3. Berg, Eric. *Stop It!* Network Publications, 1985, ages 8-10.

4. Berg, Eric. *Tell Someone!* Network Publications, 1985, ages 10-12.

5. Berg, Eric. *Touch Talk.* Network Publications, 1985, ages 5-8.

6. Berry, Joy. *Teach Me About Touching.* Children's Press, 1988, grades K-3.

7. Dayce, Francis. *Private Zone.* The Charles Franklin Press, 1983, grades 1-6.

8. Family Information Systems, Inc. *Some Secrets Should be Told.* Massachusetts Society for the Prevention of Cruelty to Children, 1982, grades 1-6.

9. Krause, Elaine. *For Pete's Sake Tell.* Krause House Publishing Co., 1983, ages 7-12.

10. Moncure, Jane Belk. *Wishes, Whispers and Secrets.* Children's Press, 1979, grades P-3.

11. Renshaw, Domeena C. *Sex Talk for a Safe Child.* American Medical Association, 1984, grades 1-6.

12. RGA Creation. *It's OK to Say No.* Playmore, Inc., 1984, ages 4-10.

13. Sanford, Linda Tschichart. *Come Tell Me Right Away.* Ed-U Press, Inc., 1982, grades 1-6.

14. Sweet, Phyllis. *Something Happened to Me.* Mother Courage Press, 1981, ages 3-12.

15. Terkel, Susan Newberg and Rench, Janice E. *Feeling Safe and Strong: How to Avoid Sexual Abuse and What to Do if it Happens to You.* Lerner Publications Co., 1984, grades 1-6.

16. Wachter, Oralee. *No More Secrets for Me.* Little, Brown and Company, 1983, ages 5-12.

17. Wheat, Patte. *The Standoffs.* Parents Anonymous, Los Angeles, 1980, ages 4-12.

Videotapes

Losses in Childhood

1. Annie and the Old One
   Phoenix/BFA Films and Video, Inc., 1976, 15 minute film, grades 1-6.

2. Baby On The Way
   Barr Films, 1978, 15 minute film, grades 1-6.

3. Coping With Depression
   Filmfair Communications, 1987, 20 minute film, grades 4-6.

4. Day Grandpa Died, The
   Phoenix/BFA Films and Video, Inc., 1970, 12 minute film, grades 4-6.

5. Death of a Friend: Helping Children Cope With Grief and Loss
   New Dimensions Film Co., 1984, 15 minute film, grades K-6.

6. Feelings
   Encyclopedia Britannica Educational Corp., 1974, 12 minute film, grades K-3.

7. Footsteps On The Ceiling
   Phoenix/BFA Films and Video, Inc., 1981, 8 minute film, grades 4-6.

8. I'm Feeling Alone
   Churchill Films, 1974, 8 minute film, grades 1-3.

9. I'm Feeling Sad
   Churchill Films, 1974, 10 minute film, grades 1-3.

10. I'm Feeling Scared
    Churchill Films, 1974, 9 minute film, grades 1-3.

11. Jasper's Hospital Experience
    AIMS Media, 1984, 20 minute film, grades 1-6.

12. Learning to Cope
    Learning Corporation of America/MTI, 1979, 24 minute film, grades 4-6.

13. Loneliness: Empty Tree House
    Guidance Associates, 1973, 10 minute film, grades 4-6.

14. Magic Moth, The
    Coronet, 1976, 22 minute film, grades 1-6.

15. My Brother Is Sick
    AIMS Media, 1984, 20 minute film, grades 1-6.

16. Strong Feelings
    National Instruction T.V., 1973, 15 minute film, grades 4-6.

17. Tenth Good Thing About Barney, The
    AIMS Media, 1987, 13 minute film, grades K-6.

18. Uncle Monty's Gone
    CRM/McGraw-Hill Films, 1985, 14 minute film, grades 4-6.

19. Who Do You Tell?
    Learning Corporation of America/MTI, 1979, 11 minute film, grades 1-6.

20. Why Is It Always Me?
    Coronet, 1983, 14 minute film, grades 4-6.

Physically Abused/Neglected Children

1. *A Kid's Guide To Self-Protection*
   Listen and Learn Company, 6 filmstrips, grades K-4.

2. After Dark
   Media Guild, 1976, 12 minute film, grades 1-6.

3. Alone At Home
   Higgin, 1983, 17 minute film, grades 1-6.

4. Always Be Careful
   Mar/Chuck Film Industries, 1981, 10 minute film, grades 4-6.

5. Animals Are Crying
   Learning Corporation of America/MTI, 1971, 15 minute film, grades 4-6.

6. Better Safe Than Sorry
   Filmfair Communications, 1986, 17 minute film, grades 4-6.

7. Boy Stuff
   Churchill Films, 1986, 16 minute film, grades 4-6.

8. *Child Abuse: Cases of Detective Duncan*
   Creative Learning, Inc., 1 filmstrip, grades K-6.

9. Child Abuse: Don't Hide The Hurt
   AIMS Media, 1978, 13 minute film, grades 1-6.

10. Clean Up Your Act
    Churchill Films, 1981, 15 minute film, grades 1-6.

11. Crime Prevention: It's Elementary
    AIMS Media, 1984, 12 minute film, grades 1-6.

12. Eating Right With Harv And Marv
    Higgin, 1976, 11 minute film, grades K-6.

13. Emergencies: What Would You Do?
    AIMS Media, 1977, 10 minute film, grades K-6.

14. Home Alone: You're In Charge
    Barr Films, 1985, 19 minute film, grades K-6.

15. I'm Feeling Alone
    Churchill Films, 1974, 8 minute film, grades 1-3.

16. In Charge At Home: Latchkey Children
    Filmfair Communications, 1986, 21 minute film, grades 1-6.

17. It Shouldn't Hurt To Be A Kid!
    AIMS Media, 1982, 15 minute film, grades 1-6.

18. Mom Deserves Some Thanks
    Barr Films, 1985, 14 minute film, grades 1-6.

19. No More Secrets
    ODN Productions, 1984, 15 minute film, grades 1-6.

20. On Your Own At Home
    Coronet, 1986, 12 minute film, grades 1-6.

21. Please Don't Hit Me, Mom
    Films Incorporated, 1981, 46 minute film, grades 5-6.

22. Sometimes It's OK To Tattle
    New Dimensions Film Co., 1980, 12 minute film, grades 1-6.

23. Standing Up For Yourself
    Coronet, 1986, 11 minute film, grades 1-6.

Sexually Abused Children

1. Boys Beware
   AIMS Media, 1980, 14 minute film, grades 4-6.

2. Child Molestation: When To Say No
   AIMS Media, 1978, 14 minute film, grades 4-6.

3. Feeling Yes, Feeling No, Part 1
   Journal Films, Inc., 1984, 14 minute film, grades K-6.

4. Girls Beware
   AIMS Media, 1979, 12 minute film, grades 4-6.

5. Never Say Yes To A Stranger
   Learning Corporation of America/MTI, 1985, 20 minute film, grades 4-6.

6. Touch
   Learning Corporation of America, MTI, 1984, 30 minute film, grades 1-6.

7. Yes, You Can Say No
   AIMS Media, 1986, 19 minute film, grades 1-6.

Films

Losses in Childhood

1. *Coping With a Death in the Family*
   Listen and Learn Company, 4 filmstrips with cassettes, grades 4-8.

2. *Dealing With Feelings*
   Random House Media, 6 filmstrips/cassettes, grades 3-6.

3. *Death: A Part of Life*
   Guidance Associates, 2 filmstrips with cassettes, grades 4-6.

4. *Exploring Your Feelings*
   Sunburst, 2 filmstrips/cassettes, grades 5-6.

5. *Family Problems: Dealing With Crisis (death, separating, divorce, and moving)*
   Walt Disney Educational Media, 6 filmstrips, grades 4-6.

6. *No One Knows For Sure* (filmstrip about loss and hope)
   Listen and Learn Company, 1 filmstrip with cassette, grades 4-6.

7. *Spring Without Dad: Coping With Death*
   Random House Media, filmstrip/cassette, grades 5-6.

Abused/Neglected Children

1. *A Kid's Guide To Personal Hygiene*
   Creative Learning, Inc., 2 filmstrips, grades K-3.

2. *Developing Self-Reliance*
   Listen and Learn Company, 4 filmstrips with cassettes, grades 4-8.

3. *Latchkey Children: When You're In Charge*
   Listen and Learn Company, 4 filmstrips with cassettes, grades 4-8.

4. *Latchkey Kids Special Responsibilities*
   Random House Media, filmstrip/cassette, grades 5-6.

5. *Nutrition: Who Cares? You Should!*
   Guidance Associates, 4 filmstrips with cassettes, grades K-3.

6. *Safety: Help Is Just A Phone Call Away*
   Marshmedia, 50 frame filmstrip/video, grades 3-6.

7. *Safety: When You're The Boss*
   Marshmedia, 50 frame filmstrip/video, grades 4-6.

8. *Your Body: An Owner's Manual*
   Guidance Associates, 12 separate programs on filmstrips, grades 4-8.

Sexually Abused Children

1. *A Kid's Guide to Self-Protection*
   Listen and Learn Company, 6 filmstrips with cassettes, grades K-4.

2. *Child Abuse: Cases of Detective Duncan*
   Creative Learning, Inc., 1 filmstrip, grades K-6.

3. *Child Sexual Abuse: You Can Always Say No*
   Random House Media, filmstrip/cassette, grades 5-6.

4. *Now I Can Tell You My Secret*
   Walt Disney Educational Media, 2 filmstrips, grades K-3.

5. *Who Do You Tell?*
   MTI Teleprograms, Inc., 11 minute film, ages 7-12.

▸ Technique #3

Title:	Say It With Feeling
Technique category:	Paper/Pencil Task
Objective:	To instruct members about some of the difficulties that can result from experiencing a trauma.

Materials needed:

- Copies of the sheet entitled "Say It With Feeling," found on page 258.
- Pencils

Procedure:

1. Pass out the sheet entitled "Say It With Feeling" to all group members.
2. Allow 5 to 10 minutes for the completion of this task.
3. Ask everyone to share their responses by going around the circle in order. The facilitator should initially share their responses to the task sheet for purposes of modeling.
4. If time allows, pose some discussion questions related to the task sheet responses.
5. Process members' positive reactions at the end of the session.

Cautions/comments:

This is an excellent technique for helping traumatized children become aware of their feelings. It is not uncommon for these youngsters to turn off all affective awareness as a way of coping. This type of sentence completion helps these youngsters become more aware of their feelings through the association of such affective states with recent experiences. The expansion of members' repertoire of feelings is the first step in helping them deal more directly with affective reactions to past trauma. Also, sentence completions typically elicit more gut level responses from children.

▸ Say It With Feeling

Instructions: Select and write a feeling out of the mouth that best completes each statement below. Feel free to draw the faces instead of writing the words.

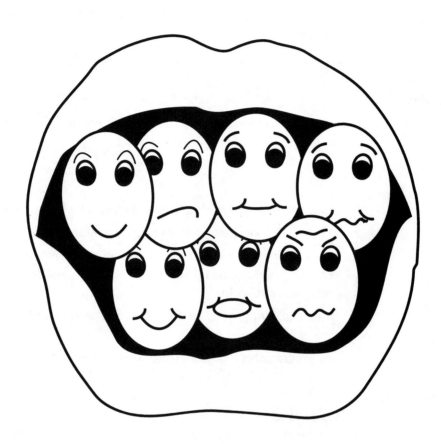

1. Today I am feeling _____.

2. When I was with my family last weekend, I mostly felt _____.

3. These days, I feel _____ about my school work.

4. At night when I am trying to go to sleep, sometimes I begin to feel _____.

5. I would like to feel _____ more in my life.

▸ Technique #4

Title:	My Ups And Downs
Technique category:	Exercise Using the Arts
Objective:	To increase members' awareness of their issues and problems related to a traumatic experience.

Materials:

- "My Ups And Downs" form found on page 260.
- Pencils

Procedure:

1. Members are told they are going to have an opportunity to participate in a creative exercise where they will be writing a poem about some of the good times and difficult times in their lives. Then, the form entitled "My Ups And Downs" is passed out.

2. Members are allowed 10 to 15 minutes to complete this task.

3. After everyone is done, each child takes a turn sharing their poem. Facilitators should be the first to share. This will create a more comfortable setting for this disclosure.

4. Throughout the above sharing, members' commonalities and significant disclosure should be reinforced.

5. At the end, everyone is asked to share in their own creative way the most enjoyable part of this artistic experience.

Cautions/comments:

This technique is usually effective in eliciting more disclosure from this group of students. These youngsters will find it less anxiety provoking to talk about their ups and downs via a poem completion. By asking for both ups and downs in members' lives, the facilitator is helping a support group become more comfortable dealing with their issues regarding a past trauma. The arts have been found to be very effective interventions to open up youngsters who are emotionally repressed due to past trauma.

▶ **My Ups And Downs**

Instructions: Complete the poem below with verses that apply to your life. Be ready to share and discuss it with your group.

My Ups and Downs

My life is full of Ups like _____

_____

And then there is the other Up of _____

_____

But there is always the Down of _____

_____

And the other Down that bothers me the most is _____

_____

All in all my life is _____

_____

_____

Signature

_____

Date

▸ Technique #5

Title:	A Penny For Your Thoughts
Technique category:	Disclosure Task
Objective:	To increase members' awareness of their issues and problems as a result of a traumatic experience.

Materials:

- At least five sentence completions prepared ahead of time that focus on increased awareness of members' problems and coping styles around a past trauma.
- Pennies

Procedure:

1. Before this group session, the facilitator will need to develop some sentence completions related to increased self-awareness of members' problems related to past trauma. Examples of such statements are listed below.

    - One thing that doesn't bother me so much anymore is . . .
    - Something upsetting that I think about almost every day is . . .
    - If only . . . didn't happen I would be so happy.
    - One way I have tried to feel better is . . .
    - The one thing others can do to help me right now is . . .

2. The session begins by introducing the saying of "A Penny for Your Thoughts." Members are told they will be playing a fun game where they will be given so much time to share their thoughts and receive a penny each time one of them does this disclosure.

3. The facilitator then briefly goes over the following rules for this game.

    - A sentence completion will be posed to the group and anyone who would like to respond can do so by taking a turn.
    - Each person who responds to a sentence completion will receive a penny for the group.
    - At the end of a designated period of time (15 to 20 minutes), the group as a whole will have to obtain a predetermined amount of pennies to win.
    - If the group acquires the number of pennies set as a goal, they win. If not, the facilitator wins.

4. The game is then played by the rules, using the sentence completions developed for each individual group.

5. Ask members to share one positive response they had to the experience.

Cautions/comments:

Usually, children enjoy this fun game of sharing their thoughts for pennies and thus winning the game. The competitive aspect of this intervention is intended to decrease the youngsters' anxiety regarding their problem disclosure. Facilitators may want to take notes regarding members' sharing content. This material can be further addressed in the following session. By keeping a list of the problems that surfaced, group leaders can modify future sessions to be more relevant to the membership's needs.

▶ Technique #6

Title:	Talk Back For Me
Technique category:	Creative Exercise
Objective:	To increase members' awareness of their difficulties in regard to their traumatic experience.

Materials:

- "Talk Back For Me" sheet found on page 264.
- Pencils

Procedure:

1. Members are told they are going to have an opportunity to participate in a creative exercise where they will make a talk back machine. Then, the form entitled "Talk Back For Me" is passed out to everyone.

2. Members are allowed 10 to 15 minutes to complete this task.

3. After everyone is done, each child takes a turn sharing their talk back machines. Facilitators should be the first to share. This will create a more comfortable setting for this disclosure.

4. Throughout the sharing, members' commonalities and significant disclosure should be reinforced.

5. At the end, everyone is asked to share in their own creative way the most enjoyable part of this creative experience.

Cautions/comments:

Creative exercises are wonderful ways for members to disclose more honestly and intimately in a group. Usually, these types of interventions offer youngsters a non-threatening way to share while at the same time increasing their own awareness level. The graphic use of a talk back machine helps children get in touch with some of the thoughts they would like to get off their mind. Also, the content that surfaces during this disclosure is often directly related to issues around past trauma. In some groups, facilitators may feel that it is better to have members do the "Talk Back For Me" sheets anonymously. The group leader can then collect the sheets and read the responses out loud.

▶ Talk Back For Me

Instructions: Make believe the talk back machine below is being programmed to say four things that are on your mind often and bother you. Write those four concerns in the spaces provided.

▸ Technique #7

Title:	The "Big Test"
Technique category:	In Vivo Experience
Objective:	To increase members' awareness of alternative ways to cope with traumatic experiences.

Materials:

- 3"x5" cards
- Pencils

Procedure:

1. This session is initiated by the facilitator explaining to the members that they are going to have a chance to brainstorm some alternative coping behaviors for one another. It is usually a good idea at this point to emphasize to the children that many of them have valuable ideas and skills to help one another handle some very difficult life problems.

2. Then, the facilitator introduces the term "The Big Test," and explains that this phrase usually means a situation that is the most difficult for a person to handle. It is a good idea to give either a personal example or real story with the "Big Test" related to facing something after a traumatic experience.

3. The youngsters are asked to relax for a few minutes, maybe even close their eyes, and think about what "Big Test" situation they would face.

4. Once everyone seems ready, the participants go around the circle one at a time sharing their "Big Test."

5. Members are asked to volunteer brainstorming ways to feel more comfortable about facing their "Big Test." As soon as a youngster volunteers, it is important to have them give more details about the situation that would be one of the toughest for them to face. Then, the group is asked to brainstorm ways for that child to cope more effectively with the big test event. At this point, the facilitator may want to note these suggestions on a 3"x5" card that can be given to the youngster at the end of this discussion.

6. This same procedure is followed for as many members' big test events that time permits being discussed. Group leaders may decide to go into another session with this same technique in order to address all members' "Big Test" situations.

7. It is important to process the youngsters' positive responses to this session.

Cautions/comments:

If a group is ready to get into this discussion, this technique can be most effective in allowing members to share coping skills with one another. Sometimes, facilitators may find that they need to share a personal example to set a more comfortable stage for this kind of sharing. Groups of children typically have a wealth of different coping behaviors that, if elicited, can be invaluable to one another. This "Big Test" concept often helps youngsters think preventively about tough situations related to a trauma.

▶ Technique #8

Title:	Pull Me Up
Technique category:	Completion Task
Objective:	To increase members' awareness of alternative ways of dealing with a traumatic experience.

Materials:

- Copies of the "Pull Me Up" sheet found on page 269.
- 3" x 5" cards prepared with coping problems relevant to members
- Scissors
- Twelve inch pieces of string
- Hole puncher

Procedure:

1. Before this session, the facilitator will need to gather some information on the specific difficulties group members are having in dealing with their traumatic experiences. Typical problem situations will need to be developed relevant to the youngsters' coping alternative needs. These should be written on 3" x 5" cards with one card prepared for each member's situation.

2. The session begins with the students being told that they will have an opportunity to learn more about alternative ways to cope with a traumatic experience via an enjoyable task. The sheet entitled "Pull Me Up" is then distributed to each group member.

3. The youngsters are asked to cut out this figure of a child. Once everyone has cut out their paper persons, a hole is punched in the top of the head of this figure. Next, a twelve inch piece of string is passed out to each child with the directions that they are to tie their string through the hole punched in the head of the paper person.

4. The facilitator then explains to the members that each of them will have an opportunity to figure out a coping alternative for the problem situation posed. It will be important to clarify that the cards contain typical difficulties children face when they have experienced a tragedy in life.

5. Next, each card is read out loud, a child volunteers to take it, and then writes on their paper person a coping behavior for the youngster in the story.

6. Once all the cards have been read and distributed, the group is given a designated period to complete this part of the exercise. Facilitators may also want to allow members to brainstorm ideas informally with one another.

7. Next, each group participant is asked to share their coping solution after the facilitator first reviews the problem written on their cards. When using this task with younger support groups, it is a good idea to have the children physically pull up their paper person as they read their answer to associate the response with a concrete action. All these paper people with coping responses can be collected and made into a group mobile. This mobile can be hung up and referred to in future sessions.

8. At the end of the session, members should be asked to share one coping solution given that was helpful to them.

Cautions/comments:

This is an excellent technique for helping group members think through and brainstorm with one another coping solutions to their difficulties. By utilizing this task in the format indicated, students are less anxious about having their unique difficulties addressed. Facilitators will notice that when the involved member's card is read, they usually pay very close attention and are eager to hear the coping suggestions given by peers.

▸ **Pull Me Up**

Instructions: Cut out the paper person below and wait for further directions from your group facilitator.

▸ Technique #9

Title:	Find The Words For You
Technique category:	Game Exercise
Objective:	To increase members' awareness of alternative ways to cope with difficulties related to a traumatic experience.

Materials:

- Form entitled "Find The Words For You" found on page 272.
- Pencils
- Blackboard
- Chalk

Procedure:

1. At the onset of this session, members are told they are going to be playing a fun wordfind game. Then, everyone is given a copy of the sheet entitled "Find The Words For You." Members are given a set period of time to complete these sheets following the directions provided.

2. Then, the rules below are reviewed with the membership.

   - Each member will get a turn in the game by going around the circle in order one after another.

   - When a member has his/her turn, they must share where one word is in the wordfind and then explain how that word is related to one of their needed coping skills.

   - This sharing continues around the circle until the contents of everyone's sheets have been shared.

   - Points will be gained by the group when words have been correctly found in the wordfind. Also, points will be obtained each time a member has been able to indicate how a word is alike or different from their coping style.

   - Points will be gained by the facilitator when words are not found in the wordfind or for every blank left at the bottom of the task sheets.

   - The one (group or facilitator) who has the most points at the end of this review wins.

3. The game is then conducted following the rules.

4. If time allows, discussion questions can be posed to the children in order to probe some of their earlier responses during the game.

5. At the end, everyone should be asked to complete the following sentence: "I really liked this session when _____."

Cautions/comments:

Participants will love playing this wordfind game. Usually, children enjoy the competitive element around this task so much that they forget about the fairly difficult or even anxiety provoking disclosure being elicited.

▸ Find The Words For You

Instructions: Circle the *10* words in the wordfind below that all have to do with ways to cope with things that have happened to you. Then, write five of these words below and explain what they have to do with your way of coping.

F	E	E	L	I	N	G	S	A	B
R	T	T	S	A	E	F	L	O	R
I	A	O	P	L	E	M	A	S	K
E	L	U	O	N	D	F	U	N	R
N	K	C	R	Y	Y	P	G	Q	S
D	S	H	T	M	O	F	H	A	G
S	E	A	S	L	P	A	S	T	E

	WORD	HOW IS THIS WORD ALIKE OR DIFFERENT FROM YOUR WAY OF COPING WITH PROBLEMS?
1		
2		
3		
4		
5		

▶ Technique #10

Title: Me Power

Technique category: Empowerment Exercise

Objective: To integrate into members' repertoire new coping alternatives.

Materials:

- Prepared list of 8 to 12 problem situations relevant to group members
- Blackboard
- Chalk

Procedure:

1. Before this session, the facilitator will need to prepare a list of problems common to the members of the group. It is important that these difficulties have surfaced in previous sessions and have been discussed for possible alternative solutions. Usually, it is best to have at least 8 to 12 such problems prepared.

2. The session begins by explaining to the members that they will be playing a fun exercise involving their "Me Power." Then, the following rules are briefly reviewed with the group.

   - A problem situation for a youngster will be posed to the entire group.

   - The group will have three minutes to come up with at least four different ways a kid could use their "Me Power" (in other words, things a kid has control over) to cope with or solve the problem posed.

   - Each round where the group comes up with four solutions in three minutes, they win. Each time they are not able to figure out four different solutions, the facilitator wins that round.

   - The one (group or facilitator) who wins the most rounds is the overall winner for the game.

3. The game is then played following the rules. It will be important to make sure the same group members are not the only ones making contributions. It is also a good idea to note contributions on a list on the blackboard to keep a count and make sure the solution suggestions are not repeats.

4. At the end of this enjoyable task, the facilitator can go back to the solution list on the board and pose some discussion questions. An example of such questions includes the following.

- Has anyone used any of these coping solutions? If yes, which ones?

- Which one of these coping behaviors was a new one for you to learn about?

- Who intends to try one of these coping behaviors in the future?

5. Members' positive responses to this intervention should be processed at the end of the session.

Cautions/comments:

This is a very effective technique for teaching members which aspects of a problem they have control over. Facilitators will find that children are invaluable resources to one another. By this point in the group, members will be sharing some of the things they have learned from previous sessions or from life experiences.

▸ Technique #11

Title: Just Call Your Helper

Technique category: Check-Ups/Assignments

Objective: To integrate into members' repertoire alternative coping behaviors.

Materials:

- A prepared list of members paired with peer helpers.
- Paper
- Pencils
- Copies of the form entitled "A Plan For My Peer Helper," found on page 277.

Procedure:

1. The preparation for this session is somewhat involved, due to its nature. Facilitators will need to determine a peer helper available in each member's school or neighborhood, who could be a good friend for them. It is usually best to contact teachers and parents for suggestions. These individuals should be asked to assist and actively support this peer pairing project. For example, parents can be requested to plan and arrange a fun event for the two kids, or teachers can be asked to have the two students work on an academic task together.

2. The session begins with participants being told that as a way of helping them maintain their changes, they are being asked to pair up with another peer. Then, the facilitator initiates a discussion in which members talk about their assignment, which is to make contact with their peer helper and begin to establish a relationship.

   In some groups, it may be helpful to structure this discussion by following the outline below.

   I. Knowledge of how to contact peer helper

   II. Ways to begin a relationship

   III. Things you and your peer helper can do together

   IV. Ways your peer helper can assist your maintenance of changes

3. Next, the facilitator passes out the form found on the following page, titled "A Plan for My Peer Helper," to each member, along with a pencil.

Participants are asked to write their plan, using some of the ideas that surfaced from the earlier discussion.

4. At the end of the session, members should be asked to share what they are looking forward to about having a peer helper.

Cautions/comments:

This is an excellent intervention for depressed and/or traumatized children. Often, these youngsters need some structured assistance for initially developing healthy relationships with peers. It is ideal if the peer helpers selected have already been through a peer helpers' training program at a school. When the group ends, these peer helpers may continue to be available to the participants and provide them some of the ongoing support they had been getting from the group. Friendships for these youngsters can be very effective in making significant and lifelong changes in their coping styles. This particular intervention is a very realistic need for most traumatized youngsters. Typically, these kids need ongoing help and support due to the nature of this at-risk problem area.

▶ A Plan For My Peer Helper

Instructions: Complete the following plan for getting together with your assigned peer helper.

1. I will first get with my peer helper by _____

    _____

    _____

    _____

2. Some things I think we can do together are:

    (1) _____

    _____

    _____

    (2) _____

    _____

    _____

3. I will stay in regular contact with my peer helper by _____

    _____

    _____

    _____

4. My peer helper can be of the most help to me by _____

    _____

    _____

▸ Technique #12

Title:	An S.O.S. Code Plan
Technique category:	Confirmation Task
Objective:	To integrate into members' repertoire new coping behaviors.

Materials needed:

- Copies of the sheet entitled "An S.O.S. Code Plan," found on page 279.
- Pencils

Procedure:

1. Pass out the sheet entitled "An S.O.S. Code Plan" to all group members.
2. Allow 5 to 10 minutes for the completion of this task.
3. Ask everyone to share their responses by going around the circle in order. The facilitator should initially share their responses to the task sheet for purposes of modeling.
4. If time allows, pose some discussion questions related to the task sheet responses.
5. Process members' positive reactions at the end of the session.

Cautions/comments:

This is a very effective technique for helping members to be prepared for difficulties around their trauma. Facilitators have to be realistic about how much of this at-risk problem area can be resolved in a short-term support group. The S.O.S. code plans provide members concrete ways to deal with trauma related problems as they surface in the future. For this reason, it is advisable to suggest that members take home and keep these plans. The concrete nature of this form will help remind youngsters of future ways to cope.

▶ An S.O.S. Code Plan

Instructions: Complete the S.O.S. Code Plan below as ways both you and the world around you will know you need help.

S.O.S. CODE FOR:

When I am _____

This means I need to talk to someone.

● ● ● — — — ● ● ●

When I am _____

This means I need to have more fun with friends.

● ● ● — — — ● ● ●

When I am _____

This means I need to get my feelings out.

● ● ● — — — ● ● ●

When I am _____

This means I need to _____

● ● ● — — — ● ● ●

▶ Bibliography

Losses in Childhood

Allan, John and Anderson, Eileen. Children and crises: a classroom guidance approach. *Elementary School Guidance and Counseling* 21(2):143-149, 1986.

Arena, Corinne et al. Helping children deal with the death of a classmate: a crisis intervention model. *Elementary School Guidance & Counseling* 19(2):107-115, 1984.

Beckman, Roberta. *Children Who Grieve and Workbook.* Doylestown, Marco, 1988.

Bernstein, J. *Books to Help Children Deal with Separation and Loss.* New York, R. R. Bowker, 1977.

Bertoia, Judi and Allan, John. Counseling seriously ill children: use of spontaneous drawings. *Elementary School Guidance & Counseling* 22(3):206-221, 1988.

Beste, H. M. and Richardson, R. G. Developing a life story book program for foster children. *Child Welfare* 60(8):529-34, 1981.

Cassini, Kathleen K. and Rogers, Jacqueline L. *Death and the Classroom.* Cincinnati, Griefwork of Cincinnati, Inc., 1990.

Cohn, Janice. *I Had a Friend Named Peter: Talking to Children About the Death of a Friend.* New York, Morrow, 1987.

Crow, Gary A. and Crow, Letha I. *Crisis Intervention and Suicide Prevention: Working with Children and Adolescents.* Springfield, Charles C. Thomas, 1987.

Fayerweather Street School Staff. *The Kids' Book About Death and Dying.* Boston, Little Brown & Co., 1985.

Gardner, Richard A. *Dr. Gardner's Fairy Tales for Today's Children.* Cresskill, Creative Therapeutics, 1974.

Haasl, Beth and Marnocha, Jean. *Bereavement Support Group Program for Children.* Muncie, Accelerated Development, 1990.

Hammond, Janice M. A parent's suicide: counseling the children. *The School Counselor* 27(5):385-388, 1980.

Heegaard, Marge. *When Someone Very Special Dies.* Minneapolis, Woodland Press, 1988.

Jewett, Claudia L. *Helping Children Cope with Separation and Loss.* Boston, Harvard Common, 1982.

Johnson, Kendall. *Trauma in the Lives of Children.* Mount Dora, Kids Rights, 1989.

Lombardo, Victor and Lombardo, Edith. *Kids Grieve Too.* Springfield, Charles C. Thomas, 1986.

Rofes, Eric E. *The Kids Book About Death and Dying: By and For Kids.* Boston, Little Brown & Co., 1985.

Rosenkrantz, L. and Joshua V. Children of incarcerated parents: a hidden population. *Children Today* 11(1):2-6, 1982.

Sandoval, Jonathan (editor). *Crisis Counseling Intervention and Prevention in the Schools.* Hillsdale, Lawrence Erlbaum Associates, 1988.

Schwarzrock, Shirley. *The Coping With Series, Revised.* Circle Press, American Guidance Service, 1984.

Staudt, M. Helping rural school children cope with the farm crisis. *Social Work in Education* 9(4):222-229, 1987.

Wass, H. and Corr, C. *Helping Children Cope With Death: Guidelines and Resources.* New York, Hemisphere/McGraw, 1982.

Wolfett, Alan. *Helping Children Cope with Grief.* Muncie, Accelerated Development, Inc., 1983.

Physically Abused/Neglected Children

Anderson, Deborah and Finne, Martha. *Robin's Story: Physical Abuse and Seeing the Doctor.* Minneapolis, Dillon, 1986.

Anderson, Deborah and Finne, Martha. *Michael's Story: Emotional Abuse and Working with a Counselor.* Minneapolis, Dillon, 1986.

Baxter, Arlene. *Techniques for Dealing with Child Abuse.* Springfield, Charles C. Thomas, 1985.

Clearinghouse on Child Abuse and Neglect, PO Box 1182, Washington, DC 20013.

Coolsen, Peter et al. *When School's Out and Nobody's Home.* National Committee for Prevention of Child Abuse, 332 South Michigan Avenue, Suite 950, Chicago, IL 60604, 1985.

Covitz, Joel D. *Emotional Child Abuse: The Family Cure.* Boston, Sigo Press, 1986.

Dean, D. Emotional abuse of children. *Children Today* 8(4):18-20, 1979.

Fairchild, Thomas N. (editor). *Crisis Intervention Strategies for School Based Helpers.* Springfield, Charles C. Thomas, 1986.

Fead, A. Kelley. *The Child Abuse Crisis: Impact on the Schools.* Alexandria, Capitol VA, 1985.

Furrer, P.J. *Art Therapy Activities and Lesson Plans for Individuals and Groups.* Springfield, Charles C. Thomas, 1982.

Garbarino, J. and Garbarino, A. C. *The Emotional Maltreatment of Children.* Chicago, National Committee for the Prevention of Child Abuse, 1980.

Garbarino, J. et al. *The Psychologically Battered Child: Strategies for Identification, Assessment, and Intervention.* San Francisco, Jossey-Bass Publishing Co., 1986.

Gil, Eliana M. *I Told My Secret: A Book for Kids Who Were Abused.* Walnut Creek, Launch Press, 1986.

Guerney, L. and Moore, L. Phone friend: a prevention-oriented service for latchkey children. *Children Today* 12(4):5-10, 1983.

Kehoe, Patricia. *Helping Abused Children: A Handbook.* Seattle, Parenting Press, 1988.

Kienzle, Patricia. *Sweet and Sour Secrets.* Doylestown, Marco, 1989.

Korbin, Jill (editor). *Child Abuse and Neglect: Cross Cultural Perspectives.* Denver, Kempe National Center, 1981.

Lane, Kristi. *Feelings Are Real.* Muncie, Accelerated Development, 1991.

Long, Lynette. *On My Own (The Kids Self-Care Book).* Washington, DC, Acropolis Books Ltd., 1984.

Morris-Vann, Artie M. *Group Counseling for Children Who Are Abused.* Oak Park, Aid-U Publishing Company, 1981.

Pall, Michael L. and Streit, Lois B. *Let's Talk About It: The Book for Children About Child Abuse.* Saratoga, R & E, 1983.

Sanders, Margo C. and DeVargas-Walker, Patricia. *Child Abuse: Empowering Victims to Become Survivors.* Vancouver, M. C. Saunders, 1987.

Sharmat, Marjorie. *My Mother Never Listens to Me.* Mount Dora, Kid Rights, 1984.

Stanek, Muriel. *All Alone After School.* Niles, Albert Whitman and Company, 1985.

Tzeng, Oliver and Jacobsen, Jamia J. (editors). *Sourcebook for Child Abuse and Neglect: Intervention, Treatment and Prevention Through Crisis Programs.* Springfield, Charles C. Thomas, 1988.

Wakcher, Bridget. *Child Abuse-Is It Happening to You?* Mount Dora, Kids Rights, 1982.

Walker, C. Eugene, et al. *The Physically and Sexually Abused Child: Evaluation and Treatment.* Elmsford, Pergamon, 1987.

Wayne, Julianne and Avery, Nancy C. *Child Abuse: Prevention and Treatment Through Social Group Work.* Boston, Charles River Books, 1979.

White, Laurie and Spencer, Steven L. *Take Care with Yourself.* Ann Arbor, Ballwing, Laurie White, 1915 Geddes Avenue, Ann Arbor, Michigan 48104.

Sexually Abused Children

Aho, Jennifer Sowle and Petras, John W. *Learning About Sexual Abuse.* Culver City, Social Studies School Service, 1985.

Baird, Kristin and Kile, Marilyn Y. *Body Rights.* Circle Pines, AGS Publishers, 1986.

Becliner, L. and Wheeler, R. Treating the effects of sexual abuse on children. *Journal of Interpersonal Violence* 2(4):415-433, 1987.

Blanchard, G. Male victims of child sexual abuse: a product of things to come. *Journal of Independent Social Work* 1(1):19-27, Fall 1986.

Briere, John and Reentz, T. Post sexual abuse trauma. *Journal of Interpersonal Violence* 2(4):435-437, 1987.

Davis, I. Lorraine. *Dealing with Child Sexual Assault and Abuse: A Resource and Planning Guide.* Madison, Wisconsin Department of Public Instruction, 1986.

Doyle, C. Helping the child victims of sexual abuse through play. *Practice* 1(1):27-38, 1987.

Edwards, D. L. and Gil, E. *Breaking the Cycle.* Los Angeles, Association for Advanced Training, 1987.

Finkelhor, David and Associates. *A Sourcebook on Child Sexual Abuse.* San Mateo, Sage, 1986.

Freeman, Lory. *It's My Body.* Seattle, Parenting Press, Inc., 1984.

Giarretto, H. *Integrated Treatment of Child Sexual Abuse: A Treatment and Training Manual.* Palo Alto, Science and Behavior Books, Inc., 1982.

Girard, Linda W. *My Body is Private.* Niles, Albert Whitman & Company, 1984.

Gordon, Sol and Gordon, Judith. *A Better Safe Than Sorry Book.* Fayetteville, Ed-U Press, Inc., 1984.

Hans, Ruth and James, Donna. *Talking About Touching.* Seattle, Committee for Children, 1984.

Hitchock, Ruth A. and Young, Dixie. Prevention of sexual assault: a curriculum for elementary school counselors. *Elementary School Guidance & Counseling* 20(3):201-207, 1986.

Holtgraves, Marnell. Help the victims of sexual abuse help themselves. *Elementary School Guidance & Counseling* 21(2):155-159, 1986.

James B. and Nasileti, M. *Treating Sexually Abused Children and Their Families.* Palo Alto, Consulting Psychologist Press, 1983.

Kile, Marilyn J. et al. *Body Rights - A Duso Approach.* Circle Pines, American Guidance Service, 1986.

Mrazek, P. B. and Kempe, C. H. (editors). *Sexually Abused Children and Their Families.* New York, Pergamon Press, 1981.

Nelson, M. and Clark, K. (editors). *The Educator's Guide to Preventing Sexual Abuse.* Santa Cruz, Network Publications, 1986.

Plummer, Carol A. *Preventing Sexual Abuse: Activities and Strategies for Those Working with Children and Adolescents.* Holmes Beach, Learning Publications, Inc., 1984.

Porter, E. *Treating the Young Male Victim of Sexual Assault: Issues and Intervention Strategies.* Orwell, Safer Society Press, 1986.

Schetky, Diane H. and Green, Arthur H. *Child Sexual Abuse.* New York, Brunner/Mazel, 1988.

Sgroi, Suzanne M. *Handbook of Clinical Intervention in Child Sexual Abuse.* Lexington, Lexington Books, 1982.

Summit, R. C. The child sexual abuse accommodation syndrome. *Child Abuse and Neglect* 7(2):177-193, 1983.

Chapter 10

Stress Management Support Group Curriculum

A complete curriculum for stress management support groups is provided in this chapter. Step-by-step instructions are outlined for the unique set-up, planning, and facilitation of this type of elementary age support group. An extensive listing of assessment scales, session themes, bibliotherapy books, videotapes/films, and "how-to-do-it" references are included as part of this practical support group guide. This chapter, along with Chapters One, Two, Three, and Thirteen, will provide complete instructions for the set-up through the termination of stress management support groups.

Treatment Guidelines

Stress levels in our society are at all-time highs. As more and more adults are affected by this national disease, so too are their offspring. We are finding that almost all adult symptoms of stress overload have impacted to a lesser, but significant degree, on elementary age children. Today for the first time, counselors are treating youngsters with severe migraines, obesity, eating disorders, substance abuse, severe physical complaints including stomachaches and ulcers, along with other anxiety-related difficulties. These are obviously not healthy times when such severe symptoms are being experienced by our younger generation.

Facilitators have a tall order when seeing these children in a stress management support group. Many times, this therapeutic experience goes counter to the messages of the greater society and more specifically those from the members' families. Even so, clinicians will find that this modality can offer many benefits to this population. In particular, the group can normalize the youngsters' feelings, provide opportunities for members to share coping alternatives, assist the children in changing their expectations of themselves, and help them develop a preventive plan for future times of stress. Children are perceptive and are often able to make significant changes in their daily living in spite of the modeling by adults around them.

Before utilizing this curriculum, the reader should review the following general treatment guidelines for working with stress management support groups with children.

1. Before a group begins, it is often helpful to get a more specific evaluation of each member's common sources of stress. Such data can be most efficiently collected by using one of the objective scales listed in the assessment instrument section of this curriculum. This information is helpful both in establishing a baseline functioning for each youngster and in providing some relevant ideas for group sessions.

2. Clinicians need to be sensitive to the types of pressure members' parents and schools are placing on them. It is not uncommon that these two sources often expect too much of these youngsters. A counselor may need to spend some of their treatment efforts in helping educate teachers and parents regarding the effect of their expectation levels on children's overall stress.

3. Support groups for this particular population are therapeutic in and of themselves when they provide fun settings for members. These youngsters need to experience enjoyment on a regular basis and process their responses to it. Facilitators should have as their primary goal the creation of an attractive, fun, and stress-free support group setting for these students.

4. These youngsters often benefit from assignments outside the group. Such interventions help members generalize knowledge and skills gained from the group to outside environments. Clinicians will have to use their expertise in developing assignments that are relevant for participants and have a high probability of being carried out successfully.

5. Group members can often serve as excellent models for each other. Members of the same group will have different areas of stress coping strengths and will be able to share these with one another.

6. Some overly stressed youngsters are also candidates for fairly serious levels of depression. Whenever a clinician feels that such a situation exists for a child, further evaluation will be necessary to determine the severity of the depression and the possibility of suicidal thoughts or plans. If a youngster is identified as seriously depressed, it is usually best to see them in individual counseling. In addition, clinicians must inform parents or guardians of a child's serious level of depression.

7. Often these children benefit from books, films, videotapes, and related techniques that provide graphic models on the subject of stress. Facilitators should look over the techniques in this curriculum and consider using them, particularly with youngsters who have few models in their natural environment who demonstrate good stress coping skills.

8. Overly stressed kids can sometimes be empowered through a group to go back and help an environment (like home or school) make some changes that could reduce the high levels of pressure. Facilitators will have to carefully assess, plan, and instruct members in this process. Readers should remember that children can have a significant impact on their environments when they are taught effective skills in approaching and handling such situations.

9. Many of these youngsters need to learn which parts of their lives they have control over. When these kids are able to differentiate where they can have impact and where they cannot, they are on the road to getting better.

10. It is extremely important for this population to have group facilitators who are handling their own stress and are able to model effective coping skills. The counselor has tremendous impact on members. Youngsters will learn far more from getting to know and watch their facilitator than almost any other single variable in the group experience.

Assessment Instruments

1. Assessment of Coping Style
2. Children's Inventory of Anger
3. Children's Version/Family Environment Scale
4. Hopeless Scale for Children
5. Inferred Self-Concept Scale

6. Quality of School Life Scale
7. Revised Children's Manifest Anxiety Scale
8. Reynold's Child Depression Scale
9. School Child Stress Scale
10. Stress Response Scale

Relevant Session Themes

Normalization of feelings

Increased sense of not being alone

Lower expectations of self

Increased skills in setting priorities

Affective awareness

Increased communication skills particularly around feelings

Skills in being aware of and taking care of one's needs

Improved self-concept

Skills for balanced lives

Understanding of the effects of overloads of stress

Skills in being able to identify and concentrate on areas of control

Increased ability to relax and have fun

Interests that turn off usual sources of stress

Skills in finding supports in environment that reinforce changes

Development of healthy peers as ongoing friends

Awareness of stress-inducing self-talk and the development of stress reduction internal messages

Awareness of one's self-expectations and priorities

Increased knowledge of how to cope effectively with stress

Increased awareness of the sources and results of one's stress level

Planning Sequence of Objectives & Techniques for Stress Management Support Group

Group Phase	Group Goals	Intervention Categories
Initial	1. To provide an attractive group setting. 2. To initiate members' participation on-task and with one another. 3. To initiate trust among the membership.	**Hello Group Techniques** (Chapter Three)
	4. To educate members about issues and difficulties related to stress overload.	**Instructive Techniques:** #1 A Living Example #2 Bibliotherapy/Video/Films #3 Words That Spell Stress
Middle	5. To increase group development goals established in initial phase (i.e., goals 1-3).	No techniques per se but follow curriculum approach.
	6. To increase members' awareness of their particular difficulties related to stress management.	**Awareness of Self Techniques:** #4 Picture Perfect #5 Out Of Balance #6 Stress Combat
	7. To provide alternative coping behaviors for handling high levels of stress.	**Alternative Coping Techniques:** #7 Stress Counter Attack #8 Build A Stress Relief Ladder #9 What's Your Secret?
	8. To assist members in the integration of new coping behaviors into their repertoire.	**Integration Techniques:** #10 Throw Me A Line #11 Stress Check #12 Prove It
Termination	9. To have members acknowledge the value of the group. 10. To assist members in validating their changes. 11. To have members brainstorm other sources of support. 12. To have members grieve the ending of group.	**Goodbye Group Techniques** (Chapter Thirteen)

▸ Technique #1

Title:	A Living Example
Technique category:	Didactic
Objective:	To instruct members regarding the causes and consequences of stress overload.

Materials:

- Structured discussion questions prepared ahead of time.

Procedure:

1. Before this session, the facilitator will need to identify a youngster (not a member of the group) who has successfully learned to manage his/her stress. This child could be a peer of a similar age to group members or an adolescent. It will be important to clearly identify what particular focus the selected youngster's presentation should address. Also, it may be helpful to have that child do at least a one-time through demonstration for the facilitator to make sure that they have a clear speaking style. The youngster should be asked to share the causes and consequences of times in life of too much stress and ineffective coping skills. It will be important that at some point the presenter indicate some specifics on how he/she was able to get their stress under control and to highlight the differences those behavioral changes made.

2. The facilitator begins the session by informing the members that they will have the opportunity to hear someone talk about personal experiences handling stress. Participants should be asked to listen carefully to the presentation and hold their questions until the end.

3. At the end of the session, members should be asked to share one thing they learned from the speaker.

Cautions/comments:

This utilization of a model peer is an excellent way to help group members see the causes and consequences of having a stress overload. Facilitators will find that the impact of a personal story is much more effective than most other instructive interventions. Also, the modeling by the selected peer helps participants feel more hopeful about learning how to cope with their own stress levels.

▶ Technique #2

Title: Bibliotherapy/Video/Films

Technique category: Bibliotherapy/Video/Films

Objective: To instruct the group about the causes and consequences of stress overload.

Materials:

- Book, film, or videotape selected from the list on page 292.
- Equipment for film or videotape, if used.
- Prepared discussion questions related to the theme of the visual aid chosen.

Procedure:

1. Before the session, the facilitator selects a book, film, or videotape from the list on page 292.
2. Session begins with the book being read or film/videotape being shown.
3. At completion of above task, members can be asked discussion questions that surface their identification with the story. Also, some disclosure can be elicited that explores the children's similar problems and struggles.
4. Members' favorite parts of the book, film, or videotape should be processed at the end.

Cautions/comments:

Typically, members will enjoy the use of bibliotherapy materials or films/video-tapes. Through these types of visual interventions, children can more easily learn about their stress management skills. In addition, youngsters in elementary grades typically identify with characters in books and films. As a result, they are often able to talk more comfortably about their similar issues via the story presented.

Readers are advised to select books that have colorful pictures on almost every page. Children as a whole find it easier to understand the message of a book page when a graphic design depicts the concept. Also, facilitators should be careful that books and films/videotapes selected are not too long. It is important to have time in the session to pose discussion questions and process reactions among the members.

▶ **Bibliotherapy**

1. Anderson, Leone. *It's OK to Cry.* The Child's World, Inc., 1979, ages 5-8.

2. Bedford, Stewart. *Tiger Juice: A Book About Stress for Kids (of All Ages).* A & S Publishers, 1981.

3. Bell, Neill. *Only Human.* Little, Brown & Company, 1983, grades 4-6.

4. Berry, Joy Wilt. *Survival Series for Kids* (set of 28 books). Children's Press, 1982-87, grades 3-6.

5. Berry, Joy. *Every Kid's Guide to Coping with Childhood Trauma.* Children's Press, 1988, grades 3-6.

6. Berry, Joy. *Every Kid's Guide to Laws that Relate to School and Work.* Children's Press, 1987, grades 3-6.

7. Berry, Joy. *Every Kid's Guide to Being Special.* Children's Press, 1987, grades 3-6.

8. Berry, Marilyn. *Help is on the Way for Listening Skills.* Children's Press, 1987, grades 4-6.

9. Berry, Marilyn. *Skills on Studying* (set of 24 books). Children's Press, 1984-87, grades 4-6.

10. Blume, Judy. *Tales of a Fourth Grade Nothing.* Dell, 1986, grades K-6.

11. Bottner, Barbara. *The World's Greatest Expert on Absolutely Nothing . . . Is Crying.* Dell, 1984, grades 3-6.

12. Cohen, Miriam. *First Grade Takes a Test.* Greenwillow, 1980, grades P-3.

13. Delton, Judy. *I Never Win!* Caroldon Books, Inc. (PO Box 17391, Pensacola, FL 32522), ages 4-7.

14. Fassler, Joan. *The Boy With a Problem: Johnny Learns to Share His Troubles.* Human Sciences Press, 1971, grades P-3.

15. Friday, Beverly and Wiles, Carol. *Patience.* Children's Press, 1986, grades P-3.

16. Giff, Patricia Reilly. *The Girl Who Knew It All.* Delacorte Press, 1979, ages 8-10.

17. Giff, Patricia R. *Today Was a Terrible Day.* Live Oak Media, 1984, grades K-3.

18. Giff, Patricia Reilly. *Next Year I'll Be Special.* Dutton, 1980, grades K-3.

19. Gross, Alan. *What if the Teacher Calls on Me?* Children's Press, 1980, grades P-3.

20. Hoban, Russell. *The Little Brute Family.* Macmillan, 1969, grades K-3.

21. Kirkland, Dianna C. *Last Year I Failed . . . but.* Aid-U-Publishers, 1981, grades P-5.

22. Kyte, Kathy S. *In Charge: A Complete Handbook for Kids with Working Parents.* Knopf, 1983, grades 5-6.

23. Laiken, Deidre S. and Schneider, Alan J. *Listen to Me, I'm Angry.* Lothrop, 1980, grades 5-6.

24. Long, Lynette. *On My Own: The Kids' Self-Care Book.* Acropolis Books, 1984, grades 4-6.

25. Odor, Ruth S. *Moods and Emotions.* Child's World, 1981, grades 2-6.

26. Ruckman, Ivy. *What's an Average Kid Like Me Doing Way Up Here?* Delacorte, 1983, grades 4-6.

27. Shreve, Susan. *The Flunking of Joshua T. Bates.* Knopf, 1984, grades 2-6.

28. Stine, Jane and Stine, Jovial. *Everything You Need to Survive Homework.* Random House, 1983, grades 5-6.

29. White, Laurie and Spencer, Steven L. *Take Care of Yourself.* Flint, Michigan, self-published, 1983, ages 3-10.

30. Wreat, Pattie. *Why Does It Hurt to Be You?* Parents Anonymous (Los Angeles), 1981, ages 4-12.

Videotapes

1. Brade's Learning Disability
   Coronet, 1 film (13 minutes), grades K-3.

2. But They Might Laugh
   National Instruction T.V., 1973, 1 film (15 minutes), grades 4-6.

3. Decisions, Decisions, Decisions!
   Barr Films, 1 film, grades 4-6.

4. Everybody's Different and That's OK
   Barr Films, 1979, 1 film reel (15 minutes), grades 1-6.

5. I'm Feeling Alone
   Churchill Films, 1974, 8-minute film, grades 1-3.

6. Learning to Cope
   Learning Corporation of America/MTI, 1979, 24-minute film, grades 4-6.

7. Less Stress
   Churchill Film, 1 film (14 minutes), grades K-6.

8. Living With Stress
   Guidance Associates, videotape (22 minutes), grades 4-6.

9. Never Say You Can't Until You Try
   Guidance Associates, 1975, 1 film reel (11 minutes), grades 4-6.

10. Productivity and Performance
    Journal Films, 1 film (24 minutes) grades K-6.

11. Seven Wishes of a Rich Kid
    Learning Corporation of America/MTI, 1 film (30 minutes), grades K-6.

12. Stress: Learning How to Handle It
    Films Media, 1 film (23 minutes), grades 4-6.

13. Up One Day - Down the Next: Why Do I Feel the Way I Do?
    Guidance Associates, videotape (60 minutes), grades 4-6.

14. What's the Good of a Test?
    Journal Films, 1 film (13 minutes), grades 4-6.

15. You Can Make It If You Try
    Barr Films, 1 film (15 minutes), grades K-6.

Films

1. *Coping With Life: Frustration and Disappointment*
   Guidance Associates, 2 filmstrips/cassettes, grades 4-6.

2. *Coping With Stress*
   Creative Learning, Inc., 4 filmstrips/video, grades 4-6.

3. *Dealing With Feelings*
   American School Publishers, 4 filmstrips/cassettes, grades K-3 and 6 filmstrips/cassettes, grades 3-6.

4. *Dealing With Feelings: Hurt, Anger, Sharing*
   Guidance Associates, 4 filmstrips/cassettes, grades 4-6.

5. *Developing Self-Confidence*
   Creative Learning, Inc., 4 filmstrips, grades 4-6.

6. *Developing Self-Esteem: Taking Pride in Who You Are*
   Guidance Associates, 1 filmstrip (7 minutes), grades K-3.

7. *Good Study Habits*
   Creative Learning, Inc., 4 filmstrips, grades 4-6.

8. *Overcoming Handicaps*
   Listen and Learn Company, 4 filmstrips/cassettes, grades 4-8.

9. *Take It Easy: Dealing With Stress*
   Sunburst, 2 filmstrips/cassettes, grades 5-6.

10. *The Group and You: Handling the Pressures*
    Sunburst, 2 filmstrips/cassettes, grades 5-6.

11. *What's So Great About Being Smart?*
    Listen and Learn Company, 1 filmstrip/cassette, grades 4-6.

▸ Technique #3

Title:	Words That Spell Stress
Technique category:	Paper/Pencil Task
Objective:	To instruct members about the causes and consequences of stress overload.

Materials needed:

- Copies of the sheet entitled "Think Of A Word," found on page 296.
- Pencils

Procedure:

1. Pass out the sheet entitled "Think Of A Word" to all group members.
2. Allow 5 to 10 minutes for the completion of this task.
3. Ask everyone to share their responses by going around the circle in order. The facilitator should initially share their responses to the task sheet for purposes of modeling.
4. If time allows, pose some discussion questions related to the task sheet responses.
5. Process members' positive reactions at the end of the session.

Cautions/comments:

This is a non-threatening way to have youngsters begin a relevant discussion on the common causes of childhood stress. Typically, members will enjoy the familiarity of this word game task. Many of the words or phrases developed by the participants are based on their own experiences.

▸ **Think Of A Word**

Instructions: Use the letters from the word "STRESS" to list things that cause kids like yourself stress. The word or phrase must begin with the letter on each line. See if you can come up with some clever ideas.

S _____

T _____

R _____

E _____

S _____

S _____

Now, in the arrow below, draw something that causes your stress load to go up.

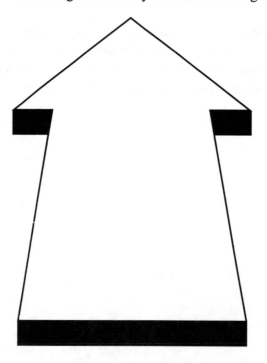

▶ Technique #4

Title:	Picture Perfect
Technique category:	Exercise Using the Arts
Objective:	To increase members' awareness of their stress related problems.

Materials:

- Copies of the sheet entitled "Picture Perfect," found on page 298.
- Pencils
- Markers
- Crayons

Procedure:

1. Copies of the sheet entitled "Picture Perfect" are passed out to members along with markers and crayons at the beginning of the session.

2. Participants are instructed to take about ten minutes to complete their picture. In particular, the youngsters should be urged to concentrate on what would be picture perfect in their lives and allow them to be less stressed.

3. All members are asked to show and clarify the meaning of their pictures in regard to their current problems with stress. While this sharing is going on, the facilitator may want to note on the blackboard the sources of stress indicated and any resulting consequences.

4. At the end of the session, members should be asked to share what they enjoyed most about this intervention.

Cautions/comments:

Picture completions are wonderful ways to elicit lots of disclosure from children. Often, they are able to say much more via this non-verbal intervention. Having the youngsters think about a picture perfect life makes them less anxious about the implications of their drawings. Usually this back door approach helps the members identify at a gut level the causes of their stress and some of the consequences.

▸ **Picture Perfect**

Instructions: Pretend you took a picture of a perfect life for you free of stress. Draw this photograph and write any changes you would want on it.

▸ Technique #5

Title:	Out Of Balance
Technique category:	Disclosure Task
Objective:	To increase members' awareness of their stress related problems.

Materials:

- Blackboard
- Chalk
- Form entitled "Out of Balance," found on page 300.
- Pencils

Procedure:

1. This session begins with members being told they will have a chance to talk about signs of being under too much stress. The facilitator directs the group to brainstorm various signs that indicate someone is under lots of stress. The list developed is written on the blackboard. When conducting younger support groups, counselors may want to make this brainstorming into a fun game.

2. Next, the youngsters are asked to complete the form entitled "Out of Balance" in a designated period of time.

3. Members take turns sharing the problems or signs they wrote in the right side pan of the scale. After this disclosure, it may also be helpful to suggest that participants be more observant over the next week of problems that seem to typically result from an overload of stress.

4. Members are asked to share what they learned from this session.

Cautions/comments:

This technique is an excellent way for children to begin being aware of what happens when they are under too much stress. It is also helpful for members to connect causes with the feelings of being overly stressed. With just a little instructing and sharing, even very young children can begin monitoring their stress level. Some youngsters may even be able to make significant changes just by this increased awareness.

▶ Out Of Balance

Instructions: Make believe you are the scale below. Fill in the right side pan with four problems or signs you experience when you are overly stressed.

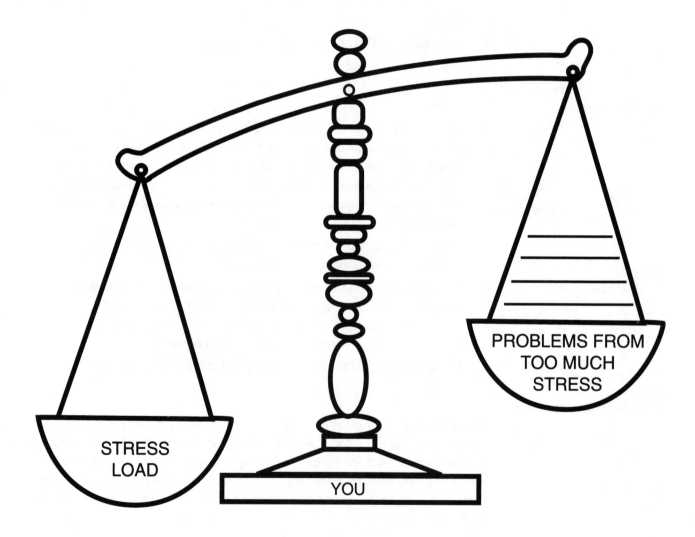

▶ Technique #6

Title: Stress Combat

Technique category: Creative Exercise

Objective: To increase members' awareness of their difficulties related to stress overload.

Materials:

- "Stress Combat" form found on page 302.
- Pencils
- Crayons

Procedure:

1. Members are told they are going to have an opportunity to create a video game. Then, the sheet entitled "Stress Combat" is distributed to everyone with the instructions reviewed.

2. Members are allowed 10 to 15 minutes to complete this task.

3. After everyone is done, each child takes a turn sharing their video games, with particular attention to the level they can beat. Facilitators should be the first to share. This will create a more comfortable setting for this disclosure.

4. Throughout the above sharing, members' commonalities and significant disclosure should be reinforced.

5. At the end of the session, members should be asked to share what the exercise taught them about their stress coping skill level.

Cautions/comments:

In this day and age, youngsters typically love anything to do with video games. So this exercise quickly elicits their attention and makes the disclosure task much more fun. The very format of this particular technique will surface considerable disclosure regarding members' stress related problems and their current coping skills.

▸ Stress Combat

Instructions: Pretend you are creating a video game based on the stresses in your life. Write the four levels for the game below. Then write or draw on the screen the level you are able to beat.

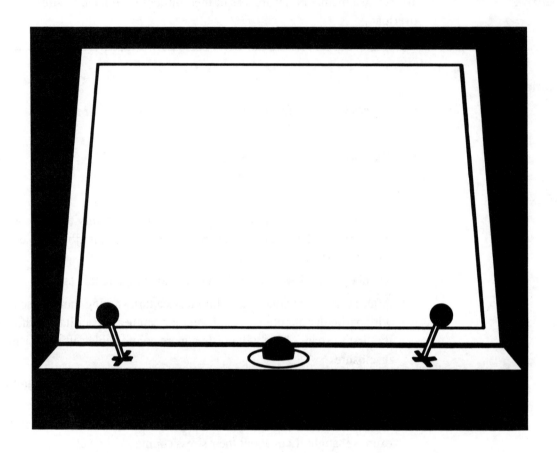

Level #1: _____

Level #2: _____

Level #3: _____

Level #4: _____

This last one means you beat the stress combat video game.

▸ Technique #7

Title: Stress Counter Attack

Technique category: In Vivo Exercise

Objective: To increase members' awareness of alternatives for coping with stress.

Materials:

- Prepared situations that would be potentially stressful to group members
- Coping alternatives indicated on 3" x 5" cards

Procedure:

1. Before this session, the facilitator will need to prepare a series of situations that would be potentially stressful to group members. It is important that these events are relevant for the youngsters. The facilitator will need to prepare some cards with types of coping responses to stress. It is usually best to label these cards with general terms so that the members can fill in specific details. Examples of such general categories for these cards are listed below.

• Self-talk	• Promise self a reward
• Self-relaxation	• Organize one's time
• Change expectations	• Ask for help
• Calm self	• Express feelings
• Positive affirmations	• Look to others as models

2. The session begins with the facilitator briefly going over the coping responses on the cards. It may also be helpful to ask the members themselves if they have other ideas on ways to cope with stress. These suggestions can be added to other cards.

3. Members are then instructed that they will be participating in a stress counter attack experience. The prepared 3" x 5" cards are laid out on the table with the coping skills showing. The youngsters are told that they will each have a one-minute time period for their turn at this experience.

4. Each child's turn consists of the facilitator reading a typical stressful situation for kids. Within one minute, the youngster must pick up the stress coping card from the table that would best counter attack the situation posed. After each member's turn, there should be a discussion on the

rationale behind the card selected. Also, participants should be encouraged to offer other ideas. This procedure is followed for all members' turns.

5. At the end of the session, participants should be asked to share what they learned from this exercise.

Cautions/comments:

This can be a very effective technique for participants understanding on more of a gut level the alternative responses they can have to stress. The youngsters will increase their repertoire of all the different ways one can effectively handle stress. Typically in a support group, children will serve as wonderful models for one another, since many of them will have different strengths in their coping skills. Facilitators are reminded to make sure that the stressful events posed are as relevant as possible to group members' experiences. The more youngsters identify with the situations, the more likely they will be to generalize the skills outside the group.

▸ Technique #8

Title: Build A Stress Relief Ladder

Technique category: Completion Task

Objective: To increase members' awareness of alternatives for coping with stress.

Materials:

- Form entitled "Build A Stress Relief Ladder," found on page 306.
- Pencils

Procedure:

1. This session begins with the group members being told they will be playing a fun beat-the-clock task. The participants are all asked to get into a relaxed position, close their eyes, and start thinking about what they are like when they are more fully rested and relaxed. The facilitator may find it beneficial to provide examples of some things kids can do to maintain a lower stress state of functioning. Such suggestions could include balanced diet, exercise, positive self-talk, fun times, getting enough sleep, alone time, expressing feelings, and getting bothersome things off one's mind.

2. The facilitator passes out copies of the "Build A Stress Relief Ladder" form. Participants are told that they will have so many minutes (e.g., ten minutes) to complete the ladder with each rung containing a way they become less stressed.

3. All group members are asked to take turns sharing the content of their stress relief ladder. Facilitators should feel free to probe youngsters during their sharing to elicit further details on their utilization of specific coping techniques.

4. At the end of the session, members should be asked to share what was most enjoyable.

Cautions/comments:

Many youngsters will find this approach quite effective in discovering their best ways to cope with stress. Also, members will serve as excellent models for one another so that they each increase their repertoire of coping alternatives. This exercise emphasizes a valuable point about the need to have a wide variety of coping skills for life stresses. In addition, many youngsters find the concrete and graphic use of the ladder a valuable tool to probe their knowledge of stress coping responses.

▶ Build A Stress Relief Ladder

Instructions: When your facilitator says begin, you will have so much time to fill in each rung of the ladder below with effective ways you can cope with stress.

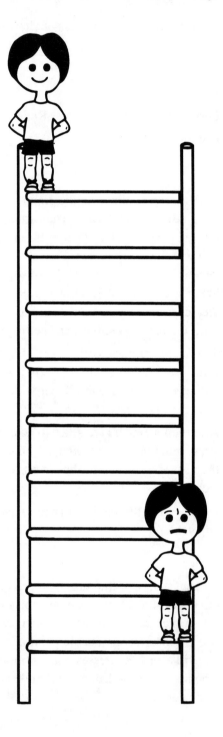

▸ Technique #9

Title:	What's Your Secret?
Technique category:	Game Exercise
Objective:	To increase members' awareness of alternatives for coping with stress.

Materials:

- 3" x 5" cards with the 12 coping strategies written on them, one to each card
- Blank 3" x 5" cards for members' ideas

Procedure:

1. Before this session, twelve 3" x 5" cards are prepared with the coping strategies listed below.

• good diet	• confidence
• exercise	• positive self-talk
• organize	• take care anger
• fun time	• relax
• ask for help	• stop worrying
• talk out feelings	• change expectations

2. At the onset of the session, members are asked to guess the content of these cards and to come up with new ideas for ways to cope with stress.

3. Next, members are told they are going to play a game of "Pass The Secret" and the rules below are then reviewed with the group.

   - All of the 3" x 5" cards will be shuffled and handed out, one to each member. Extra cards should just be left in the pile for the next round of the game.

   - Each member looks at their card and then turns it over.

   - The secret passing part then begins, with youngsters one right after another around the circle telling the content of their card and all cards of members before them.

   - By the time the series of secrets has gone around the full circle, the last child must get up and correctly give the order of them.

   - Each member turns over their card to check on the accuracy of this secret passing game.

- This same procedure can be followed for additional rounds as time permits.

4. At the end of this session, youngsters should be asked to share what was most beneficial and enjoyable about this game.

Cautions/comments:

Children usually find this secret passing activity lots of fun. The disclosure elicited is therefore less anxiety provoking. Also, the technique provides an easy attention holding format for teaching coping strategies for stress management. In addition, the sharing among the youngsters normalizes their feelings and provides excellent modeling. The memorizing of coping alternatives in this game helps members learn this very important material.

▶ Technique #10

Title: Throw Me A Line

Technique category: Empowerment Exercise

Objective: To integrate into members' repertoire new coping behaviors for stress management.

Materials:

- A real lifeline or one made from cardboard with a round preserver at the end so it can be thrown over the head of each member in this exercise

Procedure:

1. At the beginning of this session, members are informed that they are going to have an opportunity to see how much they have learned about coping with stress. Then, everyone is asked to think over their past week and recall a time when they felt overly stressed.

2. The membership is shown a lifeline that will be used in this task. The youngsters are instructed that they will each briefly describe their stressful experience and the group will have two minutes to give the presenting member a coping strategy. When a youngster comes up with a suggestion, they also get a chance at throwing the life preserver line around the member who is having their turn.

3. Everyone then shares their story and participates in the lifeline throwing. Facilitators should note and reinforce commonalities as they surface.

4. At the end of the session, the youngsters should be asked to share the best part of the intervention for them.

Cautions/comments:

Usually, children love the concrete association of a lifeline with stress coping suggestions. Also, this technique shows members on a gut level how much they have learned about handling stressful situations. The fun competitive nature of this task tends to make the sharing less difficult. In addition, by having the membership brainstorm coping strategies for real life situations, the youngsters are able to easily generalize the learning.

▶ Technique #11

Title: Stress Check

Technique category: Check-Up/Assignment

Objective: To integrate into members' repertoire new coping behaviors for stress management.

Materials:

- Copies (two per member) of the sheet entitled "Stress Log," found on page 312.
- Prepared discussion questions

Procedure:

1. Members are instructed to spend the week between sessions monitoring their stress levels in various situations. Usually, it is best to provide the youngsters with a log form like the one entitled "Stress Log." The facilitator will need to briefly outline to members how to maintain their log on their stress level. It is best to advise children to remember to do the log at the same time of day and to associate it with another regular activity so it is not forgotten.

2. Readers may want to have group members use biodots (available from Biodots International, 1-800-272-2340, about 10 cents each), which last for a week and provide color change feedback regarding one's stress level. There are very clear and concise instructions in the packet when you order the biodots from the publisher. Even young children enjoy watching their dots change color and begin to see the association of certain events with resulting stress levels.

3. When this session begins, the participants are asked to share the results of their week of monitoring. Group leaders should point out commonalities that arise during this discussion.

4. At the end of this disclosure, some structured discussion questions are posed to the group. Examples of such questions are listed below.

   - Where did you see yourself most stressed?
   - Were you surprised by the results of your logging? If yes, in what way?
   - Name some of the ways you noticed you are coping more effectively with your stress level.

5.   Participants should be asked to share what was most helpful about the self-monitoring and/or the session discussion.

Cautions/comments:

This assignment of monitoring one's stress level usually proves to be an excellent intervention for validating members' changes. This experience gives the youngsters some insight into times when they still need to work on handling their stress. Facilitators will find that students typically love using the biodots which help members be more accurate in their stress level monitoring.

▸ **Stress Log**

Instructions: Keep the log below on your stress level this next week. Use this number rating for your stress level:

1 = a little stressful   2 = stressful   3 = very stressful

Date: _____ Stress Level Today: _____

Reason for Rating: _____

_____

_____

_____

Date: _____ Stress Level Today: _____

Reason for Rating: _____

_____

_____

_____

Date: _____ Stress Level Today: _____

Reason for Rating: _____

_____

_____

_____

Date: _____ Stress Level Today: _____

Reason for Rating: _____

_____

_____

_____

▶ **Technique #12**

Title: Prove It

Technique category: Confirmation Task

Objective: To integrate into members' repertoire new coping behaviors for stress management.

Materials:

- Blank paper
- Pencils
- Form entitled "Up From Stress," found on page 315.

Procedure:

1. The session begins with the members being told they will have an opportunity to show how much they have learned about managing their stress. Then, blank sheets of paper and pencils are passed out to everyone.

2. Participants are briefly given the following rules for this game.

   - Round one will involve the members being given three minutes to write as many causes of being overly stressed as possible. Everyone who comes up with at least eight things on their list earns a point for the group. Members who do not have a minimum of eight items on their list earn a point for the facilitator. The one (group or facilitator) who has the most points at the end wins round one.

   - Round two involves all members developing a list of problems someone can have when they are under too much stress. In a three minute period, members who have at least five things on their list earn a point for the group. Members who do not have a minimum of five problems earn a point for the facilitator. Again, the one with the most points wins round two.

   - Round three involves the same type of challenge, but now members have three minutes to write down eight alternative stress coping strategies they have learned in the group. The form entitled "Up From Stress," found on the following page, is passed out to all members, along with pencils. Participants are instructed to use this form to write their eight coping strategies on the balloons. Members who do not list a minimum of eight coping strategies earn a point for the facilitator. Again, the one with the most points wins round three.

4. After each round of these challenging tasks, the facilitator should further probe members about their lists. In particular, commonalities should be noted, along with well-developed ideas on how to cope more effectively with one's stress level.

5. Members at the end of the session should be asked to indicate how this exercise reminded them about their progress in the group.

Cautions/comments:

Children typically love this series of fun games. Often, they do not even realize until the end of a support group how much they have learned about stress and ways to cope with it effectively. Facilitators should suggest that the youngsters take their lists home to serve as reminders.

Facilitators may find this task to be too high a level for kindergarten through third graders. A modified version of this technique should be planned for these groups. A suggested idea is to play the same type of competition, but instead to have all members verbally brainstorm these three lists.

▶ Up From Stress

Instructions: Write on all the balloons below eight ways you have learned to cope with stress.

YOU, STRESS FREE

▶ Bibliography

Bedford, Stewart. *Tiger Juice: A Book About Stress for Kids.* Chicago, A & N Publishers, 1981.

Benenzon, Rolando. *Music Therapy Manual.* Springfield, Charles C. Thomas, 1981.

Bielen, Peggy and McDaniel, Sandy. *Project Self-Esteem.* Torrance, CA, Jalmar Press, 1986.

Borba, Michele. *Esteem Builders.* Torrance, CA, Jalmar Press, 1989.

Borba, Michele and Borba, Craig. *Self-Esteem, A Classroom Affair.* San Francisco, Harper & Row, 1982.

Bowman, Robert. *Test Buster Pep Rally.* Minneapolis Educational Media, 1989.

Brenner, Avis. *Helping Children Cope with Stress.* New York, Lexington Books, 1984.

Brown, Bonnie M. *Stress Busters for Kids: A Parent's Guide to Helping Kids Cope With Stress.* (8316 Winder St., Vienna, VA 22180), 1990.

Canfield, J. and Keinek, P. *The Inner Classroom: Guided Fantasy in the Classroom.* New Jersey, Prentice-Hall, 1977.

Carothers, James and Gasten, Ruth. *Helping Children to Like Themselves: Activities for Building Self-Esteem.* Livermore, R. J. Associates, 1978.

Carr, R. *Creative Yoga Exercise for Children.* New York, Harper & Row, 1973.

Chandler, Louis. *Children Under Stress: Understanding Emotional Adjustment Reactions.* Springfield, Charles C. Thomas, 1988.

Cooper, JoAnn. *Helping Children Series.* Doylestown, Marco, 1990.

Drew, Naomi. *Learning the Skills of Peacemaking, Revised.* Torrance, CA, Jalmar Press, 1996.

Fairchild, Thomas N. *Crisis Intervention Strategies for School Based Helpers.* Springfield, Charles C. Thomas, 1986.

Fassler, Joan. *Helping Children Cope: Mastering Stress Through Books and Stories.* New York, Free Press, 1978.

Fugitt, E. *He Hit Me Back First!* Torrance, CA, Jalmar Press, 1983.

Furrer, P. J. *Art Therapy Activities and Lesson Plans for Individuals and Groups.* Springfield, Charles C. Thomas, 1982.

Hendricks, G. and Wells, R. *The Centering Book, Awareness Activities for Children, Parents and Teachers.* Englewood Cliffs, Prentice-Hall, 1975.

Herzfeld, Gerald and Powell, Robin. *Coping for Kids: A Complete Stress-Control Program for Students Ages 8-18.* Englewood Cliffs, Center for Applied Research in Education, 1985.

Humphrey, James and Humphrey, Joy. *Controlling Stress in Children.* Springfield, Charles C. Thomas, 1985.

Humphrey, James and Humphrey, Joy. *Reducing Stress in Children Through Creative Relaxation.* Springfield, Charles C. Thomas, 1981.

Isaacs, Susan and Ritchey, *Wendy. I Think I Can, I Know I Can.* Philadelphia, Childswork/Childsplay, 1989.

Kaufman, Gersten and Raphael, Lev. *Stick Up for Yourself.* Minneapolis, Educational Media, 1988.

Kuczen, Barbara. *Childhood Stress: How to Raise a Healthier, Happier Child.* New York, Dell, 1987.

Lane, Kristi. *Feelings are Real.* Muncie, Accelerated Development, 1991.

Lupin, M. *Peace, Harmony Awareness: A Relaxation Program for Children.* Austin, Learning Concepts, 1977.

Moser, Adolph. *Don't Pop Your Cork on Mondays.* Philadelphia, Center for Applied Psychology, 1989.

Ogburn, Keith D. *Emotional Education: How to Deal With Stress in the Classroom Before and After it Happens.* Saratoga, R & E Publishers, 1983.

Palmer, Pat. *Liking Myself.* Minneapolis, Johnson Institute, 1988.

Peale, Janet and Tade, Carla. *In A Pickle.* Circle Pines, American Guidance Service, 1988.

Sunderlin, Sylvia and McNamee, Abigail (editor). *Children and Stress.* Wheaton, Association for Childhood Education International, 1982.

Trotter, Jennie. *Stress Education Curriculum for Grades 1-6.* Atlanta, Wholistic Stress Control Institute, 1986.

Youngs, Bettie B. *A Stress Management Guide for Young People.* Del Mar, Learning Tools/Bilicki Publishers, 1986.

Chapter 11

Learning Performance Support Group Curriculum

A complete curriculum for learning performance support groups is provided in this chapter. Step-by-step instructions are outlined for the unique set-up, planning, and facilitation of this type of elementary age support group. An extensive listing of assessment scales, session themes, bibliotherapy books, videotapes/films, and "how-to-do-it" references are included as part of this practical support group guide. This chapter, along with Chapters One, Two, Three, and Thirteen, will provide complete instructions for the set-up through the termination of learning performance support groups.

Treatment Guidelines

Youngsters with learning performance problems usually have a variety of specific difficulties in terms of this at-risk area. For example, they could have learning disabilities, hyperactivity, short attention span, developmental delays, intellectual deficits, school phobia, or any number of other causes that result in not being able to perform at grade level. For this reason, facilitators will need to individually determine the causes of members' poor school performance to determine relevant content and plans for this particular type of support group.

In this country today, we have ever increasing numbers of children with serious difficulties performing at grade level. In some states, in fact, as many as 40% of all 18-year-olds never graduate from high school. It is appalling that our nation is not able to meet the varying needs of our school age children. Guidance personnel are finding more and more that these youngsters are being referred for counseling services. Facilitators have to be careful to set realistic expectations with this population in a support group program. At the same time, involved parents and teachers need to be reminded of their responsibility in this change effort. This is not to say that learning performance support groups cannot be effective; this particular problem area, by its very nature, requires the input and support of parents and school personnel.

Before utilizing this curriculum, the reader should review the following general treatment guidelines for working with children in groups who have learning performance problems.

1. Before placing a youngster in a support group, it is essential that specifics around his/her school performance problems be obtained. This gathering of assessment data can be requested from teachers and parents by any one of the rating forms suggested on the assessment instrument list found in this curriculum. Identifying the reasons behind members' school problems can provide some initial focus for group session plans. This baselining of specific school difficulties can serve as a way of determining realistic goals for individual group members.

2. Facilitators should be ready to spend lots of time in the initial sessions just trying to attract members to the support group. As a result of these students' histories, many will be difficult to attract to school-related activities like support groups.

3. Without a doubt, many of these children need to be referred for further testing. These evaluations may include a medical, neurological, psychological, or in some cases, a psychiatric. Such evaluations can sometimes surface the exact cause and extent of a learning performance problem.

4. Since members of this group may have some type of learning problem, it is essential that facilitators plan their intervention formats very carefully. Readers should feel free to modify, change, and add to the session plans in this curriculum so that their group interventions will be at the functioning levels of the students.

5. Facilitators may find when screening members for this support group that a change of school placement may also be in order. It is extremely important that when such a case arises, efforts be directed toward assisting with this placement change. Facilitators ideally want to have students who are in appropriate class settings in this support group. This greatly enhances the impact of this service.

6. Since so many of these kids have secondary problems as a result of their school difficulties, it may be advisable to place them in other group programs. In these therapeutic settings, the youngster can learn the step-by-step skills for other aspects of healthy school functioning. Support groups that may be beneficial include self-esteem building, social skills enhancement, conflict resoution, and stress management skills.

7. Counselors may find that in some cases observation in the natural settings will provide needed data on potential group members' functioning level. Often times, this observation gives the facilitator some insight into how to handle the identified youngster in a group setting. Such data can provide relevant session content ideas for a particular student's support group.

8. Compositions of these support groups needs to be made very carefully. It is important that the members of the same group have varied strengths. It is not a good idea to put too many students having problems such as hyperactivity or short attention span in the same group. These particular youngsters can have a chain effect on one another, and facilitators may not be able to maintain basic rule keeping behavior. This group usually benefits from assigned seating arrangements.

9. The use of assignments is often recommended as an essential component of these youngsters' treatment plan. It is imperative that new skills discussed and taught in the group sessions are also tried in the real world. These in vivo assignments will allow a youngster the opportunity to try out a new behavior knowing that they can turn to the group for help and support.

10. These children also greatly benefit from the therapeutic relationship with the counselor. For many of them, adult relationships have been strained, if not outright conflictive. Usually, the facilitator can be more accepting of the child because of the nature of the relationship. This corrective experience with a warm, caring, open, and supportive adult can be the impetus for a youngster's initial changes. Facilitators should always be sensitive to the kind of impact their relationship can have with this population.

Assessment Instruments

1. A.D.D. Behavior Rating Scale
2. Behavior Evaluation Scale-2
3. Burks Behavior Rating Scales
4. Child Behavior Checklist
5. Children's Perceived Self-Control Scale

6. Conners' Teacher and Parent Rating Scales
7. Coopersmith Self-Esteem Inventories
8. Hyperactivity and Withdrawal Scale
9. Impulsivity Scale
10. School Behavior Checklist

Relevant Session Themes

Normalization of feelings

Increased sense of not being alone

Improved attitude toward school

More positive self-esteem

Improved peer skills

Affective awareness

Communication skills particularly around feelings

Specific school skills for attending, staying on task, etc.

Stress management skills

Ability to seek support and help from peers

Knowledge and involvement in activities that provide success

Increased self-control

Awareness of needs and skill in getting them met

Assertiveness skills with peers and adults

Improved ability to interact with teachers

Increased motivation to perform at maximum level in school

More positive affect state

Skills in handling anger and frustration

Time management skills

Awareness of compensation skills necessary for school work

Skill in asking for help or clarification in the classroom

Planning Sequence of Objectives & Techniques for Learning Performance Support Group

Group Phase	Group Goals	Intervention Categories
Initial	1. To provide an attractive group setting. 2. To initiate members' participation on-task and with one another. 3. To initiate trust among the membership.	**Hello Group Techniques** (Chapter Three)
	4. To educate members about issues and difficulties related to learning problems.	**Instructive Techniques:** #1 Now I See #2 Bibliotherapy/Video/Films #3 Tracking Me In School
Middle	5. To increase group development goals established in initial phase (i.e., goals 1-3).	No techniques per se but follow curriculum approach.
	6. To increase members' awareness of their particular difficulties related to classroom learning.	**Awareness of Self Techniques:** #4 Lightbulbs Go Off #5 Pull My Leg #6 Read Me Like A Comic Book
	7. To provide alternative learning skills.	**Alternative Coping Techniques:** #7 Create A Scene #8 Look For The Answer #9 "X" Marks The Spot
	8. To assist members in the integration of new coping behaviors into their repertoire.	**Integration Techniques:** #10 Go It Alone #11 Me Watching Me #12 How Good?
Termination	9. To have members acknowledge the value of the group. 10. To assist members in validating their changes. 11. To have members brainstorm other sources of support. 12. To have members grieve the ending of group.	**Goodbye Group Techniques** (Chapter Thirteen)

▸ Technique #1

Title: Now I See

Technique category: Didactic Technique

Objective: To instruct members in the causes and consequences of learning performance problems.

Materials:

- Copies of pre-selected reading material on a school performance subject of relevance to the group
- Prepared discussion questions
- Form "Now I See," found on page 326.
- Pencils

Procedure:

1. Before this group session, the facilitator will need to prepare some brief reading material for the children. It is important that this latter material be relevant to the specific school performance problems of the group members. For example, if many of the youngsters have difficulty completing their homework, the group leader may choose some of the reading from Jane and Jovial Stine's book *Everything You Need to Survive Homework*. Or, if several of the members are procrastinators about their work, then material from Linda Morse's book *Working with Young Procrastinators* may be the reading of choice. These two texts are fully referenced in the bibliography at the back of this curriculum.

2. At the onset of the session, members can read the material silently or facilitators may want to read it out loud to the whole group.

3. Next, the group leader has all the members complete the sentences found on the form "Now I See."

4. The facilitator requests that each youngster share the contents of their sheet. Younger children (grades kindergarten through third) may require the use of visual aids or memory games to keep their interest during this intervention.

5. Members should be asked to share the most important point they learned in the group.

Cautions/comments:

Facilitators need to be sure the reading material presented in this session is brief and written in a way that holds members' interest. Youngsters will enjoy learning the possible causes and consequences of their school performance problems. It is extremely important that the format of this instruction is attractive enough to hold their attention. In older groups (fourth through sixth grades), facilitators may even choose to have participants take home some reading material as an assignment.

▸ Now I See

Instructions: Finish each sentence below based on what you just learned from the lesson in group.

1. I never knew that _____

    _____

2. The lesson today could really help me because _____

    _____

3. This lesson would probably _____

    _____

    for other kids.

4. If only _____

    _____

5. Now I am going to try _____

    _____

▶ Technique #2

Title:	Bibliotherapy/Video/Films
Technique category:	Bibliotherapy/Video/Films
Objective:	To educate the group regarding learning performance skills.

Materials:

- Book, film, or videotape selected from the list on page 328.
- Equipment for film or videotape, if used.
- Prepared discussion questions related to the theme of the visual aid chosen.

Procedure:

1. Before the session, the facilitator selects a book, film, or videotape from the list on page 328.
2. Session begins with the book being read or film/videotape being shown.
3. At completion of above task, members can be asked discussion questions that surface their identification with the story. Also, some disclosure can be elicited that explores the children's similar problems and struggles.
4. Members' favorite parts of the book, film, or videotape should be processed at the end.

Cautions/comments:

Typically, members will enjoy the use of bibliotherapy materials or films/videotapes. Through these types of visual interventions, children can more easily understand their learning performance problems and learn alternative coping skills. In addition, youngsters in elementary grades typically identify with characters in books and films. As a result, they are often able to talk more comfortably about their similar issues via the story presented.

Readers are advised to select books that have colorful pictures on almost every page. Children as a whole find it easier to understand the message of a book page when a graphic design depicts the concept. Also, facilitators should be careful that books and films/videotapes selected are not too long. It is important to have time in the session to pose discussion questions and process reactions among the members.

▶ Bibliotherapy

1. Berry, Joy Wilt. *Survival Series for Kids* (set of 28 books). Children's Press, 1982-87, grades 3-6.

2. Berry, Joy Wilt. *Interrupting.* Children's Press, 1986, grades P-3.

3. Berry, Joy Wilt. *Whining.* Children's Press, 1984, grades P-3.

4. Berry, Joy Wilt. *Throwing Tantrums.* Children's Press, 1984, grades P-3.

5. Berry, Joy. *Help Me Be Good Series.* Grolier Enterprises Corporation, 1987, grades 1-3.

6. Berry, Joy. *Being Destructive.* Children's Press, 1984, grades K-3.

7. Berry, Marilyn. *Help is on the Way for Listening Skills.* Children's Press, 1987, grades 4-6.

8. Berry, Marilyn. *Help is on the Way for Memory Skills.* Children's Press, 1985, grades 4-6.

9. Buerger, Jane. *Obedience.* Children's Press, Inc., 1981, ages 3-6.

10. Fiday, Beverly and Wiles, Carol. *Patience.* Children's Press, 1986, grades P-3.

11. Galvin, Matthew. *Otto Learns About His Medicine.* Magination Press, 1986, grades 1-6.

12. Gambill, Henrietta. *Self-Control.* Children's Press, 1982, grades P-3.

13. Gambill, Henrietta. *Are You Listening?* Children's Press, 1985, grades P-2.

14. Giff, Patricia Reilly. *Today Was a Terrible Day.* Viking Press, 1980, grades 2-3.

15. Gross, Alan. *Sometimes I Worry....* Children's Press, 1978, grades P-3.

16. Hargreaves, Roger. *Mr. Noisy.* Creative Education, Inc., 1980, ages 3-7.

17. Hunter, Edith Fisher. *Sue Ellen.* Houghton Mifflin Co., 1969, ages 10-12.

18. Kherdian, David. *Right Now.* Knopf, 1983, grades 1-4.

19. Kraus, Robert. *Leo the Late Bloomer.* Prentice-Hall Books for Young Readers, 1971, grades 1-6.

20. Lindgren, Barbro. *The Wild Baby.* Greenwillow, 1981, grades P-K.

21. Moser, A. *Don't Pop Your Cork on Mondays.* King of Prussia, Kansas City, Hardrack editions, 1988, grades 2-6.

22. Simon, Norma. *I Was So Mad!* Whitman, 1974, grades K-3.

23. Tester, Sylvia. *Frustrated.* Children's Press, 1980, grades P-2.

24. Wannamaker, Bruce. *Terry's Turn-Around: A Story About Obedience.* Children's Press, 1983, grades K-3.

Videotapes

1. Backwards: The Riddle of Dyslexia
   Learning Corporation of America/MTI, 1984, 32 minute film, grades 4-6.

2. Beginning Responsibility: Manners in Public
   Coronet, 1975, 11 minute film, grades 1-3.

3. Beginning Responsibility: Taking Care of Your Own Things
   Coronet, 1976, 11 minute film, grades K-3.

4. Brad's Learning Disability
   Coronet, 1982, 18 minute film, grades 4-6.

5. Developing Independence: Working On Your Own
   Coronet, 1977, 11 minute film, grades 4-6.

6. Developing Self-Esteem: Living With Disabilities
   Guidance Associates, 1985, 6 minute film, grades K-3.

7. Get It Right: Following Directions With Goofy
   Walt Disney Educational Media Company, 1972, 8 minute film, grades 1-6.

8. Getting Angry
   Phoenix/BFA Films and Video, Inc., 1966, 12 minute film, grades 1-6.

9. Give School A Chance
   Barr Films, 1979, 15 minute film, grades 1-6.

10. Going To School Is Your Job
    Journal Films, Inc., 1976, 16 minute film, grades 1-6.

11. I Can Do It
    Coronet, 1978, 14 minute film, grades 1-3.

12. I'm Mad At Me
    Churchill Films, 1974, 8 minute film, grades 1-3.

13. Lunchroom Goes Bananas
    Coronet, 1978, 12 minute film, grades 1-3.

14. No Laws Today
    Journal Films, Inc., 1982, 12 minute film, grades 4-6.

15. Rules Are For Gorillas, Too!
    Coronet, 1981, 11 minute film, grades 1-3.

16. Values: Cooperation
    Phoenix/BFA Films and Video, Inc., 1969, 11 minute film, grades 1-6.

▸ Technique #3

Title:	Tracking Me In School
Technique category:	Paper/Pencil Task
Objective:	To instruct members in the causes and consequences of learning performance problems.

Materials needed:

- Copies of the sheet entitled "Tracking Me In School," found on page 331.
- Pencils

Procedure:

1. Pass out the sheet entitled "Tracking Me In School" to all group members.
2. Allow 5 to 10 minutes for the completion of this task.
3. Ask everyone to share their responses by going around the circle in order. The facilitator should initially share their responses to the task sheet for purposes of modeling.
4. If time allows, pose some discussion questions related to the task sheet responses.
5. Process members' positive reactions at the end of the session.

Cautions/comments:

Facilitators will find that this graphic tracking of members' school history provides an avenue where there can be an increased awareness of the causes and consequences of school difficulties. At the same time, this reflection on participants' school performance will surface patterns around their coping strategies. Elementary age youngsters will find it very helpful to look back via this concrete technique. Readers may want to keep these tracking sheets for developing relevant themes for future group sessions.

▸ Tracking Me In School

Instructions: Fill in the empty boxes as you remember your school experiences.

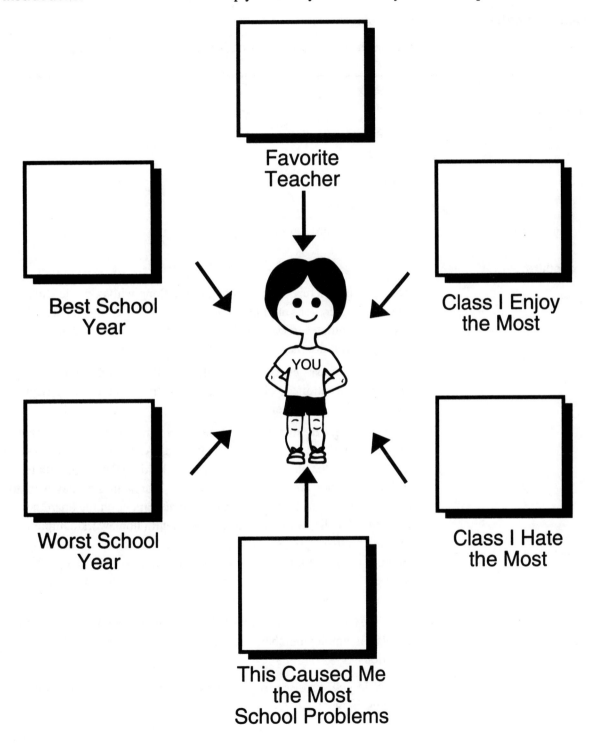

▸ Technique #4

Title:	Lightbulbs Go Off
Technique category:	Exercise Using the Arts
Objective:	To increase members' awareness of their learning performance problems.

Materials:

- Paper
- Crayons
- Scissors
- Popsicle sticks
- Lightbulb picture found on page 334.

Procedure:

1. The lightbulb picture, found on page 334, along with popsicle sticks, scissors, and crayons are passed out to each child. Members are asked to take a few minutes to color and decorate their lightbulb and then cut it out. The lightbulbs are then stapled to the popsicle stick.

2. The facilitator asks everyone to think about the meaning of the saying, "lightbulbs went off." A brief discussion is then conducted, clarifying the message of that statement.

3. Next, members are instructed to listen very carefully to a list of school problems read and noted on the blackboard. As each problem is given by the facilitator, the participants are asked to hold up their lightbulb to indicate that they are having that problem. The facilitator may want to conduct a count each time and indicate that number on the board next to the problem. The list could include problems with homework completion, reading, math, staying on-task, other classes (physical education, science, English, etc.), getting along with peers at school, getting along with teachers, being able to do work, paying attention to instructions, or enjoying school.

4. Once the list is completely covered, the facilitator conducts a structured discussion among members, asking them to share responses to such questions as:

    - Were you surprised by your lightbulb reactions or by the group's? If yes, in what way?

- Do you think you see your school problems the same way as your parents and teachers see them?

- What were some problems common to our entire group?

- Which of these problems are you most eager to solve?

- Have you made any attempts to solve one of these problems? If yes, which one and what did you do?

5. Members should be asked to share one positive effect the technique had on their motivation to solve school problems.

Cautions/comments:

Children typically enjoy this technique because it addresses their attention span and combines a fun art project with a discussion. Since members initially respond to the question regarding their school difficulties via a non-verbal (lightbulb holding up) technique, they are less anxious about the latter disclosure. In particular, facilitators will find that younger children (grades kindergarten through fourth grade) respond positively to the developmental level of this intervention.

▶ Technique #5

Title:	Pull My Leg
Technique category:	Disclosure Task
Objective:	To increase members' awareness of their learning performance problems.

Materials:

- Blackboard
- Chalk
- Timer
- Form entitled "School Problem List," found on page 337.
- Pencils

Procedure:

1. The facilitator explains that everyone will be participating in a task where they must first complete the sheet titled "School Problem List." Members are informed that they are to lie about one problem they check on this list. About 10 minutes is allowed for the completion of this task sheet.

2. The competition in the game will be that the youngsters have to see if they can "pull the facilitator's leg" by not having their lie caught. The rules for this task are noted below and should then be briefly covered with the membership.

   Game Rules:

   - Each member will get a turn in the game by going around the circle in order one after another.

   - When a member has his/her turn, they must share the full content of their school problem list.

   - After each list is read, the facilitator has to guess which problem checked is a lie and not a real difficulty for the youngster.

   - Points will be gained by the group when members are able to fool the facilitator. Points will be gained by the facilitator when he/she guesses the lie on a member's list.

   - The one (group or facilitator) who has the most points at the end of the designated period wins.

3. The game exercise is then played following the rules.

4. All participants should be asked to process the part about the session that was most fun.

Cautions/comments:

Participants will love playing this fun game that actually gives them permission to lie. At the same time, the students usually get so caught up in the competition that they forget that the disclosure they are sharing is difficult.

▸ School Problem List

Instructions: Place an "X" next to each school problem below that you are experiencing. Feel free to add ones not listed at the bottom. Remember to lie about one problem.

Problems with:

Homework

Finishing my work on time

Getting along with other students

Getting along with teachers

Work in a certain class
(Name of class: _____)

Liking school

Paying attention

Other: _____

_____

Other: _____

_____

Other: _____

_____

▸ Technique #6

Title:	Read Me Like A Comic Book
Technique category:	Creative Exercise
Objective:	To increase members' awareness of their learning performance problems.

Materials needed:

- Copies of the sheet entitled "Me In Comics," found on page 339.
- Pencils

Procedure:

1. Pass out the sheet entitled "Me In Comics" to all group members.
2. Allow 5 to 10 minutes for the completion of this task.
3. Ask everyone to share their responses by going around the circle in order. The facilitator should initially share their responses to the task sheet for purposes of modeling.
4. If time allows, pose some discussion questions related to the task sheet responses.
5. Process members' positive reactions at the end of the session.

Cautions/comments:

This is an excellent technique for providing another avenue for members to express their perceptions of their learning performance difficulties. Facilitators will be amazed at how much more disclosure surfaces from this indirect and non-threatening intervention.

▶ Me In Comics

Instructions: Complete the title of a comic book that would best describe your school performance. Then complete the sentences below about the story inside your comic book.

The hero of this comic book is _____

_____

_____

The problem the hero has to solve is _____

_____

_____

At the end, everything ends happy because _____

_____

_____

_____

_____

_____

▸ Technique #7

Title: Create A Scene

Technique category: In Vivo Experience

Objective: To increase members' awareness of alternative coping skills for their learning performance problems.

Materials:

- Any materials that the facilitator will need for the simulated situation(s)

Procedure:

1. Before the group session, the facilitator will need to develop one or a series of mini-problem situations that will be set up for all the group members to experience simultaneously. This is not role playing per se but the set-up of a simulated classroom situation where the facilitator gives each students a task. The clinician acts out the part of the teacher.

2. Participants are told at the beginning of the session that they are going to be taking part in a fun play that will actually test their skills for coping with typical school situations.

3. When working with younger groups (grades kindergarten through third), it may be helpful to add a game component to this task. For example, the facilitator could actually keep points during the play, the members earning a point each time they cope effectively with a stress and the facilitator getting the point when the coping was ineffective. Also, some groups may find it helpful to videotape the simulated situation and play it back when processing their experience.

4. When the play is completed, the facilitator will need to have some structured disclosure questions prepared, such as the ones listed below.

   - Name the stress you had to handle.
   - What effective coping response did you use?
   - Did this situation elicit real and typical feelings from you?
   - Did someone use a coping response in this play that you could use in the classroom?
   - How do you think the group as a whole handled this play?

5. Participants should be asked at the end of the session to share a coping response they intend to now begin using.

Cautions/comments:

Facilitators will be delighted to find that many youngsters are able to quickly get into simulated situations and experience typical response patterns. In order to ensure that this occurs, the group leader will need to make sure that the members are put into an experience that seems very real to them. Sometimes this goal can be accomplished by posing a test situation, promising a prize to the one with the best score or task completion, or merely developing a fun exercise everyone wants to do. This particular intervention is often a fun and non-threatening way to teach alternative coping skills. Here again, members will serve as excellent models for one another.

▸ Technique #8

Title:	Look For The Answer
Technique category:	Completion Task
Objective:	To increase members' awareness of alternative coping skills for their learning problems.

Materials:

- A prepared list of school performance problem situations relevant to members' school performance problems
- A bell
- A series of coping skills for those same problems will have to be written, one per sheet, on the form entitled "Look For The Answer," found on page 344.

Procedure:

1. Before this session, the facilitator will need to develop a series of relevant school problem situations. Then, the coping skills for these problem situations will have to be written on the form entitled "Look For The Answer." The facilitator will need to make several copies of this form so that there is one coping skill written on each magnifying glass picture.

2. The group begins by members being instructed that they are going to be participating in a fun completion task. Youngsters are given the following rules.

    - A typical school performance problem will be posed to the entire group.

    - The members will have 60 seconds to walk around the room and look at the coping skills written on the "Look For The Answer" forms. These sheets should be posted on the walls of the group room.

    - If the member who is up for a turn is able to come up with the skill, the group gets a point. If the member cannot do so in 60 seconds, the point goes to the facilitator.

    - Everyone will get a turn in this fun game by going around the circle in order.

    - The one (group or facilitator) with the most points at the end wins.

3. The game is then played following the rules. Facilitators should probe members' responses to the problem situations in order to elicit enough details for the participants to use the coping behaviors outside the group setting.

4. Have members share what they enjoyed most about this intervention at the end of the session.

Cautions/comments:

Facilitators will find that youngsters of all elementary school ages enjoy this exercise. Members are often more motivated in their problem solving skills due to the fun and competitive nature of this task. It may be helpful to review the coping skills on the sheets at the end of the session. This additional highlighting will increase the members' ability to remember this alternative coping information.

▸ **Look For The Answer**

▸ Technique #9

Title:	"X" Marks the Spot
Technique category:	Game Exercise
Objective:	To increase members' awareness of alternative coping skills for learning performance problems.

Materials:

- A large poster board with eight squares marked off as a target. Each square has a different relevant school performance problem indicated in it.
- Pennies
- Pencils

Procedure:

1. The facilitator explains that everyone will be participating in a penny tossing game. The members are then shown a large poster board with eight squares marked off. Inside each square a relevant school problem situation is written.

2. The rules for this game, as noted below, are then reviewed with all the participants.

   - Each member will get a turn in the game by going around the circle in order one after another.

   - When a member has his/her turn, they must toss a penny onto the poster board target from a designated line. The object is to get their penny on one of the eight squares. If they are able to hit a square, the member must disclose one coping solution to the school performance problem indicated in the box.

   - Once a member has hit a square on the target, they must put an "X" with their name on that square. This mark means that in the next round, that member cannot hit the same square but must aim for one of the others.

   - Points will be gained by the group when a member gets on a square and gives a coping skill that would be effective for the problem indicated. The coping skill has to be one that no one else has contributed during the game.

- Points will be gained by the facilitator when someone either does not hit a square or is not able to come up with an effective coping response to the school performance problem in the square.

- The one (group or facilitator) who has the most points at the end of the designated period wins.

3. The game exercise is then played following the rules.

4. All participants should be asked to process the part about the session that was the most fun.

Cautions/comments:

Usually, children enjoy combining this disclosure exercise with a fun movement game. The members will often come up with some very clever coping skills during this competition. It will be important, however, to only allow one member out of their seat when it is their turn; otherwise, the group could get out of control and off-task.

▸ **Technique #10**

Title:	Go It Alone
Technique category:	Empowerment Exercise
Objective:	To integrate into members' repertoire new learning performance skills.

Materials:

- Whatever materials are necessary for the facilitator's group task project

Procedure:

1. Before this session, the facilitator will need to develop a task that the group as a whole will have to complete. It will be important that this task be one that requires participants to utilize the alternative coping skills they have learned thus far in the group.

2. The session begins with the task being clearly defined and accompanying materials handed out to participants. Members are instructed that their job will be to accomplish the task without the active supervision of the facilitator. The group leader will sit to the side, taking notes on how well members handle their part of the task.

3. Groups should be given a time limit of about 15 to 20 minutes to complete this activity. It may be helpful to videotape this project so that members can see themselves and review their performance more objectively.

4. At the end of the task completion period, participants should be asked to guess the effective coping behaviors they each demonstrated. This discussion will be more enjoyable if the facilitator indicates a specific number of coping skills that he/she observed. The youngsters should be encouraged to guess all those skills from the leader's list.

5. Participants should be asked to share what was most reinforcing about this exercise.

Cautions/comments:

This is a wonderful in vivo experience for members to feel on a gut level that they have learned new coping skills. Also, the youngsters' performance will serve as excellent modeling for one another. Facilitators will often find this to be a very gratifying experience as they watch their members handle a task without their direct supervision. Participants should be reinforced for their performance and reminded that the skills utilized can now be generalized outside the group setting.

▸ Technique #11

Title: Me Watching Me

Technique category: Check-Ups/Assignments

Objective: To integrate into members' repertoire new learning performance skills.

Materials:

- Form entitled "Me At School," found on page 350.
- Prepared discussion questions

Procedure:

1. The session before this one, the facilitator will need to pass out copies of the "Me at School" form. All members are briefly instructed to complete this form following the directions indicated on the top. Younger children may require that the group leader figure out a time each school day for them to complete this form.

2. The results of this weekly monitoring of positive school performance changes are then brought back for this session. Participants are asked to share one after another the results of this assignment.

3. The facilitator poses some structured discussion questions like the ones listed below.

   - What was the most positive change you noticed in your school performance?

   - Did you learn anything new about your changes from this assignment? If yes, what?

   - How has this observation of yourself affected your motivational level to continue changing?

   - Did anyone around you indicate they noticed your changes? If yes, who and what did they notice?

     Facilitators will want to be sure all members respond to these discussion questions.

4. Participants should be asked to share the most beneficial part of the assignment.

Cautions/comments:

This assignment provides members an opportunity to watch their positive school performance changes in action. It is also extremely helpful for youngsters to have a chance to come back to their group and share these changes. Facilitators will find that by this point in the group, participants often spontaneously reinforce each other's changes. This task also gives members an opportunity to elicit assistance from the group if they still have difficulties making and/or seeing their changes.

Younger support groups (kindergarten through third grade) may need to have this assignment modified. For example, facilitators can ask involved teachers to make sure that the youngster does the rating on himself/herself each day.

▸ **Me At School**

Instructions: At the end of each school day, complete the calendar below indicating how you feel you performed on the behaviors listed. Use the scale at the bottom for your ratings.

BEHAVIORS	MON	TUES	WED	THURS	FRI
Completed school work					
Did my required homework					
Paid attention in class					
Enjoyed and tried in school today					
Other: _____ _____ _____ _____					

RATING SCALE:

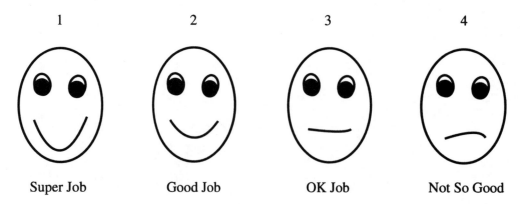

1	2	3	4
Super Job	Good Job	OK Job	Not So Good

▸ Technique #12

Title:	How Good?
Technique category:	Confirmation Task
Objective:	To integrate into members' repertoire new learning performance skills.

Materials:

- Form entitled "How Good?" found on page 352.
- Prepared discussion questions

Procedure:

1. The session before this one, the group members are all given a copy of the form "How Good?" Participants are instructed to have the teacher of the class where they made the most changes complete this evaluation form.

2. The session begins with participants being asked to share the results of their evaluation. Every member should take a turn verbally indicating the behavioral changes seen and the ratings given to them.

3. Next, the facilitator should have some prepared structured disclosure questions such as the ones listed below:

   - Were you surprised by this feedback? If yes, in what way?

   - What was most reinforcing about this evaluation?

   - How has this evaluation affected your motivation to continue making changes?

4. Members should be elicited to share the best part about getting this feedback.

Cautions/comments:

This is a wonderful technique for members to be stroked directly from their teachers for changes they have made. Facilitators may need to go to involved teachers in some cases to advise them that reinforcement of positive changes is being elicited. (Otherwise, some teachers may use this evaluation as an opportunity to indicate behaviors that still need to be addressed.) Group leaders may find a secondary benefit from this task in indirectly instructing teachers of the need to concentrate on positive feedback to these youngsters.

▶ How Good?

Teacher Name: _____ Date: _____

Student Name: _____

Instructions: Please complete the sentences below about positive changes the above student has made in your class. Thank you for taking the time to provide this valuable feedback.

1. This student's biggest positive change in the last month has been _____

   _____

2. This student seems to be working very hard at _____

   _____

3. Compared to two months ago, this student is doing _____
   in my class.

4. Now I would like this student to continue to work on _____

   _____

On this trophy, please write a word or phrase that indicates what kind of an award you feel this student deserves around this improved school performance.

▶ Bibliography

Alabiso, Fran P. and Hansen, James C. *The Hyperactive Child in the Classroom.* Springfield, Charles C. Thomas, 1977.

Berkeley, Russell. *Hyperactive Children.* New York, Guilford Press, 1981.

Borba, Michele. *Esteem Builders.* Torrance, CA, Jalmar Press, 1989.

Borba, Michele and Borba, Craig. *Self-Esteem: A Classroom Affair, Volumes 1 & 2.* San Francisco, Harper & Row, 1982.

Bowman, Robert P. *Test Buster Pep Rally.* Minneapolis, Educational Media Corporation, 1990.

Broyles, Jeffrey and Beigel-Beck, Sharon. *Children Observing Peers in School.* Doylestown, Marco, 1986.

Burton, Leon H. and Woltas, Susan N. *Pathways (Guidance Activities for Young Children).* Menlo Park, Addison-Wesley Publishing Company, 1986.

Camp, Bonnie and Bash, Mary Ann. *Think Aloud.* Champaign, Research Press, 1987.

Carroll, Jerri. *Let's Learn About Magnificent Me.* Carth, Good Apple, 1987.

Cooper, JoAnn and Martenz, Arden. *Affective Education in the Classroom.* Doylestown, Marco, 1985.

Cooper, JoAnn and Martenz, Arden. *Study Skills Series.* Doylestown, Marco, 1989.

Dennison, Susan and Glassman, Connie. *Activities for Children in Therapy.* Springfield, Charles C. Thomas, 1987.

Dennison, Susan. *Twelve Counseling Programs for Children at Risk.* Springfield, Charles C. Thomas, 1989.

DiLeo, Joseph H. *Otto Learns About His Medicine.* New York, Magination Press, 1988.

Dupont, Henry et al. *TAD: Toward Affective Development.* Circle Pines, American Guidance Service, 1974.

Faber, Adele and Mazlish, Elaine. *How to Talk So Kids Listen.* New York, Negotiation Institute, Inc., 1985.

Fairchild, Thomas N. (editor) *Crisis Intervention Strategies for School Based Helpers.* Springfield, Charles C. Thomas, 1986.

Furren, P.J. *Art Therapy Activities and Lesson Plans for Individuals and Groups.* Springfield, Charles C. Thomas, 1982.

Gittelman, M. (editor). Intervention strategies with hyperactive children. *International Journal of Mental Health* 8(1):3-138, 1979.

Gittelman, Martin (editor). *Strategic Intervention for Hyperactive Children.* Armonk, M.E. Sharpe, 1981.

Goldberg, Joan and Hymowitz, Ellen. *Mental Health Activities in the Classroom.* New York, Western Publishing, 1977.

Goldstein, Arnold. *The Prepare Curriculum.* Champaign, Research Press, 1987.

Heacox, Diane. *Up From Underachievement.* Minneapolis, Johnson Institute, 1990.

Isaacs, Susan and Ritchey, Wendy. *I Think I Can, I Know I Can.* New York, St. Martin, 1989.

Jackson, Paula. *Test Bingo.* Doylestown, Marco, 1988.

Jernberg, Ann M. *Theraplay.* San Francisco, Jossey-Bass, Inc. 1979.

Lane, Kristi. *Feelings are Real.* Muncie, Accelerated Development, 1991.

Martenz, Arden et al. *Giving Kids a Piece of the Action.* Doylestown, Marco, 1977.

McGinnis, Ellen et al. *Skillstreaming the Elementary School Child.* Champaign, Research Press, 1986.

Millman, Howard C. et al. *Therapies for School Behavior Problems.* San Francisco, Jossey-Bass, 1980.

Morse, Linda A. *Working With Young Procrastinators.* West Lafayette, Cumberland Elementary School, 1987.

Moser, Adolph. *Don't Pop Your Cork on Mondays.* Kansas City, Hardrack Editions, 1988.

Oldfield, Dick and Petosa, Richard. Increasing student "on task" behaviors through relaxation strategies. *Elementary School Guidance & Counseling* 20(3):180-186, 1986.

Peale, Janet and Tade, Carla. *In a Pickle.* Circle Pines, American Guidance Service, 1988.

Renard, Sue and Sockol, Kay. *Creative Drama.* Minneapolis, Educational Media Corporation, 1987.

Rommey, David, M. *Dealing with Abnormal Behavior in the Classroom.* Bloomington, Phi Delta Kappa, 1986.

Sheinker, Jan and Sheinker, Alan. *Metacognitive Approach to Social Skill Training.* Frederick, Aspen Publishers, 1989.

Shles, Larry. *Do I Have to Go to School Today?* Torrance, CA, Jalmar Press, 1989.

Stine, Jane and Stine, Jovial. *Everything You Need to Survive Homework.* New York, Random House, 1983.

Taylor, John. *Motivating the Uncooperative Student.* Doylestown, Marco, 1990.

Tindall, Judith. *Peer Power (Becoming an Effective Peer Helper).* Muncie, Accelerated Development, 1985.

Trotter, Jennie. *Stress Education Curriculum, Grades 1-5.* Atlanta, Wholistic Stress Control Institute, 1986.

Trower, Terry. *The Kid Counselor Curriculum.* Doylestown, Marco, 1986.

Vernon, Ann. *Thinking, Feeling, Behaving.* Champaign, Research Press, 1986.

Whittington, Ronaele et al. *Peace Begins With Me.* Honolulu, Waikiki Community Center, 1988.

Wittner, Joe and Myrick, Robert. *The Teacher as Facilitator.* Minneapolis, Educational Media Corporation, 1989.

Worzbyt, John C. and O'Rourke, Kathleen. *Elementary School Counseling.* Muncie, Accelerated Development, 1989.

Chapter 12

School Motivation/Attitude Enhancement Support Group Curriculum

A complete curriculum for school motivation/attitude enhancement support groups is provided in this chapter. Step-by-step instructions are outlined for the unique set-up, planning, and facilitation of this type of elementary age support group. An extensive listing of assessment scales, session themes, bibliotherapy books, videotapes/films, and "how-to-do-it" references are included as part of this practical support group guide. This chapter, along with Chapters One, Two, Three, and Thirteen, will provide complete instructions for the set-up through the termination of school motivation/attitude enhancement support groups.

Treatment Guidelines

Unfortunately, children today are turned off to school at younger and younger ages. It is not surprising that I have found a tremendous need across the country to offer support group programs that specifically address youngsters' school attitude and motivational levels. Unlike the population focused on in the previous chapter (learning performance support group), these children have the abilities to handle school tasks, but for any number of reasons are not motivated to do so. The good news is that these elementary age students have the academic skills to handle work at their grade level. The bad news is that they have, in some cases, been completely turned off to even attempt to perform at their ability level.

This population can be very challenging to treat in a support group program. These youngsters may need to be more actively attracted to a group because they see it as part of the school picture, which they hate. Changing members' attitudes in this modality can often positively affect their feelings toward school. Any time treatment efforts are made at this elementary school level, there is a higher probability of turning around attitude and motivation at school.

Before utilizing this curriculum, the reader should review the following general treatment guidelines for working with children in support groups who have attitude and motivational school problems.

1. It is imperative that this population of students be highly attracted to a support group. It is typically more difficult to get these youngsters involved in any type of services connected to a school.

2. Counselors need to obtain specific feedback from teachers and/or parents on the nature and extent of the school motivation difficulties. Good baselining of the problem is essential for developing realistic expectations and relevant content for support group sessions.

3. Facilitators should be careful to maintain teachers' and parents' responsibility. This is one problem area that almost always requires some follow through, both in the classroom and at home. Therefore, support group goals should be clearly defined for these involved adults. In addition, it will be helpful to instruct teachers and parents on ways they can actively support the purpose of this support group program.

4. These students will find interventions that surface reasons behind their school attitude problems to be most helpful. In some cases, facilitators may find that this increased awareness among members is the initial step in making significant progress with this at-risk problem.

5. Interventions involving assignments are not only helpful but essential when support groups focus on this problem area. Assignments should be well thought out and should in the beginning be realistic so that the members complete them successfully. These techniques should also indirectly elicit parents' and teachers' ongoing support of the group program.

6. Sometimes we forget the obvious with these youngsters. It can be extremely helpful at the time of referral or during an initial group session to ask members their perception of their school attitude difficulties. Facilitators will usually gain significant insight about members from such an exploration. In addition, the material that surfaces could very well provide some relevant material for group sessions.

7. Facilitators should never underestimate the value of having these children enjoy a support group program. Even if there is not a lot of direct sharing about their attitude problems, these youngsters gain tremendously from being in a school program that they like. Goals for these support groups, therefore, should be kept realistic and be evaluated relative to members' baseline functioning.

8. Counselors should be aware that some of these students may have underlying depression, which greatly contributes to the school attitude and motivational problems. In such cases, the facilitator will need to notify involved adults. Also, a referral for further evaluation of this problem may be necessary. In particular, group leaders should watch for any signs of suicidal thoughts among these students.

9. Sometimes it is necessary to go beyond the individual child's situation and look at the total school environment. Counselors may find, for example, that a number of students are experiencing a similar problem because of environmental issues. The bottom line is that children can only be expected to adapt to a certain level of inappropriate or unrealistic school demands — at some point, the cause of the situation needs to be addressed.

10. Facilitators should never underestimate the impact they can have on these youngsters. For some of these children, a corrective relationship with a warm, caring, and open adult can initiate a student's first steps in changing their attitude and motivation at school.

Assessment Instruments

1. About Me and My School Work
2. Attitude Toward School Questionnaire
3. Child Behavior Checklist
4. Conners' Teacher and Parent Rating Scales
5. Devereux Elementary School Behavior Rating Scale
6. Dropout Scale
7. Quality of School Life Scale
8. School Attitude Survey: Feelings I Have About School
9. School Behavior Checklist
10. School Child Stress Scale

Relevant Session Themes

Normalization of feelings

Increased sense of not being alone

Affective awareness

Communication skills, particularly ones for sharing feelings

Increased awareness of underlying causes for school attitude difficulties

Improved social skills with peers and teachers

Increased state of feeling happy at school

Increased feelings of self-worth

Accurate awareness of one's strengths in school

Specific skills for completing school tasks

A balancing of one's daily activities

Assertiveness skills

Increased ability to be aware of needs and have them met

Identification of at least one aspect of school that is of interest or a source of success

Planning Sequence of Objectives & Techniques for School Motivation/Attitude Enhancement Support Group

Group Phase	Group Goals	Intervention Categories
Initial	1. To provide an attractive group setting. 2. To initiate members' participation on-task and with one another. 3. To initiate trust among the membership.	**Hello Group Techniques** (Chapter Three)
	4. To educate members about issues and difficulties related to school motivation/attitude problems.	**Instructive Techniques:** #1 Hidden Pictures/Hidden Problems #2 Bibliotherapy/Video/Films #3 Next Came . . .
Middle	5. To increase group development goals established in initial phase (i.e., goals 1-3).	No techniques per se but follow curriculum approach.
	6. To increase members' awareness of their particular difficulties related to their school motivation and attitude.	**Awareness of Self Techniques:** #4 A Rap Song On School #5 Trash It #6 You Win
	7. To provide alternative coping behaviors for their school motivation and attitude.	**Alternative Coping Techniques:** #7 Shadowing A Peer #8 Work It Out #9 Opposite Day
	8. To assist members in the integration of new coping behaviors into their repertoire.	**Integration Techniques:** #10 Dial ... For A Positive School Attitude #11 On Location #12 Attitude Adjustment Quiz
Termination	9. To have members acknowledge the value of the group. 10. To assist members in validating their changes. 11. To have members brainstorm other sources of support. 12. To have members grieve the ending of group.	**Goodbye Group Techniques** (Chapter Thirteen)

▶ Technique #1

Title: Hidden Pictures/Hidden Problems

Technique category: Didactic Technique

Objective: To instruct members about difficulties that can result from school attitude/motivational problems.

Materials:

- Copies of a hidden picture game sheet from a children's magazine or a book
- Pencils

Procedure:

1. At the beginning of this session, members are informed that they are going to have a chance to learn more about difficulties that can happen as a result of their school problems. Then, the intervention of "Hidden Pictures/Hidden Problems" is introduced.

2. Members are given a designated period of time to look over a sheet or page from one of the hidden picture task games found in magazines like *Highlight* or in one of the *Search for Waldo* books.

3. Participants are instructed that in this fun learning task, they must do the following when it is their turn:

   - Share a hidden problem that results from a school attitude or motivational difficulty.

   - Next, that same member must tell the location of a hidden item in the picture task sheet that no one else has found yet in the group.

4. The members then take their turns in this exercise by going around the circle one right after another. After all the hidden pictures have been located, the facilitator asks the group to do a memory review game. All the youngsters are asked to share one of the hidden problems given during the game. These are listed on a blackboard by the facilitator to enhance members' learning.

5. Participants should be asked to share the number one point they learned from this experience.

Cautions/comments:

Fun didactic techniques are usually effective ways to teach young children. Facilitators will find that members at this age are able to make the more concrete association of hidden pictures with hidden problems. The enjoyable parts of this exercise tend to increase students' ability to stay on task and come up with some well thought out responses.

▶ Technique #2

Title: Bibliotherapy/Video/Films

Technique category: Bibliotherapy/Video/Films

Objective: To instruct the group about difficulties that can result from school attitude/motivation problems.

Materials:

- Book, film, or videotape selected from the list on page 365.
- Equipment for film or videotape, if used.
- Prepared discussion questions related to the theme of the visual aid chosen.

Procedure:

1. Before the session, the facilitator selects a book, film, or videotape from the list on page 365.
2. Session begins with the book being read or film/videotape being shown.
3. At completion of above task, members can be asked discussion questions that surface their identification with the story. Also, some disclosure can be elicited that explores the children's similar problems and struggles.
4. Members' favorite parts of the book, film, or videotape should be processed at the end.

Cautions/comments:

Typically, members will enjoy the use of bibliotherapy materials or films/videotapes. Through these types of visual interventions, children can more easily learn about their school attitude/motivation issues. In addition, youngsters in elementary grades typically identify with characters in books and films. As a result, they are often able to talk more comfortably about their similar issues via the story presented.

Readers are advised to select books that have colorful pictures on almost every page. Children as a whole find it easier to understand the message of a book page when a graphic design depicts the concept. Also, facilitators should be careful that books and films/videotapes selected are not too long. It is important to have time in the session to pose discussion questions and process reactions among the members.

▸ Bibliotherapy

1. Adams, Barbara. *The Not-Quite-Ready-for-Prime-Time Bandits.* Dell, 1986, grades 3-6.

2. Adler, C. S. *The Once in a While Hero.* Putnam Publishing Group, 1982, grades 3-6.

3. Bates, Betty. *Everybody Say Cheese.* Dell, 1986, grades 3-6.

4. Berenstain, Stan and Berenstain, Janice. *The Berenstain Bears Go to School.* Random, 1978, grades P-2.

5. Berry, Joy. *Teach Me About School.* Children's Press, 1988, grades K-3.

6. Berry, Joy. *Every Kid's Guide To Laws That Relate To School And Work.* Children's Press, 1987, grades 3-6.

7. Berry, Joy. *Teach Me About Listening.* Children's Press, 1988, grades K-3.

8. Berry, Marilyn. *Skills On Studying (set of 24 books).* Children's Press, 1984-87, grades 4-6.

9. Blume, Judy. *Tales of a Fourth Grade Nothing.* Dell, 1986, grades K-6.

10. Bottner, Barbara. *The World's Greatest Expert on Absolutely Everything...Is Crying.* Dell, 1984, grades 3-6.

11. Buckley, William F., Jr. *The Temptation of Wilfred Malachey.* Workman Pub., 1985, grades 4-6.

12. Carlson, Nancy. *Loudmouth George and the Sixth Grade Bully.* Live Oak Media, 1986, grades K-3.

13. Chapman, Carol. *Herbie's Troubles.* Dutton, 1981, grades P-1.

14. Christian, Mary B. *But Everybody Does It: Peer Pressure.* Concordia, 1986, grades 4-7.

15. Cleary, Beverly. *Ramona the Brave.* Morrow, 1975, grades 3-7.

16. Cohen, Miriam. *First Grade Takes a Test.* Greenwillow, 1980, grades P-3.

17. Cohen, Miriam. *Will I Have a Friend?* Macmillan, 1967, grades K-1.

18. Cohen, Miriam. *Liar, Liar, Pants on Fire!* Greenwillow, 1985, grades K-2.

19. Coleman, William L. *Getting Ready for My First Day of School.* Bethany House, 1983, grade K.

20. Conford, Ellen. *Lenny Kandell, Smart Aleck.* Little, 1983, grades 4-6.

21. Cooney, Nancy E. *The Blanket That Had to Go.* Putnam Pub. Group, 1981, grades 4-8.

22. Cross, Gillian. *The Demon Headmaster.* Merrimack Pub. Cir., 1983, grades 3-7.

23. Delton, Judy. *The New Girl at School.* Dutton, 1979, grades K-3.

24. Elliott, Dan. *Grover Goes to School.* Random, 1982, grades 1-3.

25. Frandsen, Karen G. *I Started School Today.* Children's Press, 1984, grades P-3.

26. Gaeddert, LouAnn. *The Kid with the Red Suspenders.* Dutton, 1983, grades 2-4.

27. Giff, Patricia Reilly. *The Girl Who Knew It All.* Delacorte Press, 1979, ages 8-10.

28. Giff, Patricia R. *Fourth Grade Celebrity.* Delacorte, 1984, grades 4-6.

29. Giff, Patricia G. *Next Year I'll Be Special.* Dutton, 1980, grades K-3.

30. Giff, Patricia Reilly. *Today Was a Terrible Day.* The Viking Press, Inc., 1980, ages 6-7.

31. Gilson, Janie. *Do Bananas Chew Gum?* Lothrop, Lee & Shepard Company, 1980, ages 9-11.

32. Gormley, Beatrice. *Fifth Grade Magic.* Avon, 1984, grades 3-7.

33. Gross, Alan. *What If The Teacher Calls On Me?* Children's Press, Inc., 1980, ages 5-7.

34. Gross, Alan. *The I Don't Want To Go To School Book.* Children's Press, Inc., 1982, ages 5-9.

35. Hallinan, P. K. *Just Open A Book.* Children's Press, 1981, grades P-3.

36. Haywood, Carolyn. *B is for Betsy.* Harcourt-Brace-Jovanovich, 1986, grades 1-4.

37. Hermes, Patricia. *Friends Are Like That.* Harcourt-Brace-Jovanovich, 1984, grades 4-6.

38. Hobby, Janice Hale with Gabrielle and Daniel Rubin. *Staying Back.* Triad Publishing Company, 1982, ages 6-12.

39. Hogan, Paula Z. *Sometimes I Don't Like School.* Raintree Publishers, Inc., 1980, ages 6-9.

40. Hurwitz, Johanna. *Tough-Luck Karen.* William Morrow & Company, Inc., 1982, ages 10-13.

41. Kirkland, Dianna C. *Last Year I Failed...but.* Aid-U Pub., 1981, grades P-5.

42. *Little Monster at School.* Western Pub., 1978, grades P-3.

43. Luttrell, Ida. *One Day at School.* Harcourt-Brace-Jovanovich, 1984, grades P-3.

44. Moncure, Jane B. *A New Boy in Kindergarten.* Childs World, 1976, grades P-3.

45. Morton, Jane. *Running Scared.* Elsevier/Nelson Books, 1979, ages 10-14.

46. Naylor, Phyllis Reynolds. *Getting Along With Your Teachers.* Abingdon, 1981, grades 4-6.

47. Quackenbush, Robert M. *First Grade Jitters.* J. B. Lippincott Company, 1982, ages 5-7.

48. Reuter, Margaret. *You Can Depend On Me.* Children's Press, 1980, grades K-3.

49. Roos, Stephen. *My Horrible Secret.* Delacorte, 1983, grades 4-6.

50. Roy, Ron. *Frankie Is Staying Back.* Houghton Mifflin, 1981, grades 2-5.

51. Ruckman, Ivy. *What's an Average Kid Like Me Doing Way up Here?* Delacorte, 1983, grades 4-6.

52. Shreve, Susan. *The Flunking of Joshua T. Bates.* Knopf, 1984, grades 2-6.

53. Steptoe, John. *Jeffrey Bear Cleans up His Act.* Lothrop, 1983, grades K-3.

54. Stevenson, James. *That Dreadful Day.* Greenwillow, 1985, grades K-3.

55. Stewart, Marabelle Young and Buchwald, Ann. *What To Do When And Why.* McKay, 1975, grades 4-6.

56. Stine, Jane and Stine, Jovial Bob. *Everything You Need To Survive Homework.* Random House, 1983, grades 5-6.

57. Tester, Sylvia Root. *We Laughed A Lot, My First Day of School.* Children's Press, 1979, grades P-2.

58. Weiss, Leatie. *My Teacher Sleeps in School.* Penguin, 1985, grades P-3.

59. Wiseman, Bernard. *Morris Goes to School.* Harper & Row Junior Books, 1970, grades K-3.

60. Young, Karen Rosann. *Best Behavior Books (series of 6 books).* Children's Press, 1986, grades P-3.

Videotapes/films

1. Balthazar the Lion
   Wombat Productions, Inc., 1973, 1 film reel (12 minutes), grades K-6.

2. Beginning Responsibility: Getting Ready for School
   Coronet, 1969, 1 film reel (11 minutes), grades 1-3.

3. Behave, Bernard
   Barr Films, 1983, 1 film reel (11 minutes), grades 1-3.

4. Being on Time Game, The
   Alfred Higgins Productions, 1978, 1 film reel (11 minutes), grades 1-3.

5. But They Might Laugh
   National Instructional T.V., 1973, 1 film reel (15 minutes), grades 4-6.

6. Day in the Life of Bonnie Consolo, A
   Barr Films, 1975, 1 film reel (17 minutes), grades 4-6.

7. Developing Independence: Working on Your Own
   Coronet, 1977, 1 film reel (11 minutes), grades 4-6.

8. Drop Out Now - Pay Later
   Handel Films Corporation, 1972, 1 film reel (24 minutes), grades 4-6.

9. Everybody's Different and That's OK
   Barr Films, 1979, 1 film reel (15 minutes), grades 1-6.

10. Following Instructions Game
    Alfred Higgins Productions, 1978, 1 film reel (11 minutes), grades 1-3.

11. Getting Organized Game
    Alfred Higgins Productions, 1978, 1 film reel (11 minutes), grades 1-3.

12. Give School a Chance
    Barr Films, 1973, 1 film reel (15 minutes), grades 1-6.

13. Going to School is Your Job
    Journal Films, Inc., 1976, 1 film reel (16 minutes), grades K-3.

14. I Can Do It
    Coronet, 1978, 1 film reel (14 minutes), grades 1-3.

15. If At First You Don't Succeed...
    Filmfair Communications, 1976, 1 film reel (15 minutes), grades 4-6.

16. Louis James Hates School
    Learning Corporation of America/MTI, 1980, 1 film reel (11 minutes), grades 1-6.

17. Magic Man
    Lucerne Films and Video, 1980, 1 film reel (24 minutes), grades 1-6.

18. Never Say You Can't Until You Try
    Guidance Associates, 1975, 1 film reel (11 minutes), grades 4-6.

19. What's the Good of a Test?
    Journal Films Inc., 1965, 1 film reel (13 minutes), grades 4-6.

Films

A Kid's Guide to Getting Along at School
Spoken Arts, 1988, 6 filmstrips and 3 cassettes, grades K-3.

Back to School With Winnie the Pooh
Walt Disney Educational Media, 5 filmstrips, grades K-3.

Being a Good School Citizen
Creative Learning, Inc., 4 filmstrips, grades K-4.

Getting Along With Teachers and Classmates
Random House Media, filmstrip/cassette, grades 5-6.

Good Study Habits
Creative Learning, Inc., 4 filmstrips, grades 4-6.

▶ Technique #3

Title:	Next Came . . .
Technique category:	Paper/Pencil Task
Objective:	To instruct members about difficulties that can result from school attitude/motivational problems.

Materials needed:

- Copies of the sheet entitled "Next Came . . ." found on page 371.
- Pencils

Procedure:

1. Pass out the sheet entitled "Next Came . . ." to all group members.
2. Allow 5 to 10 minutes for the completion of this task.
3. Ask everyone to share their responses by going around the circle in order. The facilitator should initially share their responses to the task sheet for purposes of modeling.
4. If time allows, pose some discussion questions related to the task sheet responses.
5. Process members' positive reactions at the end of the session.

Cautions/comments:

This is a very effective intervention for helping members become more aware of how a poor school attitude affects all parts of your life. The sharing of ideas among the participants will usually have a greater impact on these students.

▶ Next Came . . .

Instructions: Write or draw in the spaces below some difficulties a kid who does not like school could have at home, with friends, and with self.

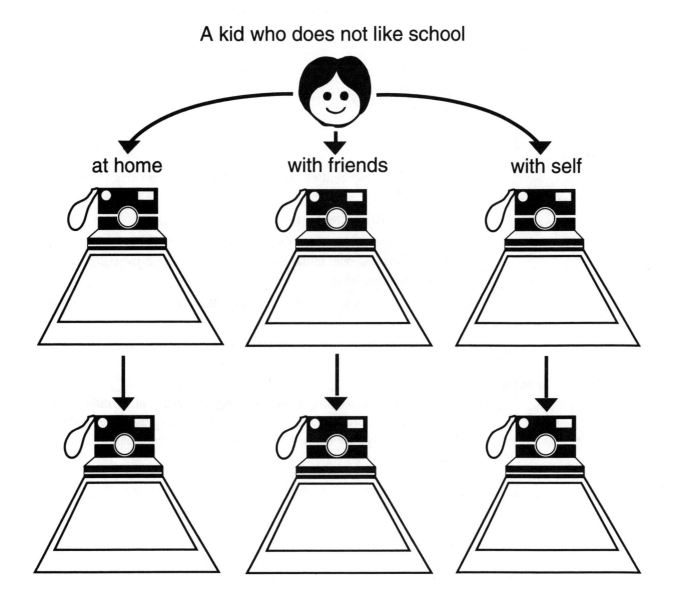

A kid who does not like school

at home   with friends   with self

▶ Technique #4

Title: A Rap Song On School

Technique category: Exercise Using the Arts

Objective: To increase members' awareness of their difficulties related to school attitude/motivational problems.

Materials needed:

- Copies of the sheet entitled "Here's the Rap On Me and School," found on page 373.
- Pencils

Procedure:

1. Pass out the sheet entitled "Here's the Rap On Me and School" to all group members.
2. Allow 5 to 10 minutes for the completion of this task.
3. Ask everyone to share their responses by going around the circle in order. The facilitator should initially share their responses to the task sheet for purposes of modeling.
4. If time allows, pose some discussion questions related to the task sheet responses.
5. Process members' positive reactions at the end of the session.

Cautions/comments:

This is an excellent technique for surfacing awareness of specifics related to members' school attitude problems. Many of these students will enjoy this more indirect and creative avenue for expressing their feelings related to school motivational issues.

▸ A Rap Song On School

Instructions: Complete the following rap song on your attitude and interest in school.

Here's the Rap on Me and School

First of all I'll tell you what's so cool about school

_____

_____

_____

But my attitude of late is not so great about

_____

_____

_____

And my interest in this school debate is

_____

_____

_____

All in all, my motivation in school is

_____

_____

_____

_____   _____
Signature   Date

▸ **Technique #5**

Title:	Trash It
Technique category:	Disclosure Task
Objective:	To increase members' awareness of their difficulties related to school attitude/motivational problems.

Materials:

- Form entitled "School Problems to Trash," found on page 376.
- Pencils
- Trash basket

Procedure:

1. The session begins with participants being told they will have a chance to participate in a movement task where they will be indicating their school attitude problems anonymously and throwing them into a trash basket.

2. Next, the sheet entitled "School Problems to Trash" is passed out to each member. The group is given a designated period of time to complete this sheet (about 5-10 minutes) following the directions provided on the top.

3. Once everyone has completed their sheets, the students are asked to fold them up in any form they like so they can be easily thrown into a trash basket. Members then each take a turn throwing from their seats or in a standing position to a designated spot in the room. It is not necessary to keep any scores on who gets their paper in the basket unless the facilitator feels a particular group needs this competition component to keep members' attention.

4. After everyone has thrown their sheets, the facilitator takes each of them out of the trash and reads the responses out loud to the group. It will be important during this sharing to note commonalities that surface from these disclosures.

5. At the end of this session, members should be asked to complete the phrase below:

    "This exercise was a good way for me to . . ."

Cautions/comments:

This is a very non-threatening and fun way to have members begin disclosing their views of their school attitude problems. Active groups particularly enjoy the idea of being able to fold up their sheets and throw them into a trash basket. Facilitators are cautioned to be sure that only one member at a time is allowed to move, so that the group does not get out of control.

▸ School Problems To Trash

Instructions: Write on this trash bag a school attitude problem you would like to get rid of and throw away.

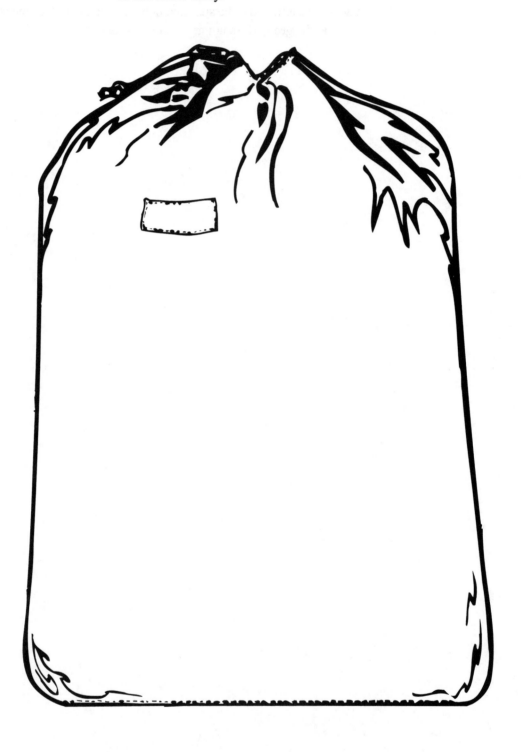

▸ Technique #6

Title: You Win

Technique category: Creative Exercise

Objective: To increase members' awareness of their difficulties related to school attitude/motivational problems.

Materials:

- Form entitled "A School Sweepstakes Winner," found on page 378.
- Pencils

Procedure:

1. Members are told they are going to have an opportunity to participate in a creative exercise where they make believe they have won a sweepstakes contest. Then, the form entitled "A School Sweepstakes Winner" is passed out, instructions reviewed, and everyone is asked to complete it.

2. Members are allowed 10 to 15 minutes to complete this task.

3. After everyone is done, each child takes a turn sharing what sweepstakes winnings they would most desire. Facilitators should be the first to share. This will create a more comfortable setting for this disclosure.

4. Throughout the sharing, members' commonalities and significant disclosure should be reinforced.

5. At the end, everyone is asked to share in their own creative way the most enjoyable part of this creative experience.

Cautions/comments:

This is an excellent technique for helping members become more aware of their school difficulties by asking instead what they want as a positive change. Students will typically find this intervention a less threatening way to share their views of such problems. Depending on a group's level of functioning, facilitators may be able to probe members' responses on the task sheet for more specifics related to their perception of their school motivational issues.

▸ A School Sweepstakes Winner

Instructions: Let's make believe you just won a sweepstakes contest at your school. You will need to select one winning attribute from each category below. Circle the number of the one you most desire in each category.

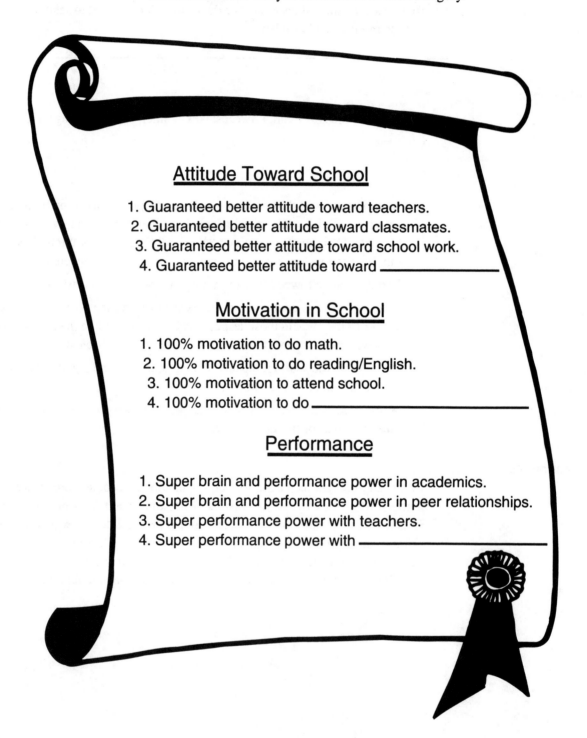

Attitude Toward School

1. Guaranteed better attitude toward teachers.
2. Guaranteed better attitude toward classmates.
3. Guaranteed better attitude toward school work.
4. Guaranteed better attitude toward _____

Motivation in School

1. 100% motivation to do math.
2. 100% motivation to do reading/English.
3. 100% motivation to attend school.
4. 100% motivation to do _____

Performance

1. Super brain and performance power in academics.
2. Super brain and performance power in peer relationships.
3. Super performance power with teachers.
4. Super performance power with _____

▶ Technique #7

Title:	Shadowing A Peer
Technique category:	In Vivo Experience
Objective:	To increase members' awareness of alternative coping behaviors for school attitude problems.

Materials:

- Form entitled "Shadowing A Peer," found on page 381.

Procedure:

1. Before this group session, the facilitator will need to assign each member a peer model to shadow for one school day. Usually, it is best for the group leader to choose peers who can demonstrate skills needed by the group members. It will be necessary to brief all peer models before the shadowing day so they understand the purpose of this task. Also, permission will need to be obtained from the members' parents and school so that they can spend an entire day shadowing another child whose schedule may vary from their usual one.

2. The session before this one, all participants are given the sheet entitled "Shadowing a Peer." They are instructed to read over the requested information ahead of time so that they will know what to ask or observe about their peer model. The members are then instructed to bring these sheets to this session.

3. At the beginning of the session, each youngster takes a turn reading out loud the results of their day of shadowing via the responses on this task sheet. Facilitators will want to note commonalities among members' observations. It will also be important to point out skills particularly relevant to problems discussed earlier in a group.

4. Members' responses to this task should be processed at the end of the session, with a particular emphasis on the number one thing they learned from this shadowing experience.

Cautions/comments:

This is an intervention that takes considerable time to set up but is well worth the extra energy. Facilitators will be amazed at how much group members can learn just from observing a peer's school behavior throughout one day.

Readers are cautioned to make sure peer model selections include youngsters who not only have effective school skills but are willing to help members in their pursuit of new coping skills. Also, it is important to make the rationale behind this assignment clear to parents and teachers so that they support this intervention from start to finish.

▶ Shadowing A Peer

Instructions: During your day of shadowing a peer model, be sure to obtain the following information.

1. Name two things you have in common with your peer model.

_____

_____

2. Name one skill your peer model showed today in regard to school attitude.

_____

_____

3. Name one skill your peer model showed today in regard to school performance.

_____

_____

4. What is one quality about your peer model you most admire?

_____

_____

5. Ask your peer model to complete the sentence below:

I keep a positive school attitude by:

_____

_____

_____

▶ Technique #8

Title: Work It Out

Technique category: Completion Task

Objective: To increase members' awareness of alternative coping skills for dealing with school attitude problems.

Materials needed:

- Copies of the sheet entitled "School Problem List," found on page 383.
- Pencils

Procedure:

1. Pass out the sheet entitled "School Problem List" to all group members.
2. Allow 5 to 10 minutes for the completion of this task.
3. Ask everyone to share their responses by going around the circle in order. The facilitator should initially share their responses to the task sheet for purposes of modeling.
4. If time allows, pose some discussion questions related to the task sheet responses.
5. Process members' positive reactions at the end of the session.

Cautions/comments:

This is an effective intervention for members to become more aware of which parts of a school problem are within their control. Many of these students unknowingly spend lots of energy thinking about issues related to their school difficulties that, for the most part, they can never change. This task is a helpful learning experience that teaches the skill of zooming in on aspects of problems that are within one's control.

▸ School Problem List

Instructions: Select a problem from the list below by circling the number of the one you most want to work on this school year. Then, answer the questions below the list regarding the problem you selected.

School Problem List
1. All the work is too hard
2. Problems with math
3. Problems with reading
4. Too much homework
5. Don't like school
6. No friends at school
7. Teachers are not nice
8. Other_____

Parts of this problem within my control:

1. _____

2. _____

Parts of this problem outside my control:

1. _____

2. _____

▶ **Technique #9**

Title: Opposite Day

Technique category: Game Exercise

Objective: To increase members' awareness of alternative skills for dealing with school attitude problems.

Materials:

- Blackboard
- Chalk
- Timer

Procedure:

1. Before this session, the facilitator will have to develop a series of ineffective coping responses relevant to members' experiences around school attitude/motivational problems. It is usually best to have about three developed for each member.

2. This session begins with participants being told that they will be doing a fun game in the group. Then, the facilitator explains that everyone will be participating in a game called "Opposite Day." The rules for this task are noted below and should be briefly covered with the membership.

Game Rules:

- Each member will get a turn in the game by going around the circle in order one after another.

- When a member has his/her turn, they must share the opposite reaction to a school attitude/motivational coping behavior posed by the facilitator. A designated period of time will need to be established by the facilitator for this game. Also, a predetermined number of responses will have to be established ahead of time. All of the latter details will then have to be given to the group during this rule coverage time.

- Points will be gained by the group when members are able to accurately give an opposite coping behavior in response to the ineffective one posed by the facilitator. Usually, it is best to give a time limit for each child's response time.

- Points will be gained by the facilitator when a member either cannot come up with an opposite reaction or the one developed does not fit the criteria indicated.

- The one (group or facilitator) who has the most points at the end of the designated period wins.

3. The game exercise is then played following the rules.

4. At the end of this fun competitive task, members can be asked to share further regarding their disclosures made during the game.

5. All participants should be asked to process the part about the session that was most fun.

Cautions/comments:

Elementary age children typically love this opposite day experience. They get into the fun and competition of the game so much that their anxieties around the disclosure are greatly reduced. Facilitators will be amazed at how much these youngsters have to offer one another in terms of effective coping skills. For this reason, readers may want to allow members to seek assistance from each other when they have difficulty coming up with an opposite response.

▶ Technique #10

Title:	Dial . . . For A Positive School Attitude
Technique category:	Empowerment Exercise
Objective:	To integrate into members' repertoire new coping skills for school attitude/motivational problems.

Materials needed:

- Copies of the sheet entitled "Dial . . . For A Positive School Attitude," found on page 387.
- Pencils

Procedure:

1. Pass out the sheet entitled "Dial . . . For A Positive School Attitude" to all group members.
2. Allow 5 to 10 minutes for the completion of this task.
3. Ask everyone to share their responses by going around the circle in order. The facilitator should initially share their responses to the task sheet for purposes of modeling.
4. If time allows, pose some discussion questions related to the task sheet responses.
5. All participants should be asked to share how the technique helped them feel more confident about their progress in the group.

Cautions/comments:

The use of this graphic exercise often validates for members all that they have learned from this type of support group. This technique also helps the children focus on the ways they can improve their school attitude and motivation.

▶ Dial . . . For A Positive School Attitude

Instructions: Write or draw in the four bursts things you can call on to have a positive school attitude.

▸ Technique #11

Title:	On Location
Technique category:	Empowerment Exercise
Objective:	To integrate into members' repertoire new school attitude and motivation skills.

Materials:

- Form entitled "Interview With a Teacher or Parent," found on page 389.
- Pencils

Procedure:

1. The sheet entitled "Interview With a Teacher or Parent," found on the following page, is duplicated and distributed to members the session before this one. Participants are instructed to conduct their interviews with a parent or teacher of their choice. In some younger groups (kindergarten through third grade), it may be necessary to help the children structure an exact time when they will do their interviews. Members are asked to bring back their interview sheets to this session.

2. The meeting begins with each participant taking a turn sharing the results of their interview. At the completion of each member's turn, it is a good idea to ask them what was most helpful about this experience. Facilitators will also want to point out commonalities that surface during this sharing time.

3. Members can be asked to process their reactions to the feedback they received during their interviews.

Cautions/comments:

This is an excellent way for members to find out what changes others have noticed in their school attitude and motivation. Also, the highly structured nature of the interview generally reduces members' anxiety regarding its completion. Typically, most children respond to this intervention as an assignment they would receive in a class.

▸ Interview With A Teacher Or Parent

Instructions: Conduct the interview below with a teacher or a parent who has observed your changes at school as a result of your group experience.

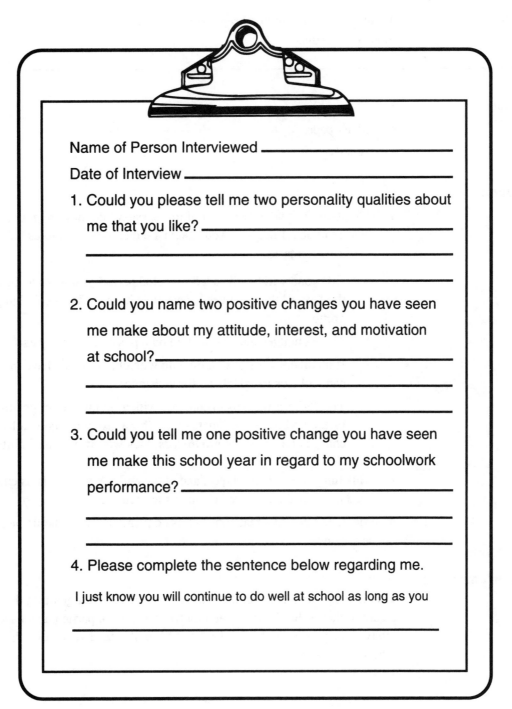

Name of Person Interviewed _____

Date of Interview _____

1. Could you please tell me two personality qualities about me that you like? _____

_____

_____

2. Could you name two positive changes you have seen me make about my attitude, interest, and motivation at school? _____

_____

_____

3. Could you tell me one positive change you have seen me make this school year in regard to my schoolwork performance? _____

_____

_____

4. Please complete the sentence below regarding me.

I just know you will continue to do well at school as long as you

_____

▸ Technique #12

Title: Attitude Adjustment Quiz

Technique category: Confirmation Task

Objective: To integrate into members' repertoire new school attitude and motivation skills.

Materials:

- Blank paper
- Pencils

Procedure:

1. Members are told at the onset of this session that they are going to have a chance to do a fun quiz. Youngsters are then given the rules below for this confirmation task.

   - Everyone will be given a designated period of time (5 to 10 minutes) to think of all the positive changes they have made since joining the group.

   - These changes must be written on a piece of paper by each member.

   - If members get stuck coming up with changes they have made, they can feel free to ask others for assistance.

   - The entire group has to come up with a set number of positive changes by the end of the designated time (for a group of eight, at least 35 changes total). If the group does, they win; if not, the facilitator wins.

2. This fun game is then played, and at the end everyone's list is checked out loud to see if the observed changes are accurate.

3. Members' positive reactions to this confirmation task should be processed at the end.

Cautions/comments:

This is a fun way for members to review all the changes they have made in regard to their school attitude and motivation. Also, participants have an opportunity to help one another remember and reinforce changes that they may have otherwise forgotten.

▸ **Bibliography**

Additional References

Balsanek, Judith A. Group intervention for underachievers in the intermediate school. *Social Work in Education* 8(1):26-32, 1986.

Barth, R. P. Social promotion and nonpromotion: non-solutions to underachievement. *Social Work in Education* 9(2):81-95, 1987.

Barth, R. P. Reducing nonattendance in elementary schools. *Social Work in Education* 6(3):151-66, 1984.

Bland, Mary et al. The effects of small-group counseling on underachievers. *Elementary School Guidance & Counseling* 20(4):303-305, 1986.

Borba, Michele. *Esteem Builders.* Torrance, CA, Jalmar Press, 1990.

Borba, Michele and Borba, Craig. *Self-Esteem: A Classroom Affair, Volumes 1 & 2.* San Francisco, Harper & Row, 1982.

Brulle, Andrew R. et al. School phobia: its educational implications. *Elementary School Guidance & Counseling* 20(1):19-28, 1985.

Coffee, Charlotte. Group work and the school attendance game. *School Social Work Journal* V:79-81, 1981.

Cooper, JoAnn et al. *Helping Children Series,* One booklet on *Motivation in School.* Philadelphia, Marco Publications, 1989.

Cowen, Emory et al. *New Ways in School Mental Health: Early Detection and Prevention of School Maladaptation.* Human Science Press, 1975.

Dobson, J. et al. The relationship between children's self-concepts, perceptions of school and life changes. *Elementary School Guidance and Counseling* 17:100-107, 1982.

Dolfi, M.A. and Edleson, J. L. Increasing student self-referrals for social work services: a program evaluation. *Social Work in Education* 7(3):160-170, 1985.

Fairbanks, Nancy McDowell. Involving children in the IEP: the car-in-the-garage technique. *Social Work in Education* 7:171-182, 1985.

Farnum, M. K. and Powell, B. H. Stress-reduction techniques to be used in schools. *Social Work in Education* 9(1):71-76, 1986.

Fisher, Gary and Cummings, Rhoda. *The Survival Guide for Kids with LD.* Minneapolis, Johnson Institute, 1989.

Greene, Lawrence J. *Kids Who Hate School: A Survival Handbook on Learning Disabilities.* New York, Fawcett, 1987.

Heacox, Diane. *Up From Underachievement.* Minneapolis, Johnson Institute, 1990.

Hellwege, Nancy. *Helping Children Reach Their Potential.* (self-published) 7701 SW 6 Street, North Lauderdale, FL 33068.

Kirkland, Dianna C. *Group Counseling for Children Who Failed.* Oak Park, Aid-U Publishing Company, 1985.

Moser, Adolph. *Don't Pop Your Cork on Mondays.* Kansas City, Hardrack Editions, 1988.

Morse, Linda A. *Working With Young Procrastinators.* West Lafayette, Cumberland Elementary School, 1987.

Parker, Harvey. *Goal Card Program.* Plantation, A.D.D. Warehouse, 1990.

Parker, Harvey. *Listen, Look and Think: A Self-Regulation Program for Children.* Plantation, A.D.D. Warehouse, 1990.

Peale, Janet and Tade, Carla. *In a Pickle.* Circle Pines, American Guidance Service, 1988.

Taylor, John. *Motivating the Uncooperative Student.* Doylestown, Marco Products, 1990.

Thyer, Bruce A. and Sowens-Hoag, K. M. The etiology of school phobia: a behavioral approach. *School Social Work Journal* 10(2):86-98, 1986.

Trotter, Jennie. *Stress Education Curriculum.* Atlanta, Wholistic Stress Control Institute, 1986.

Welsh, B. L. and Goldberg, G. Insuring educational success for children-at-risk placed in new learning environments. *School Social Work Quarterly* 1(4):271-283, 1979.

Worzbyt, John and O'Rourke, Kathleen. *Elementary School Counseling.* Muncie, Accelerated Development, 1989.

Zoff, S. B. Program for disadvantaged elementary school students. *Social Work in Education* 4(1):19-29, 1981.

Chapter 13

Goodbye Group Plans

The Goodbye Group Plans are introduced and described in this chapter. These session interventions are intended to be used at the end of any support group as part of the termination phase. This package of ten-session plans in this chapter will give the reader a wide range of intervention possibilities. As indicated in Chapter Two, the total length and purpose of a children's support group will determine the number of sessions spent in this final closure phase.

This last section of the book provides specific objectives for these plans, along with practical treatment guidelines. The ten-session plans are then outlined in a step-by-step format with detailed instructions. The material in this chapter is relevant and necessary for the therapeutic closure of any of the support group programs found in the nine curriculum chapters of this book.

Termination Phase Objectives

Readers may recall from Chapter Two (Table I) that there are four specific objectives addressed in the termination phase of a group. These objectives are as follows:

1. To have member acknowledge the value of the group
2. To have members validate their progress in the group
3. To have members brainstorm other sources of support
4. To have members grieve the ending of group

These objectives are the essential ingredients for a healthy closure experience in the termination phase. The goals are extremely important for a therapeutic closure to be attained among the membership. It is imperative that facilitators remember that all support groups spend some of their ending session(s) focusing completely on these objectives. Children's groups need to have time at the end to acknowledge the group's value, to validate their progress, look for other supports, and grieve the termination of this experience.

In Table II in Chapter Two, timing guidelines were given for the utilization of the Goodbye Group Plans. For example, six- and eight-session groups require only that a part of the final meeting use interventions from this curriculum. A twelve-session group needs the entire last meeting to focus on these objectives, with a plan selected from one of the ten interventions provided in this chapter.

This is not to say that support groups go through the termination phase in one or two sessions; the point is that the need to do some relationship closure at the end of support group programs is critical. A more therapeutic children's group requires about four to six sessions in this phase. In fact, depending on the length of such a group, more sessions may be necessary to address the goals of this phase. Readers who intend to run groups more therapeutic in nature should feel free to use as many of the plans from this chapter as is necessary.

Treatment Guidelines for Goodbye Plans

The primary purpose of these plans is to provide ways that a group can attain a healthy closure. Following are some specific treatment guidelines for use when conducting support groups in this termination phase.

1. Facilitators generally need to take on a more directive role such as the one they had in the initial phase. Most groups want to avoid termination issues and require the clinician to redirect them to face and discuss their reactions to the group's ending.

2. Members need to be stopped from disclosing further about new problems. At this point in a group, children begin to be even more open about their difficulties. Such responses are usually their way of saying that they are not ready for their group to end. It is helpful for facilitators to process such responses in a sensitive manner.

3. Group members can become very emotional in this ending phase. Facilitators need to be ready to deal with some participants' strong emotional reactions to a support group's ending. Sometimes, it is not until this termination that clinicians realize how important a group has become to particular members.

4. Youngsters should be aware of the ending date of a group and reminded of it as they get closer to that time. Many children have trouble remembering future dates and need to be reminded on a regular basis.

5. Some participants will break down in these ending sessions. In fact, it is not usual for children in close-knit groups to act out significantly at this point. The clinician needs to process such reactions in a sensitive fashion.

6. Often, this ending of a group will spontaneously remind members of other times they have had to say goodbye to significant people in their lives. If time permits, processing such disclosure could be very beneficial to the involved member(s). Where time is not available for such probing, the clinician may need to see the involved members outside the group in an individual session.

7. As much as possible, participants should be given opportunities in the group to experience the progress they have made. Usually, children do better validating their growth through in vivo situations as opposed to verbal discussions. Many of the techniques suggested in this chapter are examples of these interventions.

8. By this point in the group, facilitators may see an extremely increased attention span as well as improved verbal discussion skills among the membership. Since the youngsters are going through this ending experience together, it often results in these types of behavioral changes.

9. It is sometimes helpful to give participants outside assignments as a way of helping them experience their changes. These assignments can include eliciting feedback from other peers or significant adults, attempting a difficult task addressed in the group, etc.

10. Group leaders should be honest with their feelings and openly share them with the group. This disclosure will provide excellent modeling for members and will often spontaneously elicit similar disclosure from them.

Facilitators will want to keep the above treatment guidelines in mind when conducting any of the ten support groups in this termination phase.

Goodbye Group Curriculum

The next several pages contain a selection of ten interventions for the Goodbye Group Plan package. Both the session objectives and interventions are indicated for all ten plans on the chart entitled "Goodbye Group Session Plans." Facilitators will need to select interventions from this package for their last meeting(s) of any one of the support group programs. Experienced group clinicians should feel free to use these planning ideas as guides for developing other interventions. Obviously, this selection of session plans is not exhaustive of therapeutic techniques for this final stage of a group.

Goodbye Group Session Plans

Session 1 *Objective:* Members acknowledge their changes *Technique:* I.D. On Me Now (A Picture Completion)	**Session 4** *Objective:* Members solidifying their changes *Technique:* If My Heart Could Talk	**Session 7** *Objective:* Final integration of changes into members' repertoire *Technique:* Check It Out
Session 2 *Objective:* Members reflecting on value of group *Technique:* Remember To Write	**Session 5** *Objective:* Helping members prepare for future difficulties *Technique:* When This Happens, I'll Just . . .	**Session 8** *Objective:* Members summarizing knowledge & skills gained in group *Technique:* Testing Your Memory
Session 3 *Objective:* Members exploring other sources of support *Technique:* People Who Will Look Out For Me	**Session 6** *Objective:* Helping members to terminate in a healthy way *Technique:* Same Feeling, Different Time	**Session 9 & 10** *Objective:* Members' final preparation for being on their own *Technique:* Sign On The Dotted Line and Party Time

▶ Technique #1

Title: I.D. On Me Now

Technique category: Exercise Using the Arts

Objective: To elicit members' perceptions of the changes they have made in group.

Materials needed:

- Copies of the sheet entitled "I.D. On Me Now," found on page 398.
- Pencils
- Crayons
- Markers

Procedure:

1. Pass out the sheet entitled "I.D. On Me Now" to all group members.
2. Allow 5 to 10 minutes for the completion of this task.
3. Ask everyone to share their responses by going around the circle in order. The facilitator should initially share their responses to the task sheet for purposes of modeling.
4. If time allows, pose some discussion questions related to the task sheet responses.
5. Process members' positive reactions at the end of the session.

Cautions/comments:

This exercise provides members a non-verbal avenue to identify changes they have made as a result of the group. By this termination phase of the group, youngsters need to be able to specifically identify how this experience was helpful to them.

▶ I.D. On Me Now

Instructions: Complete the picture below of all the changes you have made as a result of your support group experience.

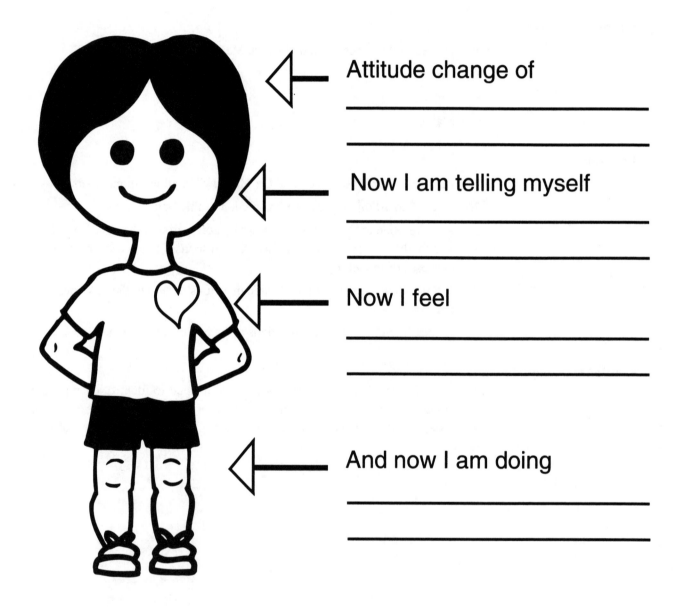

Attitude change of

_____

_____

Now I am telling myself

_____

_____

Now I feel

_____

_____

And now I am doing

_____

_____

▶ Technique #2

Title: Remember To Write

Technique category: Paper/Pencil Task

Objective: To have members reflect on the value of the group.

Materials needed:

- Copies of the sheet entitled "Goodbye Letter Completion," found on page 400.
- Pencils

Procedure:

1. Pass out the sheet entitled "Goodbye Letter Completion" to all group members.

2. Allow 5 to 10 minutes for the completion of this task.

3. Ask everyone to share their responses by going around the circle in order. The facilitator should initially share their responses to the task sheet for purposes of modeling.

4. If time allows, pose some discussion questions related to the task sheet responses.

5. Process members' positive reactions at the end of the session.

Cautions/comments:

This exercise offers a chance for members to tell one another what the group experience has meant to them. Even seasoned facilitators will sometimes be surprised to find how much a support group has meant to members who have seemed relatively untouched by the experience. When working with some younger participants (third grade and under), it may be advisable to develop a goodbye letter form that would involve more drawing completions.

▸ **Goodbye Letter Completion**

Instructions: Complete this letter to your group. Be sure it expresses how you have felt about your experience in this support group.

Date:_____

Dear Group,

I liked this group because_____

_____

It really helped me_____

_____

All in all, this group_____

_____

Thanks for giving me the symbolic gift below.

_____
Signature

▶ Technique #3

Title: People Who Will Look Out For You

Technique category: Game Exercise

Objective: To help members explore other sources of support when the group ends.

Materials:

- Form entitled "People Who Will Look Out For Me," found on page 403.
- Pencils

Procedure:

1. The membership is informed that in today's session, a fun game is going to be played. Then the form entitled "People Who Will Look Out For Me" is handed out to all members.

2. Next, youngsters are given the following rules:

   - The members will be given a designated period of time to complete these task sheets. It will be important to emphasize that the people listed will also potentially help the youngsters maintain their changes.

   - Everyone will have to write these supportive people's names on the incomplete picture form.

   - When the time is up, everyone's answers will be checked to see how realistic their list of supports is for them.

   - The person who completes their form fastest and has the most realistic list wins this game.

3. The game is then played, making sure members are encouraged to come up with their own list of supportive people. While the youngsters are sharing their lists, the facilitator may want to write general name categories (i.e., parents, siblings, neighbors, etc.) on the blackboard and tally the content of members' lists.

4. Have the participants share at the end how this discussion will help them after the group terminates.

Cautions/comments:

It is extremely important during this last phase that members have an opportunity to explore who outside the group will help them continue with some of their newly acquired behaviors, attitudes, and values. Facilitators will need to be sensitive to members who may have trouble coming up with potential supportive people in their environment. In these cases, the membership should be elicited to come forward with other ideas and even brainstorm some creative possibilities. Clinicians will never cease to be amazed at how resourceful peers can be for one another.

▶ People Who Will Look Out For Me

Instructions: When your facilitator says "Go" in this fun game, write down the names of all people who will look out for you and who you can turn to for help.

▸ Technique #4

Title:	If My Heart Could Talk
Technique category:	In Vivo Experience
Objective:	To have members solidify the changes they made as a result of the group.

Materials:

- Form entitled "If My Heart Could Talk," found on page 406.

Procedure:

1. Two weeks before this session, youngsters are asked to prepare a speech that explains the changes that they have experienced as a result of the group. Some facilitators may want to spend a few minutes instructing a group on guidelines for good speech preparation and presentation. Younger groups (third grade and under) may require an outline form to follow as a way to help them in their speech preparation. The form entitled "If My Heart Could Talk" can be used for these youngsters.

2. Members should be told that they will each be rated on their speech. One possible rating system to use is indicated below.

Speech Content:	1 to 10 points
Type of Preparation:	1 to 10 points
Presentation Style:	1 to 10 points
	———————
Total:	3 to 30 points

   Higher numbers indicate higher performance in each of the areas.

3. The session is held with the speeches given by each member. Facilitators or outside people such as teachers rate the presentations. It may be a good idea to have a trophy for the person who gets the highest total rating. This often adds to the attractiveness of the technique for members.

4. Members' response to this intervention should be processed at the end of the session.

Cautions/comments:

Generally, children love this task and are able to identify through it all the changes they have made in the group. Youngsters who are shy about giving speeches may need to be the last ones to present and should be given lots of support to do so. Also, facilitators should emphasize that this speech is supposed to be "from the heart" so that the content will be on more of a gut level. This focus will assist members in talking about attitude and value changes along with the behavioral ones.

▶ If My Heart Could Talk

Instructions: Complete the lines below with what your heart would say about how the group has helped you.

It would say:

It would say:

> If my heart could talk...

It would say:

It would say:

▸ **Technique #5**

Title: When This Happens, I'll Just . . .

Technique category: In Vivo Experience

Objective: To help members prepare for future difficulties in regard to their at-risk problem area.

Materials:

- Blank lined paper
- Pencils

Procedure:

1. This session begins with the facilitator passing out a lined blank sheet of paper and pencil to each member. Youngsters are instructed to think of two situations they are most fearful of facing on their own once the group has ended. Everyone is asked to write these on their sheet of paper. Groups with younger members (kindergarten through third grade) may need to do this part of the exercise verbally rather than having to rely on their spelling and writing skills.

2. After everyone has come up with two anxiety provoking situations, the facilitator has each member take a turn presenting one from their list. After each one is posed, the group as a whole is asked to brainstorm potential responses to the feared event. These situations are presented to the members as: "When this happens, I'll just . . ."

3. It will be important to check with the child presenting the potential problem situation to see if the coping responses seem to be both practical and realistic. Once this list of alternatives has been developed for each youngster, it should be written down by the child or the facilitator. Participants can use this written reminder of how to handle difficult situations after the group ends.

4. Members should be asked to share how this brainstorming of coping responses was helpful for them.

Cautions/comments:

Inevitably, members will have some fears around certain situations related to the group content in this ending phase. This intervention is an excellent way of addressing those fears directly and with the invaluable help of one's peers. After this brainstorming exercise, youngsters usually feel more comfortable about facing their most feared situations.

▸ **Technique #6**

Title: Same Feeling, Different Time

Technique category: Brainstorming Exercise

Objective: To help members learn and experience a healthy termination.

Materials:

- Blackboard
- Chalk

Procedure:

1. The facilitator begins this session by explaining to the group that a brief story is going to be shared of a time when he/she had to say goodbye to someone. It is extremely important that this be a true story and one where there was a special relationship with the person who left. Group leaders want to share not only the details around this departure but also their affective reactions and subsequent responses.

2. After this sharing has been completed, members are requested to think of all the times in their lives thus far they have had to say goodbye to someone. The facilitator then writes on a blackboard the names of the individuals who have left members over the years.

3. When this listing is done, the youngsters are asked to share how some of those terminations are similar to the group ending. Members need to be instructed to think of these similarities in terms of their affective reactions as opposed to the content or description of what occurred. This sharing should also be noted on the board, in a list next to the names of people members have had to say goodbye to in the past.

4. At the end of this session, the group leader can explain to the members that special or difficult goodbyes often remind us of other ones. Members are then asked to share how this discussion has assisted their termination from the group.

Cautions/comments:

If a group has been together for a long time (12 sessions or more) or has become very close, members spontaneously start to recall earlier goodbyes in their lives. Sometimes the group can provide a corrective experience for some of these unresolved goodbyes in members' lives. The facilitator's sharing at the onset of this session usually establishes a mood in the group that easily surfaces disclosure at the youngsters' gut level. Members may remember earlier terminations that still upset them. In some cases, it may be necessary to process and work through these feelings in an individual session or two with the involved youngster. (Obviously, the group would be a more ideal setting for this processing but time may not permit such discussion.)

Facilitators are cautioned to use this technique only when there is enough time in the termination phase to fully process members' responses and reactions. Generally, only support groups that have existed for longer than three months and have three or more sessions in the termination phase should use a technique like this one.

▸ Technique #7

Title: Check It Out

Technique category: Assignment

Objective: To have members solidify the changes they have made in group.

Materials:

- Form entitled "Check It Out," found on page 411.
- Pencils
- Blackboard

Procedure:

1. At the end of the session before this one, all group members will need to be given an assignment. Their task will be to request feedback from significant people in their lives regarding their positive changes. This data can be logged on the form entitled "Check It Out." Participants should be asked to bring this completed sheet to this session.

2. When the session begins, all participants are asked to look over the information they have collected on their "Check It Out" form. Then, members are instructed to take turns going around the circle sharing their results with everyone.

3. At the end of the session, members should be asked to complete the sentence below:

    "This session was just perfect for me because . . ."

Cautions/comments:

Members will find this to be a valuable task for eliciting people outside the group to give them feedback regarding their changes. By asking youngsters to view this as an assignment, it will be more comfortable for them to request this type of feedback.

▶ **Check It Out**

Instructions: Ask the people below to give you their view of your changes. Feel free to have each person write their answers in the space provided.

ANOTHER CHILD

Name of Child: _____

One positive change you have seen in me: _____

_____

_____

A TEACHER

Name of Teacher: _____

One positive change you have seen in me: _____

_____

_____

A FAMILY MEMBER

Name of Family Member: _____

One positive change you have seen in me: _____

_____

_____

▶ Technique #8

Title:	Testing Your Memory
Technique category:	In Vivo Exercise
Objective:	To help members summarize the knowledge and skills they learned in group.

Materials:

- A test prepared ahead of time with questions focused on positive changes among the members
- Blank paper
- Pencils
- Form entitled "Who Done It?" found on page 414.

Procedure:

1. Before this session, the facilitator prepares a test on positive changes made among the membership. The format of this test can vary, depending on the age of members and preferred style of the group leader. Questions could be true or false, require members' names as answers, elicit essay responses, or combine these three types of answers. Facilitators do want to be sensitive to the grade level of members when developing the test format. Younger groups (kindergarten through third grade) may find the form "Who Done It?" to be an easier format to follow. It is extremely important that the group leader is fairly certain that most participants will pass the test with flying colors.

2. The session begins with members being told that today they will be tested on how much they have learned about their own and other members' changes in the group. As youngsters prepare their papers, it is a good idea to process members' responses to this testing situation.

3. Next, the test is administered, with answers being checked at the end.

4. Members should be asked to share what was most reinforcing about this test experience.

Cautions/comments:

This is a great way to assist members in identifying their changes as a result of the support group. It will be important to help relieve youngsters' anxieties around testing so that they can attend to the content of the questions. Facilitators should emphasize that only the members will know their own scores after the answers are checked. Youngsters should be assured that no grades will be given and logged anywhere. The children need to understand that the purpose of this test is to see how aware they are of their positive changes and progress achieved through the group experience.

▸ **Who Done It?**

Instructions: Write down the name of the group member who made the changes indicated in your facilitator's test questions. Remember, you could be the answer to some questions.

1. Name of Group Member: _____

2. Name of Group Member: _____

3. Name of Group Member: _____

4. Name of Group Member: _____

5. Name of Group Member: _____

6. Name of Group Member: _____

7. Name of Group Member: _____

8. Name of Group Member: _____

9. Name of Group Member: _____

10. Name of Group Member: _____

▸ Technique #9

Title:	Sign On The Dotted Line
Technique category:	Paper/Pencil Task
Objective:	To help members prepare for ways to maintain changes

Materials needed:

- Copies of the sheet entitled "Contract," found on page 416.
- Pencils

Procedure:

1. Pass out the sheet entitled "Contract" to all group members.
2. Allow 5 to 10 minutes for the completion of this task.
3. Ask everyone to share their responses by going around the circle in order. The facilitator should initially share their responses to the task sheet for purposes of modeling.
4. If time allows, pose some discussion questions related to the task sheet responses.
5. Process members' positive reactions at the end of the session.

Cautions/comments:

This is an excellent technique for helping members summarize the changes they have made as a result of the group experience. It will be important to have the youngsters take their contracts home to serve as reminders once the group ends. If some participants have trouble completing their contracts, it will be valuable to have other members assist them. This brainstorming can serve as excellent peer feedback regarding positive changes the member has made.

▶ **Contract**

I, _____, do hereby agree to the following:

I will work on having a positive attitude toward_____

_____

_____

I will remember that two things I have control over are:

      1. _____

      2. _____

I will ask _____ when I feel I need help.

I will work on changing my behavior in regard to _____

_____

_____

By signing this contract, I am making the above commitment to myself.

                            _____

                            Signature   Date

▶ Technique #10

Title: Party Time

Technique category: In Vivo Experience

Objective: To have members celebrate their group progress.

Materials:

- Whatever activities are planned for this party will determine the materials needed

Procedure:

1. Before this session, facilitators can individualize the party plans to the needs of the participants and their own styles. Possible activities include a snack or a shared meal, a field trip to a special place, distribution of Certificates of Participation in the group, small gifts given by the facilitator that have symbolic meanings, or a planned sharing time in which members tell each other what they have come to like about one another.

2. Have members process their response both to the party and to the group in general at the end of this session.

Cautions/comments:

Kids, like most of us, love a good party and particularly one that signifies the celebration of an accomplishment (group participation). Just as grieving is essential in this last phase of group, so is the sharing of the joy that all members have benefitted from the experience. Unfortunately, we no longer do enough celebrating of milestones in life. Therefore, many of these youngsters will secondarily benefit from this experience, which teaches how important celebrations of milestones are to us.

Dennison Ideal Group Index

Please provide a rating based on the scale below for either a current or potential group therapy program:

1 = Not at all   2 = Somewhat   3 = Definitely yes

____ 1. Screen all clients for the group.

____ 2. Have an ideal number of clients for the group.

____ 3. Run a true assessment phase of the group.

____ 4. Appropriate and conducive setting that is consistent.

____ 5. Co-facilitator for the group.

____ 6. Time in schedule for both planning and processing.

____ 7. Good meeting time, length of sessions, and frequency.

____ 8. Materials for group activities with continued funding.

____ 9. Money available for other reinforcers (snacks, field trips).

____ 10. Facilitator able to time members out of group.

____ 11. Realistic expectations of group from referring party/significant others.

____ 12. Facilitator excited about the group.

Reference For Total Scoring

Total of 12-15 points: Think twice about doing this group.

Total of 16-24 points: Keep your expectations of this group realistic and remember the group's development may be slow and may plateau after a while.

Total of 25-36 points: This should be an ideal group therapy program to both set up and facilitate.

©Dennison 1985

Group Screening

Name of Child: _____

Date: _____ Potential Group: _____

Feedback from Significant Others

Please indicate with a check if child displays any of the following behaviors.

_____ Psychotic behaviors that are not controlled with medication (hallucinations, loses contact with surroundings, talks to people not present, etc.)

_____ Severe paranoid behavior that is not controlled with medication

_____ Severely narcissistic behaviors where child cannot typically share with others in a group setting

Observations in Group

Rate child on each of the behaviors below as seen in group.

BEHAVIORS	PERFORMANCE 1 = low 2 = age appropriate 3 = high	COMPATIBLE WITH GROUP Yes or No
In-seat Behavior		
Attention Span		
Social/Emotional Level		
Comprehension Level		
Ability to Share/Take Turns		
Contact with Reality		

Based on the above data, this group facilitator recommends: _____

_____

_____

_____   _____
Group Facilitator Signature   Date

Pre/Post Evaluation Of Group Progress

Name of Child: _____

Date: _____ Pre or Post Evaluation (circle one)

Person Doing Evaluation: _____

Relationship to Child: _____ Parent _____ Teacher _____ Other: _____

Group Program: _____

Using the scale listed below, please rate this child on the following behaviors in regard to the problem area.

   1 = Low level

   2 = Fair level

   3 = Expected level

   4 = Good level

   5 = High level

PROBLEM AREA:	
RATING	BEHAVIOR
	General knowledge of difficulties and issues related to this problem area
	Awareness of own difficulties related to this problem area
	Awareness of alternative ways to handle his/her difficulties regarding this problem area
	Coping skills to handle difficulties related to this problem area

Activity Interest Questionnaire

Name of Child: _____ Date: _____

Group: _____

Please indicate with a ✔ in the far left column the three activities below you most like to play or do. If your favorite ones are not listed, add them on the space provided. If you would like, write the specific kind of game you like to the right of the categories.

✔	TYPE OF ACTIVITY	SPECIFIC GAME
	Board games	
	Card games	
	Brainstorming games	
	Drawings	
	Clay projects	
	Sand activities	
	Painting	
	Poetry	
	Reading books of interest	
	Watching films or videotapes	
	Movement games	
	Memory games	
	Sports games	
	Feeling games	
	Paper/pencil fun task sheets	
	Animal activities	

✔	TYPE OF ACTIVITY	SPECIFIC GAME
	Puppets	
	Plays or performances	
	Relaxation activities	
	Sentence completions	
	Story completions	
	Cartoon activities	
	Creative tasks	
	Academic games	
	Music	
	Other:	

Objectives/Progress Report for Group

Name of Child: _____

Dates in Group: _____

Group Facilitator(s): _____

Objectives of Group

1. To provide an attractive setting where child will fully participate on task and with other group members.

2. To educate child about difficulties that can result from:

   _____

3. To increase child's awareness of his/her specific difficulties in regard to:

   _____

4. To provide child with coping alternatives.

5. To assist child's integration of new knowledge and skill into his/her repertoire.

6. To have child experience a healthy group termination.

Assessment Methods

___ Screening Report (if applicable, see attached form)

___ Formal assessment utilizing the following scales:

   _____

___ Informal feedback from significant others (specifically:

   _____)

Group Model Plan Utilized

___ Dennison Support Group Model

___ Other Models Incorporated: _____

   _____

Specific Goals for Child

Beyond the above group objectives, the following goals were set for this child:

1. _____

2. _____

Status on Five Group Objectives: ____ Attained

                                              ____ Not Attained

Comments: _____

_____

_____

_____

_____

_____

Child's Specific Goal Status: ____ Attained

                                              ____ Not Attained

Comments: _____

_____

_____

_____

_____

_____

Recommendation as a Result of Child's Participation in this Group:

____ Terminate from counseling support services

____ Place in another group program (specify type: _____)

____ Other: _____

_____

_____   _____
Signature of Facilitator   Date

Publisher Listing of Assessment Scales

About Me and My School Work
   Edward Earl Gotts
   Appalachia Educational laboratory
   PO Box 1348
   Charleston, West Virginia 25325

A.D.D. Behavior Rating Scale
   Ned Owens and Betty White Owens
   Ned Owens, Inc.
   2186 Promenade
   Richardson, Texas 75080

Aggression Inventory
   Guy T. Doyal
   Dept. of Educational and Clinical Psychology
   Wayne State University
   Detroit, Michigan 48202

Assessment of Coping Style
   Herbert F. Boyd and G. Deville Johnson
   Charles Merrill Publishing Co.
   1300 Alum Creek Drive
   Columbus, Ohio 43216

Attitude Toward School Questionnaire
   G. P. Strickland, R. Hoepfner, and S. P. Klien
   Monitor
   PO Box 2337
   Hollywood, CA 90028

Behavior Evaluation Scale - 2
   Stephen McCarney and James Leigh
   Hawthorne Educational Services
   PO Box 7570
   Columbia, MO 65205

Behavior Problem Checklist
   Herbert Quay
   PO Box 248074
   University of Miami
   Coral Gables, FL 33125

Bellevue Index of Depression
   Dr. Theodore A. Petti
   University of Pittsburgh
   School of Medicine
   Pittsburgh, PA 15213

Burks Behavior Rating Scales
   Harold Burks
   Arden Press
   8331 Alvarado Drive
   Huntington Beach, CA 92646

Checklist of Children's Fears
   James W. Croake and Nancy Catlin
   James W. Croake
   Virginia Polytechnic Institute and
      State University
   Blacksburg, VA 24060

Child Behavior Checklist
   Thomas M. Achenbach and Craig Edelbrock
   Thomas M. Achenbach
   Department of Psychiatry
   University of Vermont
   Burlington, VT 05401

Children's Action Tendency Scale
   Robert H. Delaty
   Division of Child Psychiatry
   Children's Memorial Hospital
   2300 Children's Plaza
   Chicago, Illinois 60614

Child's Attitude Toward Father and Mother Scales
Walter Hudson
The Dorsey Press
224 South Michigan Avenue, Suite 440
Chicago, Illinois 60604

Children's Inventory of Anger
W. M. Nelson and A. J. Finch
Unpublished manuscript, Xavier University

Children of Alcoholics Screening Test
John W. Jones
Camelot Press
Attention: Dr. John W. Jones
1812 Rolling Green Curve
Mendola Heights, MN 55118

Children's Perceived Self-Control Scale
Laura Lynn Humphrey
Department of Psychiatry
Northwestern University Medical School
320 E. Huron
Chicago, IL 60611

Children's Version/Family Environment Scale
C. J. Pino, Nancy Simons and Mary Jane
Slawinowski
Slosson Educational Publications, Inc.
PO Box 280
East Aurora, NY 14052

Conners' Teacher Rating Scale
Keith Conners
Children's Hospital National Medical Center
111 Michigan Avenue, N.W.
Washington, DC 20010

Conners' Parent Rating Scale
Keith Conners
Children's Hospital National Medical Center
111 Michigan Avenue, N.W.
Washington, DC 20010

Coopersmith Self-Esteem Inventories
Stanley Coopersmith
Consulting Psychologists Press, Inc.
577 College Avenue
Palo Alto, CA 94306

Culture Free Self-Esteem Inventories for Children
and Adults
James Battle
Special Child Publication
4535 Union Bay Place, N.E.
Seattle, WA 98105

Devereaux Elementary School Behavior Rating Scale
George Spivack and Marshall Swift
Devereaux Foundation Press
PO Box 400
19 S. Waterloo Road
Devon, PA 19333

Dropout Scale
George Demos
Western Psychological Services
12031 Wilshire
Los Angeles, CA 90025

Family Relations Test
Eva Bene and James Anthony
NFER Nelson Publishing Company
Darville House
2 Oxford Road East
Windsor, Berkshire
SL4 1DF England

Hare Self-esteem Scale
Bruce R. Hare
The Free Press
866 Third Avenue
New York, NY 10032

Hopelessness Scale for Children
Alan E. Kazdin
Alan E. Kazdin, Ph.D.

Professor of Psychiatry and Psychology
Western Psychiatric Institute and Clinic
3811 O'Hara Street
Pittsburgh, PA 15213

How I Perceive Myself
Eui-Do Rim
Research for Better Schools, Inc.
1700 Market Street
Philadelphia, PA 19103

Hyperactivity and Withdrawal Scale
R. Bell, M. Waldrop and G. Waller
Richard Bell
Child Research Branch
National Institute of Mental Health
Building 15K
9000 Rockville Pike
Bethesda, MD 20014

Impulsivity Scale
Paul Hirschfield, Brian Sutton-Smith and
B. G. Rosenberg
Dr. Paul Hirschfield
Hirschfield and Associates, S29
Pharr Road
Atlanta, GA 30305

Inferred Self-Concept
E. L. McDaniel
Western Psychological Services
12031 Wilshire Blvd.
Los Angeles, CA 90025

Iowa Social Competency Scale: School Age
Damaris Pease
Child Development Department
101 Child Development Building
Iowa State University
Ames, Iowa 50011

Kiddie S.A.D.S.
W. Y. Chambers and J. Puig-Antich
Western Psychiatric Institute and Clinic
3811 O'Hara Street
Pittsburgh, PA 15213

Louisville Behavior Checklist
Lovick C. Miller
Western Psychological Services
12031 Wilshire Blvd.
Los Angeles, CA 90025

Matson Evaluation of Social Skills with Youngsters
Johnny L. Matson
Northern Illinois University
Dekalb, IL 60115

Perception-of-Relationship (PORT)
Barry Bricklin
Western Psychological Services
12031 Wilshire Blvd.
Los Angeles, CA 90025

Piers-Harris Self-Concept Scale
Ellen V. Piers and Dale B. Harris
Counselor Recordings and Tests
PO Box 6184, Ackler Station
Nashville, TN 37212

Pupil Evaluation Inventory
E. G. Pekasik, R. J. Peinz, D. E. Liebert,
S. Weintraub and J. M. Neale
John M. Neal
Department of Psychology
State University of New York
Stony Brook, NY 11794

Quality of School Life Scale
Joyce L. Epstein and James M. McPortland
The Riverside Publishing Company
8420 Bryn Mawr Avenue
Chicago, IL 60631

Revised Children's Manifest Anxiety Scale
   Cecil Reynolds and Bert Richmond
   Western Psychological Services
   12031 Wilshire Blvd.
   Los Angeles, CA 90025

Reynolds Child Depression Scale
   William Reynolds
   Psychological Assessment Resources, Inc.
   PO Box 998
   Odessa, FL 33556

Rochester Teacher Rating Scale
   Gerald Rubenstein and Lawrence Fisher. A
   measure of teachers' observation of student
   behavior. *Journal of Consulting and Clinical
   Psychology* 42:310, 1974.

School Child Stress Scale
   Justin Pikunas
   335 Briggs Bldg.
   University of Detroit
   Detroit, Michigan 48221

School Attitude Survey: Feelings I Have
      About School
   Harold Burks
   Arden Press
   8331 Alvaredo Drive
   Huntington Beach, CA 92646

School Behavior Checklist
   Lovick C. Miller
   Western Psychological Services
   12031 Wilshire Blvd.
   Los Angeles, CA 90025

Self-Concept Adjective Checklist
   Alan Y. Politte
   Psychologists and Educators, Inc.
   Sales Division
   211 West State Street
   Jacksonville, IL 62650

Self-Concept as a Learner Scale
   Walter B. Waetjen
   Cleveland State University
   Cleveland, Ohio 44115

Self-Concept Scale for Children
   Lewis P. Lipsett
   Department of Psychology
   Brown University
   Providence, RI 02912

Self-Perception Inventory
   Soares, Louise and Anthony Louise Soares
   Professor of Psychology, Research and Statistics
   University of Bridgeport
   Bridgeport, CT 06602

Social Adjustment Inventory for Children
      and Adolescents
   Karen John and G. Davis Gammon
   Karen John
   Depression Research Unit
   909 Howard Avenue, Suite 2-A
   New Haven, CT 06519

Social Behavior Assessment
   Thomas M. Stephens
   Cedars Press, Inc.
   PO Box 29351
   Columbus, Ohio 43229

Social Skills Rating System
   Frank Gresham and Stephen Elliott
   American Guidance Service
   Circle Pines, MN 55014

Stress Response Scale
   Louis A. Chandler
   5D Forbes Quadrangle
   Pittsburgh, PA 15260

What I Think and Feel
  Cecil R. Reynolds and Bert Richmond
  Cecil R. Reynolds
  Department of Educational Psychology
  University of Georgia
  Athens, GA 60602

Young Children's Social Desirability Scale
  LeRoy H. Ford and Barry M. Rubin. A social
  desirability questionnaire for young children.
  *Journal of Consulting and Clinical
  Psychology* 35:195-204, 1970.

Publishers of Films and Videotapes

AAIMS Media
6901 Woodley Avenue
Van Nuys, CA 91107
800-367-2467

Barr Films
Box 5667
3490 E. Foothill Blvd.
Pasadena, CA 91107
213-681-6978

Churchill Films
662 N. Robertson Blvd.
Los Angeles, CA 90069
800-334-7830

Creative Learning, Inc.
Box 324
Warren, RI 02885
401-245-0326

Coronet Instructional Films
3710 Commercial Avenue
Northbrook, IL 60062

CRM/McGraw-Hill Films
2999 Overland Avenue, Suite 211
Los Angeles, CA 90064
213-870-5912

Encyclopedia Britannica Educational Corporation
425 N. Michigan Avenue
Chicago, IL 60611
800-621-3900

Eye Gate
3314 E. Broadway
Long Beach, CA 90803
310-438-3569

Filmfair Communications
10900 Ventura Blvd.
Studio City, CA 91604
818-766-9441

Films Incorporated
440 Park Avenue South
New York, NY 10016
800-223-6246

Guidance Associates
Box 3000
90 S. Bedford Road
Communications Park
Mount Kisco, NY 10549
800-431-1242

Handel Films Corporation
8730 Sunset Blvd. West
Hollywood, CA 90069
213-657-8990

Alfred Higgins Productions
9100 Sunset Blvd.
Los Angeles, CA 90069
213-272-6500

Johnson Institute
7205 Ohms Lane
Edina, MN 55439
800-231-5165

Journal Films
930 Pitner Avenue
Evanston, IL 60202
800-323-5448

Leane Leighton
Dimensional Sound
301 W. 54 Street
New York, NY 10019
212-247-6010

Learning Corporation of America/MTI
1350 Avenue of the Americas
New York, NY 10019
800-323-6301

Listen and Learn Company
133665 Pescadero Road
Lahonda, CA 94020
415-366-6033

Lucerne Films and Video
37 Ground Pine Road
Morris Plains, NJ 07950
800-633-7344

Mar/Chuck Film Industries
2211 Vinewood
Ann Arbor, MI 48104
313-763-6044

Marshmedia
Box 8082
Shawnee Mission, KS 66208
800-821-3303

Media Guild
11722 Sorrento Valley Road, Suite B
San Diego, CA 92121
619-755-9191

MTI Teleprograms, Inc.
1443 Park Avenue
New York, NY 10029
800-CALL-MTI

National Instruction T.V.
PO Box 40130
Albuquerque, NM 87196
800-468-3453

New Dimensions Film Company
PO Box 1352
Fair Oaks, CA 95628
916-961-4807

ODN Productions
74 Varick Street, Suite 304
New York, NY 10013

Phoenix/BFA Films
468 Park Avenue South
New York, NY 10016
800-221-1274

Pyramid Films and Video
Box 1048
Santa Monica, CA 90406
800-421-2304

Random House Media
201 E. 50 Street, 31st Floor
New York, NY 10022
800-733-3000

Spoken Arts
310 North Avenue
New Rochelle, NY 10801
914-636-5482

Sterling Educational Films
241 East 34 Street
New York, NY 10016
212-683-6300

Sunburst Communications, Inc.
39 Washington Avenue
Pleasantville, NY 10570
800-431-1934

Walt Disney Educational Media
500 S. Buena Vista Street
Burbank, CA 91521
800-423-2555

Wombat Productions, Inc.
250 W. 57 Street, Suite 919
New York, NY 10019
212-315-2502

At Last . . . You Can Be That
"MOST MEMORABLE" PARENT/TEACHER/CARE-GIVER
To Every Person Whose Life You Touch (Including Your Own!)

HELP KIDS TO: ❖ IMPROVE GRADES ❖ INCREASE CLASS PARTICIPATION ❖ BECOME MORE ATTENTIVE
ENCOURAGE & INSPIRE THEM AND YOU TO: ❖ TACKLE PROBLEMS ❖ ACHIEVE GOALS
AND
IMPROVE SELF-ESTEEM — BOTH THEIRS AND YOURS

Our authors are not just writers, but researchers and practitioners. Our books are not just written, but proven effective. All 100% tested, 100% practical, 100% effective. Look over our titles, choose the ones you want, and send your order today. You'll be glad you did. Just remember, our books are "SIMPLY THE BEST."   *Bradley L. Winch, Ph.D., JD — President and Publisher*

Sandy Mc Daniel &
Peggy Bielen

NEWLY REVISED

Naomi Drew, M.A.

Bettie B. Youngs, Ph.D.

V. Alex Kehayan, Ed.D.

Project Self-Esteem, Expanded (Gr. K-8)

Innovative *parent involvement program.* Used by over 2000 schools/400,000 participants. Teaches children to respect themselves and others, make sound decisions, honor personal and family value systems, develop vocabulary, attitude, goals and behavior needed for *living successfully ,* *practicing responsible behavior* and *avoiding drug and alcohol use.* VHS, 1½ hrs. $149.95

0-915190-59-1, 408 pages, **JP-9059-1 $39.95**
8½ x 11, paperback, illus., reprod. act. sheets

Learning The Skills of Peacemaking:
Communicating/Cooperation/Resolving Conflict (Gr. K-8)

A completely revised and expanded how-to guide for teachers and parents for bringing the skills of peacemaking to real-life situations. New section on how to create a peer mediation program, training guide, mediation scripts, role plays, and 59 activities to teach kids the skills they need to get along. Activities now coordinated with major content areas.

1-880396-42-4, 272 pages, **JP9642-4 $24.95**
8½ x 11, paperback, illus., reprod. act. sheets

You & Self-Esteem: The Key To Happiness & Success (Gr. 5-12)

Comprehensive *workbook* for young people. Defines *self-esteem* and its importance in their lives; helps them identify why and how it adds or detracts from their vitality; shows them how to protect it from being shattered by others; outlines a *plan of action* to keep their self-esteem *positive.* Very useful. Companion to *6 Vital Ingredients.*

0-915190-83-4, 160 pages, **JP-9083-4 $16.95**
8½ x 11, paperback, biblio., appendices

Self-Awareness Growth Experiences (Gr. 7-12)

Over *593 strategies/activities* covering affective learning goals and objectives. To increase: self-awareness/self-esteem/social interaction skills/problem-solving, decision-making skills/coping ability /ethical standards/independent functioning/ creativity. Great *secondary resource.* Useful in counseling situations.

0-915190-61-3, 224 pages, **JP-9061-3 $16.95**
6 x 9, paperback, illus., 593 activities

Esteem Builders (Gr. K-8)

Teach self-esteem via curriculum content. Best K-8 program available. Uses 5 building blocks of self-esteem (*securiity/ selfhood/affiliation/mission/ competence*) as base. Over 250 grade level/curric. content cross-correlated activities. Also assess. tool, checklist of educator behaviors for modeling, 40 week lesson planner, ext. bibliography and more.

Paperback, 464 pages, **JP-9053-2 $39.95**
Spiral bound, **JP-9088-5 $49.95**, 8½ x 11, illus.

Michele Borba, Ed.D.

NOT JUST AUTHORS BUT RESEARCHERS AND PRACTITIONERS.

6 Vital Ingredients of Self-Esteem: How To Develop Them In Your Students (Gr. K-12)

Put self-esteem to work for your students. Learn practical ways to help kids manage school, make decisions, accept consequences, manage time, and discipline themselves to set worthwhile goals...and much more. *Covers developmental stages from ages 2 to 18, with implications for self-esteem at each stage.*

0-915190-72-9, 192 pages, **JP-9072-9 $19.95**
8½ x 11, paperback, biblio., appendices

Bettie B. Youngs, Ph.D.

NOT JUST WRITTEN BUT PROVEN EFFECTIVE.

Partners for Change: Peer Helping Guide For Training and Prevention (Gr. K-12)

This comprehensive *program guide* provides an excellent *peer support program* for program coordinators, peer leaders, professionals, group homes, churches, social agencies and schools. *Covers 12 areas,* including suicide, HIV / Aids, child abuse, teen pregnancy, substance abuse, low self esteem, dropouts, child abduction. etc.

Paperback, 464 pages, **JP-9069-9 $44.95**
Spiral bound, **JP-9087-7 $49.95**, 8½ x 11, illus.

V. Alex Kehayan, Ed.D.

100% TESTED — 100% PRACTICAL — 100% GUARANTEED.

Unlocking Doors to Self-Esteem (Gr. 7-12)

Contains *curriculum content objectives with underlying social objectives.* Shows how to teach both at the same time. *Content objectives* in English/Drama/Social Science/Career Education/Science/Physical Education. *Social objectives* in Developing Positive Self-Concepts/Examining Attitudes, Feelings and Actions/Fostering Positive Relationships.

0-915190-60-5, 224 pages, **JP-9060-5 $16.95**
6 x 9, paperback, illus., 100 lesson plans

C. Lynn Fox, Ph.D. &
Francine L. Weaver, M.A.

ORDER FROM: B.L. Winch & Associates/Jalmar Press, Skypark Business Center, 2675 Skypark Drive, Suite 204 , Torrance, CA 90505
CALL TOLL FREE — (800) 662-9662 • (310) 784-0016 • FAX (310) 784-1379 • Add 10% shipping; $3 minimum   6/95

DISCOVER materials for positive self-esteem.
CREATE a positive environment in your classroom or home by opening a world of understanding.

Good Morning Class - I Love You (Staff)

Contains thought provoking quotes and questions about *teaching from the heart*. Helps love become an integral part of the learning that goes on in every classroom. Great for new teachers and for experienced teachers who sometimes become frustrated by the system. Use this book to begin and end your day. Greet your students every day with: "*Good morning class - I love you.*"

Esther Wright, M.A.

0-915190-58-3, 80 pages, **JP-9058-3 $7.95**
5¹/₂ x 8¹/₂, paperback, illus./**Button $1.50**

**Enhancing Educator's Self-Esteem:
It's Criteria #1 (Staff)**

For the educator, a *healthy self-esteem* is job criterion No. 1! When high, it empowers us and adds to the vitality of our lives; when low it saps energy, erodes our confidence, lowers productivity and blocks our initiative to care about self and others. Follow the *plan of action* in this great resource to develop your self-esteem.

0-915190-79-6, 144 pages, **JP-9079-6 $16.95**
8¹/₂ x 11, paperback

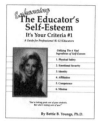

Bettie B. Youngs, Ph.D.

NOT JUST AUTHORS BUT RESEARCHERS AND PRACTITIONERS.

I Am a Blade of Grass (Staff)

Create a school where all — students, teachers, administrators, and parents — see themselves as both learners and leaders *in partnership*. *Develop* a new *compact for learning* that focuses on results, that promotes *local initiative* and that *empowers* people at all levels of the system. How to in this *collaborative curriculum*. Great for self-esteem.

Elaine Young, M.A.
with R. Frelow, Ph.D.

0-915190-54-0, 176 pages, **JP-9054-0 $14.95**
6 x 9, paperback, illustrations

Stress Management for Educators: A Guide to Manage Our Response to Stress (Staff)

Answers these significant questions for educators: *What is stress?* What causes it? How do I cope with it? What can be done to manage stress to moderate its negative effects? Can stress be used to advantage? How *can educators be stress-proofed* to help them remain at *peak performance?* How do I keep going in spite of it?

0-915190-77-X, 112 pages, **JP-9077-X $12.95**
8¹/₂ x 11, paperback, illus., charts

Bettie B. Youngs, Ph.D.

NOT JUST WRITTEN BUT PROVEN EFFECTIVE.

He Hit Me Back First: Self-Esteem Through Self-Discipline (Gr. K-8)

By whose authority does a child choose right from wrong? Here are *activities* directed toward *developing* within the child an *awareness* of his own *inner authority* and ability to choose (will power) and the resulting sense of *responsibility*, freedom and *self-esteem*. 29 separate activities.

Eva D. Fugitt, M.A.

0-915190-64-8, 120 pages, **JP-9064-8 $12.95**
8¹/₂ x 11, paperback, appendix, biblio.

Let's Get Together! (Gr. K-6)

Making friends is *easy* with the activities in this thoroughly researched book. Students are paired, get to know about each other, produce a book about their new *friend*, and present it in class. Exciting activities help discover commonalities. Great *self-esteem booster*. Revised after 10 years of field testing. Over 150 activities in 18 lessons.

0-915190-75-3, 192 pages, **JP-9075-3 $19.95**
8¹/₂ x 11, paperback, illustrations, activities

C. Lynn Fox, Ph.D.

100% TESTED — 100% PRACTICAL — 100% GUARANTEED.

Feel Better Now: 30 Ways to Handle Frustration in Three Minutes or Less (Staff/Personal)

Teaches people to *handle stress as it happens* rapidly and directly. This basic requirement for *emotional survival* and *physical health* can be learned with the methods in this book. Find your own recipe for relief. Foreword: Ken Keyes, Jr. "*A mine of practical help*" — says Rev. Robert Schuller.

Chris Schriner, Rel.D.

0-915190-66-4, 180 pages, **JP-9066-4 $9.95**
6 x 9, paperback, appendix, bibliography

Peace in 100 Languages: A One-Word Multilingual Dictionary (Staff/Personal)

A candidate for the Guinness Book of World Records, it is the *largest/smallest dictionary ever published*. Envisioned, researched and developed by *Russian peace activists*. An-cient, national, local and special languages covered. A portion of purchase price will be donated to joint U.S./Russian peace project.

0-915190-74-5, 48 pages, **JP-9074-5 $9.95**
5 x 10, glossy paperback, full color

By:
M. Kabattchenko,
V. Kochurov,
L. Koshanova,
E. Kononenko,
D. Kuznetsov,
A. Lapitsky,
V. Monakov,
L. Stoupin, and
A. Zagorsky

ORDER NOW FOR 10% DISCOUNT ON 3 OR MORE TITLES.

NEW

The Learning Revolution (Adult)

A revolution is changing your life and your world. Here's a book that tells how this revolution is taking shape in America and how it can give us the world's best educational system by the year 2000. That revolution is gathering speed -- a revolution that can help us learn anything five times faster, better, and easier. A must reading for parents, teachers and business people.

Gordon Dryden,
Jeannette Vos, Ed.D.

1-880396-34-3, 528 pages, **JP9634-3 $29.95**
6 x 9, hard-cover, many quotes, biblio.

Hilde Knows: Someone Cries for the Children (Staff/Personal)

We're all aware of the growing problem of child abuse. In this book, a dashshund, is kidnapped from her happy family. The dog sees child abuse firsthand, when the parents abuse their daughter. Psychiatrist Dr. Machlin, outlines how caring adults can use the book with a child.

1-880396-38-6, 48 pages, **JP9638-6 $6.95**
7 x 8¹/₂, fully illustrated

Lisa Kent
Illust. by Mikki Machlin

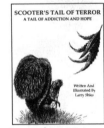

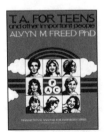